THE COMPLETE BOOK OF WALKING

THE COMPLETE BOOK OF WALKING

For Slimming Down, Shaping Up
and Feeling Great

by

RAYMOND DREYFACK

FARNSWORTH PUBLISHING COMPANY, INC.
Rockville Centre, New York 11570

for Jacob—
may he ever
walk tall

THANK YOU

I acknowledge with gratitude the efforts on my behalf and information made available from the following individuals and organizations: Dr. Joseph P. Bertucci, Dr. Matthew Guidry, Dr. Louis C. Galli, Dr. Vincent Giudice, Dr. Jerome Abrams (Chiropractor), Dr. Mark W. Green, Dr. Arthur Greenspan, Dr. Paul Ruegsegger, Dr. James Lawrence Evans, Jr., Dr. Elias Savitsky, Joseph Paquette, Ph. D., Irving Russin. And: The Walking Association (Dr. Robert B. Sleight), Alden Shoe Co. (Floyd Gilmore), The President's Council on Physical Fitness and Sports, J.C. Penney Company (James Schwaninger), Travelers Insurance Company (Lenore Skilton), The National Park Service (Duane Enger), Department of Commerce (William Dawson), The Strang Clinic (Ira L. Neiger), The Life Extension Institute (Delores R. Floss), The Executive Health Examiners Group (Carmen Moynehan), Scholl, Inc., Allen Edmonds Shoe Company, Johnson & Murphy Shoe Company, The Appalachian Mountain Club. Plus the scores of backpackers and walkers who were kind enough to share their thoughts and experiences with me.

Research Associate: Yseult Cleirens, Ph.D.

THE PAINLESS ROAD TO GOOD HEALTH

A recent issue of *Executive Health Report* states: "Not running, not jogging, but *walking* is your most efficient form of exercise and the only one you can safely follow *all* the years of your life!"

An increasing number of health and fitness experts agree and are campaigning to get Americans back on their feet. Formal and informal walking and hiking clubs are mushrooming throughout the nation. A nationally known shoe company, in cooperation with the President's Council on Physical Fitness and Sports, has developed an ambitious program of walking tours in America. Scholl, Inc., has launched an educational program to help Americans use their feet more efficiently, and has introduced a healthfully beneficial walking program of its own.

Predicting a powerful new trend, C. Carson Conrad, executive director of the President's Physical Fitness Program, states that, "Within the next 3 years we expect that walking will become the 'in' thing that jogging is today." Many doctors, journalists and health clinic administrators are predicting it will happen much sooner than that.

If so, walking—not just strolling or meandering in the aimless manner of most people, but *pace walking,* the disciplined, vigorous exercise detailed herein may well become something more than the fads running and jogging are today. Or *religion* might be a more appropriate word. Indeed, I can call to mind "born again" addicts who, having taken up running six or eight weeks ago, now worship it as if a shrine. One publication, *Marathoner*, actually refers to running as the "Holy Grail." New Jersey cardiologist George Sheehan who, along with Dr. Kenneth Cooper (the "aerobics" man), is counted among the high priesthood of running, has even stated that the "runner puts himself above the law, above society."

That is something to swallow.

Under ideal conditions running *is* a fine exercise and, like anything else, properly and sensibly managed, can yield beneficial results. But if you're a sinner, you won't save your soul by running. If you make a pilgrimage to the Boston Marathon, you may come back bone-weary and aching, but you won't be purified or healed of chronic ailments.

Ascribing good health and long life to the True Runner may make some kind of sense, but attributing spiritual endowments as well may be going too far. Running, however beneficial to some, falls far short of the utopian subculture which rhapsodic practitioners claim it to be. The fact is, as Frank Trippet so aptly expressed it in a *Time Magazine* essay, America has "become overrun with runners running every which way, including off at the mouth."

This book will offer no euphoric tributes to walking. Walking will not be touted as a religious experience. If you're nearsighted, it won't correct your vision. If you stutter, it won't help your speech. If you're shy and withdrawn, walking won't make you an extrovert.

What walking *can* do is, from a health standpoint, the same thing running can do for you and, in many cases, a whole lot better and—from both a physical and financial standpoint—far less painfully. As many doctors and clinics could testify, innumerable joggers, using their feet more than their heads, are hurting themselves trying to stay healthy. Since the running craze took over, orthopedists, podiatrists, chiropractors and chiropodists have been doing a land office business treating everything from knees and ankles to backs and toes. Many runners persist despite their doctors' advice to slow down. As Mt. Sinai Hospital's Dr. Burton L. Berson states the case: "Runners are fanatics. You can't tell a runner to cut back."

In my personal experience as a physician I have seen many runners ruin their ankles and knees, and a number of deaths as a result of jogging have been reported.

As the evidence in this book will disclose, more and more doctors today are recommending walking—*pace walking* as outlined in these chapters—for its therapeutic effect on the cardiovascular system and lungs. But it can also help relieve back problems, tension headaches, and a host of other physical ailments, not to mention the psychological benefits.

I recommend pace walking to all of my qualified patients. Since a continuing pace walking program burns calories, it can trim your waistline every bit as effectively as running or jogging, less expensively than fat farms and health clinics featuring running programs, and much more safely than crash diets. A conscientiously administered walking program following the precepts outlined in this book will make you look just as good as you feel. As one female afficionado expressed it: "Walking will do more for your looks than all the cosmetics and beauty treatments you could purchase."

Like any other activity or enterprise, it's a mistake to assume you know how to walk properly because you've been doing it for years. There's a great deal to learn, several pitfalls to sidestep. Engaged in sensibly and thoughtfully, pace walking can bring new dimensions of health and joy to your life. And in the safest and most painless way possible.

Joseph P. Bertucci, M.D., F.A.C.C.
Cardiologist

Table of Contents

Illustrations

1

THE BENEFITS AND DANGERS OF EXERCISE

"All muscles need exercise.
The heart is no exception."

California Heart Association

The cardiovascular system includes the blood vessels and the heart. According to the American Heart Association, cardiovascular diseases claim more American lives than all other death causes combined. More than 29 million Americans have some major form of heart and blood vessel disease. Hypertension (high blood pressure) afflicts about 24 million; coronary heart disease, 4,120,000; rheumatic heart disease, 1,800,000; and stroke, 1,840,000.

Heart attack, usually triggered by the blockage of any artery that supplies the heart muscle with blood, is the nation's number one killer. Although it appears to be a sudden, unpredictable event, this is rarely the case. Often, it is the result of a slowly developing disease of the coronary arteries (atherosclerosis), with the arterial channels being narrowed and congested by fatty deposits so that the heart muscle supplied by the blocked artery fails to get its essential quota of oxygen and other nutrients. This is a continuing and, fortunately, often a reversible process.

This book will show how, *by pace walking,* you can slow, halt, and in many cases *reverse* the ravages of time and a sedentary life upon the cardiovascular system. It will show you how, *through pace walking,* you can improve your oxygen intake, endurance and general feeling of well being.

This may seem hard to believe. After all, you've been walking most of your life, haven't you?

Well, yes and no. Even though you've been walking most of your life, there's a great deal more to walking than setting one foot in front of the other. The kind of walking most of us routinely do on a day-to-day basis doesn't benefit our health very much. A program of pace walking, on the other hand, can make you feel younger, stronger, and more energetic, and will trim down pounds of excess fat in the process.

Most people take walking for granted and so don't do it efficiently. This book will tell you *how to* pace walk, tell you everything you need to know about pace walking. After reading this book you will understand why hundreds of doctors rate pace walking as the safest and most healthful of all exercises, bar none.

RISK FACTORS

There are some risk factors we can do nothing about. Although there is no conclusive evidence that heart disease is hereditary, for example, many doctors believe that a tendency toward this problem appears to be inherited. Men seem to be more prone to heart attacks than women. The older one gets, the greater the chance one has of being stricken by heart disease. And black Americans are twice as likely to have high blood pressure as whites, a leading precursor to heart attacks and strokes.

Other risk factors—serum cholesterol, high blood pressure, and diabetes—are controllable by medical supervision consisting of close monitoring, diet and drugs.

And some of the most significant risk factors are controllable by the individual himself. Specifically:

- As the American Heart Association makes clear, cigarette smoking significantly increases the risk of heart attack and stroke. The death rate from cardio-vascular disease of cigarette smokers who stop is nearly as low as that of people who have never smoked.

- A nutritious diet, low in saturated fat and cholesterol, consumed at a low calorie level to maintain optimal body weight, will lower the risk of heart disease.
- Reducing stress, a prime contributor to heart ailments, by changing one's life patterns, habits and philosophy, will also help to cut down the odds of cardiovascular illness.
- Finally, numerous studies prove that people leading sedentary lives run a higher risk of heart disease than those who get regular exercise of the type that is recommended by a physician and which in some cases is medically supervised.

The therapeutic value of proper exercise in particular has captured the attention and interest of medical practitioners in recent years—the major factor accounting for the unprecedented popularity of running and jogging. Virtually every doctor or health clinic could cite evidence based on individual experience that people who start and stick with supervised exercise programs register significant drops in cholesterol count, blood pressure, pulse rate, body weight and body fat.

Too few people, unfortunately, take advantage of this opportunity that is available to everyone to improve the state of their health, the way they feel, and the length of their lives. Notes Dr. Malcolm Carruthers, "Most of the known risk factors in heart disease—such as high blood fat levels, high blood pressure, sugar intolerance and rapid blood clotting—have been found to decrease in suitable physical training schemes. The subjects also look and feel better, cope more easily at home and at work and sleep more soundly at night."

As C. Carson Conrad, executive director of the President's physical fitness program, tells us: "Half of America doesn't do anything for exercise. Inactivity is a major culprit in degenerative diseases."

If half of America doesn't do anything for exercise as Conrad claims, it would appear that a fair portion of the half that does exercise does so in a way that causes them more harm than good. It stands to reason that if you've been chair-bound and inactive for years, suddenly romping out on an ambitious exercise program like a youth of 15 could seriously strain poorly toned muscles and could even be fatal.

As James R. White, exercise physiologist of the Sun Valley Executive Health Institute, states: "Irregular exercise is hazardous and may be more counterproductive than no exercise."

WEEKEND JOCKS

According to *Time,* an estimated 12 million Americans were hurt in recreational athletics in 1963. By 1971 that figure had climbed to 17 million. It reached 20 million in 1977.

I know a man who at age 50 plays doubles tennis for an hour one evening per week. From time to time he also takes on his son, age 27, in tough singles competition. His son runs him all over the court so that he winds up gasping for breath. Recently he did this one time too often, suffered a "mild heart attack" and was rushed to the hospital. When his doctor found out what triggered it, he commented, "He's a lucky guy. This may be the best thing that could have happened to him."

Not everyone is so lucky. Although the majority of weekend jocks who get carted off to the hospital may not wind up in boxes, a sobering number do drop dead on tennis, handball, paddleball, squash courts and playing fields.

One reason is that it's not always easy or pleasant for a person of 35 or more to face the realization that he's no longer 20 and, especially if he doesn't engage in regular exercise, that his body can no longer take the strain and abuse it once did.

Most of the injuries range from shock-jolted knee joints and ankles to shoulder, back and hip problems, and result from what doctors refer to as the "overuse syndrome" —trying to force underused muscles, tendons and joints in bodies out of condition to respond in a way they're simply not geared to respond. Nor is overuse necessarily confined to the more strenuous or competitive sports. While games like tennis and paddleball rack up the lion's share of the injuries, an exercise as seemingly harmless as bicycle riding gets its own toll of casualties, mainly lower-back injuries from the prolonged bent-over position.

Sports like tennis and basketball are responsible for a great many injuries because they require sudden lurches, stops and sharp pivots that inflict excessive strain on ankles and knee joints, and extra pressure on tendons.

GYM AND SPA WORKOUTS

A few weeks ago a corporate athletic director I know was at my side as I watched a 30 year old engineer working out in the company gym. He had adjusted an exercise board to a 25 degree angle off the floor and was lying on it face up with his legs slanted upwards and his feet hooked around a horizontal bar. In this position he was jerking himself upwards repeatedly in a frenetic series of situps which made me wince with every upward snap of his back.

The athletic director remarked, "See that hard snapping motion? If he keeps that up I'd give him no more than three months before he throws his back out of shape." Shaking his head, he strolled over to speak with the man.

Gym and spa workouts, or calisthenics at home, are supposed to be good body-building, muscle toning, and waist-slimming exercises. Right?

Not necessarily. Often as not, as experience proves, they can do you more harm than good. For example, even that old standard waistline reducer, touching your toes without bending your knees, can trigger anything from back sprain to a heart attack. More risky yet is wrestling with heavy barbells or trying to pull up your own weight on a high chinning bar if you're out of condition. Many newly converted fitness addicts, seeking to get back into shape, tackle such feats with a determination they might consider foolhardy if they considered the realities of their physical capabilities and age.

Another invitation to trouble is the passion for pushups some hopeful body builders seem to display. Dr. Carruthers notes it is a mistake to assume that you can measure a person's fitness by the number of pushups he can do. He says, "The thrust needed to hoist yourself to this totally unnatural posture is anything up to your total body weight. If anyone suggested that raising your similarly-sized wife up to arms length while lying on your back as many times as you could before you collapsed was a good way of starting an exercise program, people might justifiably say he was mad."

HOW OLD? HOW ACTIVE?

Where then, does this leave *you?* How can a person tell what kind of exercise and/or athletic activity his or her body can withstand? Your safest bet, of course, is to let your doctor help you decide by giving you a stress test and physical exam, a subject I will discuss in detail later on.

Apart from this, there are some common sense rules and standards anyone can apply for himself. One thing you can't afford to ignore is your age. The fact that a forty or fifty-year-old body can't take the punishment a twenty-year-old body can absorb is a reality you might not enjoy facing, but doing so could help you to safeguard your health and well-being.

Another reality is equally important. If you have been leading a sedentary life for any period of time, the chances are strong that your physical stamina and endurance have diminished along with the speed of your reflexes. Prolonged inactivity slowly and gradually undermines one's circulatory system in general and the capillaries in particular.

A controlled program of realistic and sensible activity will gradually open up capillaries by making you breathe harder and can gradually increase your functional capacities up to a reasonable limit depending on your age and condition. But if you are 35 or older and have been chairbound for years, the best advice you could get is, "Train, don't strain!"

Despite today's running/jogging mania and the mushrooming of exercise clinics and spas all over the country, most Americans are still out of shape and, according to some surveys, executives may be the most unshapely of all. Commenting on out-of-condition executives, Professor Henry L. Taylor of the University of Minnesota's physiology department notes: "Indications are that about the hardest thing you can do to your heart is to pick up a couple of suitcases and run for an airplane."

An equally taxing exertion is to trudge up and down hilly golf courses lugging clubs as some golfers do, especially if you are fat, flabby, and past forty.

RUNNING/JOGGING

I repeat, I am not against running or jogging per se. I *am* opposed to running or jogging for people who shouldn't be doing it. More to the point, I am opposed to ill conceived and ill advised running programs and, most important, to running programs entered into over-ambitiously instead of slowly and gradually, a precaution that is applicable to any kind of exercise, including pace walking. In some cases, I agree it might be a good idea for walkers to convert into runners, or to supplement their walking with running if they wish, if the circumstances and conditions are right for it, a subject I will deal with in a subsequent chapter.

In the meantime, it is a good idea for anyone who is presently running or jogging, or planning to do it, to become familiar with some of the perils and pitfalls involved. One problem many runners and would-be runners encounter is that at first blush it is difficult to think of running or jogging as potentially harmful as opposed, for example, to a sport like tennis, where you can get whacked in the eye by a ball, trip on a ball while in play, or get clouted by a wildly swung racquet, your own or your partner's. And needless to say, when compared against contact sports like football, soccer, or basketball, running appears positively mild.

Mild it may seem; risk-free it is not. The running world was recently shocked by the death of Rep. Goodloe E. Byron (D-Md.), a marathon runner who died of an apparent heart attack while making the popular run along the Chesapeake and Ohio Canal. A non-smoker and veteran of six Boston Marathons, the congressman had been running for years and at 48 was regarded as a model runner.

Nor is this an isolated case. *Medical Tribune* Correspondent Mark Grant, in a recent article for doctors, wrote: "The 44-year-old Director of New York's Creedmore Hospital collapses and dies while jogging along a pretty Long Island road. An HEW program analyst drops dead during a three-mile mass run in Washington to protest HEW red tape. The head of the Miami Heart Institute himself collapses and dies while jogging at age 46. These reported cases and many others like them across the nation constitute a challenge to the widely popularized theory that jogging is an immunogen for cardiovascular disease."

This doesn't imply that running will kill you any faster or more easily than any other activity, or lack of activity. People have been known to drop dead reading a newspaper. It doesn't mean reading is dangerous.

Dr. William Haskell, Professor of Cardiology at Stanford University Medical School, has conducted studies which show that the risk for cardiacs (people with heart problems) in *supervised* jogging programs is no greater than that for cardiacs who do no exercise at all, Grant writes further. In fact, Dr. Haskell's record of unsupervised jogger deaths shows that about half of them had seen their doctor some time within the previous month, and that most of them had a history of some kind of problem.

Know Yourself. Whatever form of exercise or athletic activity you indulge in, the importance of understanding your physical limitations cannot be overseated. In running in particular it's a good idea to keep in mind that the average person loses from two to four quarts of water an hour while running, and that he is particularly vulnerable when the temperature goes above 70. At this time the body gradually dehydrates and your blood flow slows. In fact, some doctors attribute running deaths more to heat than to exertion.

Dr. Vincent Giudice, a nationally known orthopedist and member of the American College of Sports Medicine, makes another key point: "From the orthopedic point of view, many people are able to walk under normal conditions of walking. When they incur the added stress of an accelerated gait such as the one used in running or jogging, and sustain it for a longer period of time than is customary, symptoms start to develop which may appear in the back, hip, knee, or foot. The musculature is unable to cope with the added stress."

Experience proves this can apply to young people as well as middle agers. Dr. Giudice calls to mind a recent case where a high school boy who had joined the cross country team hobbled into his office. "His knee had blown up to the size of a grapefruit, a malfunction that might never have revealed itself under ordinary conditions."

Much on the increase are injuries that result from running and jogging, particularly when it's done on hard surfaces. Each time your foot strikes the concrete, shock waves are transmitted from the heel and up through the ankle, leg, knee, thigh, hip and back. The longer and harder you run, the more shock impacts you receive. The human body isn't built for this kind of abuse. Something has to give and usually does. As a consequence, the runner often suffers from an ankle that is twisted or sprained, inflammation of the knee (which is one of the more frequent complaints), pulled hamstring muscles, stress fractures of the leg bone, low back pain, or simple foot blisters.

Bronx chiropractor Jerome Abrams points out further that the spine acts like a shock absorber. Especially for people who are overweight, out of condition, or have poor muscle tone, the repeated shock vibrations of running or jogging can throw the vertebrae out of alignment, raising the potential for low back problems and sciatica. The more heavily one comes down when one runs or jogs, the greater the risk of injury, and the more you weigh, the more heavily you are apt to come down.

It stands to reason that if hidden physical problems exist, they are more likely to surface if you indulge in prolonged strenuous exercise such as running or jogging. A panel of medical experts consulted by *The New York Times Magazine,* in preparing a guideline chart titled "The Best Exercise For You," described jogging as "hard on joints and ligaments . . . an activity that requires preconditioning," and cautioned people over 40 in particular to have a checkup and stress test before doing it.

COMMON DILEMMA

This brings us right back to where we started. On the one hand, our occupations and living habits, usually centered around the automobile, have gotten us out of condition, exacting a heavy toll in terms of sapped energy, muscle detoning, weakening of the cardiovascular system, and stamina decline, a problem the right exercise and activity can play a major role in correcting. On the other hand, most of the exercises and sports people engage in hold the peril of bodily injury. So it would appear that we're in the midst of a damned-if-you-do-and-damned-if-you-don't situation. Actually, it is not nearly so bad as it may seem.

The greatest danger of injury lies in attempting too much prematurely, embarking on an over-ambitious exercise or athletic program before you are ready to do so. If you haven't been working out regularly, there's no reason you can't start an exercise program in your local gym, spa, or at home, providing you check first with your doctor to guard against specific activities that might be harmful to you. Deep knee bends, for example, aren't recommended for people with a heart problem history because the exercise tends to bring up one's blood pressure.

If you are out of condition, there's no reason you can't *gradually and patiently* work yourself back into condition to play tennis, paddleball, or any other sport that appeals to you—if you do it intelligently, in moderation, and with your doctor's okay. As far as the more strenuous sports are concerned, no one knows better than you how much punishment your body can take.

How you feel before, during and after an activity can be highly significant. I'm a regular walker, for example. I swim, and I also play tennis because I'm something of a nut about the game. Recently while on vacation I was lured into a pickup game of basketball, one hoop, four players on each team, most of them younger than I am. Well, I once played basketball fairly regularly. But that was more than twenty years ago. After five minutes I was panting like a steam locomotive with a broken-down engine and knew enough to say, "Thanks a lot, but I've had it!"

If any activity of any kind results in chest pains, dizziness, or what seems like utter exhaustion, persisting in it would be foolhardy. The idea in exercising is to accelerate your pulse rate to a reasonable degree, not beat your heart to death. So far as tennis is concerned, the kind of game you play is a factor. Usually the more skilled and experienced you are as an athlete, the less energy you will waste chasing after balls. If you are a semi-skilled tennis player up against a highly skilled player in singles competition, he could run you ragged in a matter of minutes. In fact, some doctors say that any person past forty who plays singles isn't using his head, and every year a quota of middle-aged players drop dead on the courts to bear out this contention.

This may not necessarily hold true for the player who has been playing several times a week for years and is in top physical condition. Still, many tennis afficionados find doubles as enjoyable as singles, useful as a calorie chaser, and a whole lot less taxing.

Of course, getting back to the main theme of this book, the walker has few if any of the problems and concerns outlined in this chapter—despite the fact that there is a right and wrong way to walk just as there is a right and wrong way to do virtually anything. As almost every doctor will confirm, a continuing program of pace walking can bring your cardiovascular system, lungs, and the rest of your physical apparatus into shape as effectively as any running, playing, or exercise program you could devise, or pay others to devise for you—and with a bare minimum of the dangers and pitfalls.

A great many people are under the mistaken impression that the faster and more vigorous the activity, the more beneficial it is from the standpoint of health. This is not the case at all.

Thus the key point of this chapter—and of pace walking itself—is, in planning your own personal exercise or reconditioning program, to heed the much-quoted advice of Charles B. Wilkinson, who served as a special physical fitness consultant to President John F. Kennedy: "Don't try to remake in a week's time a body that took years to wreck."

2

PACE WALKING: WHAT IS IT?

The concept of pace walking will be expanded upon throughout the book. But here in brief is its essence.

In a nutshell, pace walking is walking that is tailored BY YOU to your individual need, capability and desire to achieve maximum health and enjoyment. Here's how it works.

Talk with any physician and he will tell you that to get the greatest possible health benefit out of walking it must be vigorous and brisk. Some programs may be more specific, recommending a given rate of speed—say 110 steps per minute; or will suggest you walk a set number of miles per hour—say 3, or 3½.

The problem is that brisk walking means different things to different people. The rate one person can handle comfortably might cause another person to pant and wheeze. That's why pace walking specifies no rate of speed in terms of steps per minute or miles per hour. Ultimately, pace walking will be as brisk as you can make it. But it varies with the individual. It's a rate of speed you arrive at yourself.

How? Quite simply. You start walking at a moderate rate you are comfortable with and you maintain it for as long as you continue to feel comfortable with it. You time yourself as you walk. All you need is a watch with a sweep second hand. See how many steps you complete in a minute. Repeat the timing two or three times to make sure it's consistent. Continue walking at this rate for a few days or a week until it becomes second nature to you.

When you feel you can easily sustain this speed, increase it a little, but not too much. Fight back impatience. Remember that gradual progress is the ideal. Do this by lengthening your stride a bit and exerting a little more energy.

Continue to time yourself periodically. Let's say your rate went up 8 steps per minute. Sustain that rate for a week, or two weeks if necessary, until you feel you can do so with ease. Don't force it; you have your whole life ahead of you.

When you feel a natural urge to accelerate, lengthen your stride to its *maximum comfortable and natural length.* Exert a little more energy if the extra effort feels good and you're sure you aren't over-taxing your system. The idea is to achieve—but not to *exceed*—your maximum capacity. When you reach what you feel to be your limit, stop. This is your personal ideal walking pace.

If your maximum natural rate happens to be 115 steps per minute, and your companion's is 125, don't let it disturb you. It doesn't mean he or she is getting greater health benefit out of walking than you are. If you each pace walk at your maximum natural rate, you will both derive the same maximum health benefit.

The concept is easy to grasp. A person who is 6' 4" tall may take fewer (but longer) steps-per-minute than a person who is 5' 4". A 62-year-old cannot be expected to keep up with a 22-year-old—unless the oldster has been pace walking for years and the young person has been inactive, in which case Pop will probably outpace *him.* The individual who smokes, who is recovering from illness, or whose heart is "de-trained" from too many sedentary years may have a lower initial natural rate than the individual with healthy lungs, trained heart and no history of illness (although even heart patients have reconditioned themselves to the point where they can equal or outpace supposedly healthier people).

The important point about pace walking is this: The walking program that suggests you walk 120 steps per minute, or 4 miles per hour, is designed as a general guide. *Pace walking is designed specifically for you!*

Keep in mind that as you get into the habit of vigorous walking, it will become easy to increase your rate as time passes and the exercise continues to tone and strengthen your muscles and build up your oxygen intake capacity. Ultimately, pace walking will give you the endurance to sustain your maximum natural rate for extended periods without risk or exhaustion. And there is no better indication than this of good health and fitness.

Of course, this is only a brief inkling of what pace walking is all about. The following chapters will tell you how, when, and where to most advantageously apply pace walking —or *modified* pace walking—in a variety of healthful and otherwise beneficial ways. Remember, though, as we discuss walking, that it is only *pace* walking if you make it so. You've made the decision to attain fitness. Do it at your *own* pace.

3

PACE WALK AND BE HEALTHY

"Walk and be healthy. The best way
to lengthen out our days is to
walk steadily and with a purpose."

Charles Dickens

We use almost every muscle in our body when we walk; in fact, more than half of our God-given equipment is employed primarily for walking. Maybe Nature is trying to tell us something.

The variety of benefits one could derive from walking would fill not one book, but several. But in this era of renewed health awareness, by far the most sought after gain is better health and longer life. More specifically, it centers on the expanding desire of millions of Americans to strengthen their heart and lungs and thus offset the adverse health effects of sedentary living in a society too much dominated by rich food, television and the wheel.

Simple as the solution may seem—"Exercise!"—it leaves many people with a problem. Engaging blindly or recklessly in the wrong kind of exercise, especially if you're not in the pink of condition, could result in serious injury and, in extreme cases, death, as a growing number of people appear to be learning the hard way. Inadequate exercise, on the other hand, will almost certainly undermine your cardiovascular system in a slow and insidious way. So where is one to turn?

To the only safe and sensible alternative, in the opinion of *Executive Health Report,* * a monthly health newsletter whose editorial board includes several of the nation's most distinguished physicians. "Walking," they maintain, "is by far the best and safest exercise of all . . . and the one you can follow all the years of your life. So . . . walk as if your life depended upon it . . . for it does!"

Strong language, and here is why.

YOUR HEART NEEDS A HAND

Your heart is a four-chambered double pump. It beats approximately 100,000 times a day and moves 4,300 gallons of oxygen-supplied blood to all portions of your body via one of Nature's great marvels, your circulatory system. The heart rests only a fraction of a second between beats, recirculating about eight pints of blood on a continuing basis. The right side of your heart receives blood from your body and pumps it through the pulmonary artery to your lungs where it gets a fresh supply of oxygen. The left side of your heart receives oxygen-laden blood from your lungs and pumps it through the aorta to the rest of your body.

During the aging process, the smoking process, the cholesterol ingesting process, and the sedentary process, the linings of the arteries become thickened and clogged by deposits of fat, cellular debris, clotting substances and calcium. As the buildup gets heavy, arteries lose their ability to expand and contract. This makes it difficult for the blood to flow through, thus heightening the risk of a blockage or clot. This slow and progressive disease, called atherosclerosis, paves the way for heart attack and stroke. If the blockage occurs in a coronary artery, the result is coronary thrombosis, a common form of heart attack. If it occurs in the brain, the result is cerebral thrombosis, a common type of stroke.

The older you are, the more you smoke, the more fatty foods and alcohol you ingest, the more inactive your life

*P.O. Box 589, Rancho Santa Fe, Cal.

on the one hand and stressful on the other, the greater the likelihood that you are a candidate for atherosclerosis. There would be no point in telling you this, however, if there wasn't something you could do about it. As medical evidence demonstrates, heart disease is reversible in a number of ways:

1. If you eat and drink moderately and switch to a diet low in saturated fat and cholesterol, it will relieve one of the key risk factors many doctors associate with cardiovascular illness. It is believed that walking in some measure helps to lower the cholesterol count.

2. If you stop smoking, it will lower the accumulation of deposits in your veins and arteries. According to the American Heart Association, "the death rate from cardiovascular disease of cigarette smokers who stop is nearly as low as that of people who have never smoked." Can walking help you stop smoking? Possibly. Many people say they smoke because they're nervous, which makes them more nervous than ever. Walking briskly is one of the best relaxants known. To the extent that walking helps you relax, it may also help you cut down your smoking.

3. In the same way, walking can help you reduce the stress you are under, thus lowering another major risk factor relating to heart attacks and strokes.

4. Finally, even if you made no other change in your life but to undertake a regular and sensible pace walking program, a program tailored to your individual needs, it would produce a substantial improvement in your cardiovascular system, and would probably lengthen your life in the process.

The trend in progressive medical thinking today is all in the direction of preventive medicine. Encompassing exercise, nutrition, and smoking, alcohol, and drug control, a preventive medicine program is usually not only the most effective health alternative, but the least expensive as well.

For many years diet and exercise were regarded as the two main changes to make in one's life in an effort to stave off heart trouble, with diet getting most of the play. In recent years, however, exercise has gradually relegated diet to the number two spot from the standpoint of potential benefit to be derived. Dr. Warren Guild, a Boston specialist in sports medicine who also teaches at the Harvard Medical School, explains why: "Exercise has come to the fore in cardio-vascular medicine because many of its benefits, which were once 'only hunches,' have proved out in laboratory analysis." He ticks them off at the end of his fingers: "Exercise converts fatty tissue to beneficial muscle tissue. Exercise can burn up fatty tissue. Exercise strengthens the heart's collateral circulation. And exercise has been proven to reduce blood cholesterol levels."

If you left your car sit unused for an extended period, then started it up, the machinery would groan and grunt a while before responding, then do so in a slow and sickly way. Our human machinery responds the same way. If we don't use it enough, the whole works tends to slow down and its life-giving lubricant drags itself through our veins. If we stand or sit for too long, our transportation system gets sluggish. The heart is forced to work harder to convey the oxygen-filled blood to the body and remove the wastes that keep our system in balance.

Virtually all doctors agree that exercising priority should go to the heart and lungs, with other health benefits regarded as byproduct plusses. Like any other muscle, we exercise the heart by increasing the load it must carry. This is accomplished by moving our legs at a sufficient pace to bring our musculature into significant action.

COOPERATIVE VENTURE

Good health is, more than any other single strategy, a cooperative venture between you and your heart. If you treat your heart well, it will do the trouble-free job for which Nature designed it.

Brisk, fast-paced, lively walking is the best favor you could do for your heart; the evidence has been accumulating for years. Physicians' enthusiasm for exercise started in the early 1950s when Dr. J.N. Morris discovered that London bus drivers had more coronary heart disease than conductors who moved back and forth to take the tickets. Later, farmers in Grand Forks, North Dakota were found to have less heart disease than town dwellers. And a study of 2,000 postal workers in Washington, D.C. revealed significantly fewer cases of heart trouble among walking carriers than clerks.

However, it's easy to oversimplify both the heart's need and its remedy, a solution that may work most of the time for most people but not all the time for everyone. The seemingly logical conclusion millions of born-again runners, gymnasts and other athletes appear to be reaching goes something like this: "My life has been too sedentary, so I'll start a program of action, and the more action the better."

It doesn't work this way. When it comes to exercise, neither 'faster' nor 'more' necessarily means better. There are many good things in life that you can get too much of, and exercise is no exception.

Too much exercise, or too strenuous exercise as we have seen, can do some people more harm than good. Doctors pinpoint in particular a group of individuals they refer to as "silent coronaries," silent because they are walking around with atherosclerotic conditions without even realizing it since no special symptoms surface. The first sign of their illness arrives with a serious heart attack. How many silent coronaries are included in this country's population is an item of speculation among some physicians, and how many of the individuals who drop dead on handball or tennis courts, or while running, fall into this category is anybody's guess. Some medical estimates state that as many as one person in fifty may have unknown heart problems, but this is largely surmise.

Yet even the silent coronary's heart, weakened or not, requires the therapy of moderate exercise, most doctors believe. Certainly no program or regimen could fill this prescription more precisely than walking, which places just the desired stress on the cardiovascular and respiratory system so important to its maintenance.

Although a physical check-up is generally advisable for anyone over the age of 35 who is contemplating beginning a walking program, it is *particularly* advised for those who have a heart problem and know about it. Even then, the walker with a history of heart problems should try to avoid walking along heavily traveled highways where carbonmonoxide fumes, injurious to heart patients, are excessive. And needless to say if, after prolonged walking, you feel chest pains or find yourself gasping for breath, it is time to stop walking and check in with your doctor. One thing is for certain: Heart trouble and heroics do not make compatible companions.

STEP AT A TIME

Composer Igor Stravinsky's publisher once urged him to hurry the completion of a new composition.

Angrily, Stravinsky replied, "Hurry! I never hurry. I have no *time* to hurry."

A good philosophy to keep in mind when you exercise. The sudden realization that one has been undermining one's body for years with a recipe of sweets, fats, cigarettes, booze, high stress and low activity, might understandably touch off the impulse to undo the damage in days or weeks. Take a tip and subdue your impatience. This is the core of pace walking—you have plenty of time to achieve your objective and, if you take your time, achieve it a lot more efficiently.

The best bet for executives and other chair bound people who aren't accustomed to exercise, advises Dr. Louis C. Galli, a podiatrist and doctor of sports medicine who runs the Medical Committee for the New York Marathon, "is to start on a program of walking. It uses the muscles all over the body; everything comes into play."

C. Carson Conrad, executive director of the President's physical fitness program, agrees. "These sedentary citizens simply need to know that 3 miles of brisk walking a day will accomplish the same thing as 3 miles of jogging. The key word is 'brisk,' which means neither racing nor sauntering. It doesn't make too much difference if you walk briskly 3 miles, or jog 3 miles, or jog and walk, or run 3 miles," he adds. "They all provide appropriate ways to get circulatory performance."

One situation in which a "step at a time" is clearly essential is where the individual is post-operative or is recovering from an illness or injury. This also applies in some cases where professional athletes are injured. "It is better to start walking right away instead of staying in bed a few weeks," notes Dr. Galli, "because it helps to start everything functioning again right away."

Surgeons know better than anyone the importance of getting the patient on his feet again as quickly as possible after an operation to avoid the formation of an embolus, or clot, in a vein or artery that could break loose and block a vital passageway to the lungs, heart or brain. On top of that, when the patient starts walking even in limited measure, his convalescence is hastened, with circulation, muscle tone, digestion, bowel movements, and all the rest of his functioning restored to normal.

In relatively recent years doctors also learned that walking is one of the most helpful treatments for heart attack victims. One reason is that the heart has the capability to make its own repairs by developing new artery branches which take over the job of the blocked artery branch.

"Usually," states *Executive Health Report,* "some weeks after suffering a first heart attack, a patient is allowed to walk at a very leisurely pace a few hundred yards a day for several weeks. When this can be accomplished easily, the distance is increased to half a mile; then gradually, week by week, the patient is allowed to walk a little farther a little faster until (some months later) he is able to cover 3½ miles in an hour, and begins to feel like a new man!"

Similar experience has been recorded for people with angina. According to one study conducted by Dr. A.A. Kattus and his associates at the University of California at Los Angeles, some 75% of the 50 patients under observation improved, and (in some), evidence of angina disappeared. Pictures showed that where arteries had been plugged, the heart, by expanding small arteries, had built "new bridges of circulation around them.''

Research cardiologists make a potent point in response to such evidence: *If a well planned walking program can improve a sick heart, why wait for a heart attack before you start to take care of your heart?*

HEADACHE RELIEF

Headache pain plagues virtually every one of us at one time or another, even if only on rare occasion. But for tens of millions of Americans it is the supreme tormentor. Yet headaches are so varied and personal in both their causes and effects that any promise or claim of relief should be taken with the proverbial grain of salt. It is unsafe to generalize. The only thing common to headaches is the place that you feel them.

An American Medical Association pamphlet prepared by the Committee on Classification of Headache of the National Institute of Neurological Diseases and Blindness identifies 15 general types of headache. Two in particular—vascular headaches of the migraine type, and muscle-contraction headaches, plus a combination of these two—account for the great majority of headaches most Americans suffer.

The vascular headache victim suffers from a swelling of the head shell, a sick feeling as from a fever or hangover. The muscle-contraction headache is what the name implies, with the pain caused by tightening muscles, a condition which may be frequent and regular.

Headache relief by means of exercise is by no means new or unique. Dr. Otto Appenzeller, Ph.D., who is associated with the neurology department and headache clinics at the University of New Mexico, speculates that endurance training may spur the body to produce an important enzyme and that this might prevent blood vessels in the brain from expanding and pressing up against nerves.

In an article for the journal *Headache,* co-authored by Dr. Appenzeller and an associate, Dr. Ruth Atkinson, M.D., a patient is described who suffered excruciating headaches that were unrelieved by antihistamines and pain-killers. He fortunately uncovered a curious fact, that the headaches occurred only during inactive periods an hour or two after dinner while he was reading, watching TV, or conversing casually. They never happened while he was working around the house or was engaged in athletic activity. One day with this pattern in mind, when he felt the pressure starting to build in his head, he tried running as an experiment to relieve it. Within ten minutes the pressure disappeared, and he has been using this therapy successfully ever since.

For some, the key to headache relief may be running, swimming, or some other form of exercise. For others it may be walking.

Some headache sufferers get relief with the aid of an oxygen breathing mask. Oxygen, as Dr. Kenneth H. Cooper and other *aerobics* afficionados who stress the importance of oxygen intake point out, is a general key to good health and well being. When we walk briskly, we process more oxygen through our body via our circulatory system. If you are a headache victim, exercise is clearly one avenue of help that is well worth exploring.

Some headaches are hereditary, and for these there is no known cure. And if a headache is caused by a sinus condition or brain tumor, walking is unlikely to do any good. Nor can a person with acute migraine symptoms run. In fact, notes Dr. Mark W. Green, Director, Headache Clinic of Montefiore Hospital in The Bronx, "strenuous exercise is very bad for the migraine-prone individual."

In Mexico City, he recalls, while training for the Olympics several athletes developed headaches due to the combination of altitude and hard physical exertion. This caused the veins to dilate (expand) because of the increased oxygen absorption requirement. Strenuous exercise made the veins dilate even more.

Where strenuous exercise is inadvisable, walking often fills the bill. Getting into a walking program, counsels Dr. Green, can be useful on a preventive basis to relieve headaches and in some cases even stave off their onset. It can be especially beneficial for headaches that are caused by depression. When the well-being which accrues from pace walking alleviates the depression, the headache tends to dissipate.

Dr. Arthur Greenspan of New York City's Mount Sinai Headache Clinic, who is a Diplomate of the American Board of Psychiatry and Neurology, and Chairman of the American Association of Sports Psychology, states: "For people with high blood pressure who are subject to headaches, the best exercise is long walks. Even with medication, if the doctor prescribes it, walking will help put the circulatory system in better condition and lower the blood pressure, which will make the headache go away.

"Tension headaches," he adds, "are due to anxiety and nervousness. If exercise relieves and reduces the tension, the headache disappears. Walking can do that. I always encourage my patients who suffer from depressions to walk instead of just sitting there brooding. I encourage all kinds of exercise, but most of my patients walk."

Dr. Paul Ruegsegger says, "For those who are out of condition with muscle atrophy due to the headache pattern, walking is highly recommended."

YOUR ACHING BACK

I can testify from personal experience that a conscientious walking program is, under most conditions, the best kind of preventive maintenance you can practice to avoid painful low back problems. As a writer, my own back problem gradually developed by my sitting at a typewriter over a period of years. Prolonged, uninterrupted standing or sitting is bad for your system in general because it hinders your body's natural circulation flow. On top of this, sitting for long periods is bad for your vertebrae, which need constant toning and conditioning.

Orthopedic doctors and chiropractors may see eye to eye on very little else, but they do agree it is beneficial for the back for the deskbound individual to get up every hour or so and take a short walk even if it is only around the room a few times. The same thing applies if you take long trips in a car.

Taxi and bus drivers, as an example, are especially prone to back problems. While traveling, getting out of the car every hour or so to stretch your legs, then walking back and forth for five minutes or so, will help you keep backaches at bay.

I am living proof that back problems respond well to exercise, a phenomenon proven by Dr. Hans Krause, a New York City orthopedic physician who recently reported the results of a YMCA exercise program he developed for people with back pain. The exercise training greatly reduced the pain, with an excellent response recorded in 29 percent of the cases, and a good response reported in 36 percent of those studied.

Eighty percent of the back problems suffered by more than five million Americans are the result of poor physical condition, according to Dr. Daniel G. Miller, President and Medical Director of the Preventive Medicine Institute (Strang Clinic). "The chief villians," he says, "are weak back and abdominal muscles," conditions that respond well to exercise. "Tension," he adds, "is actually the second most common cause of back pain because it leads to prolonged tensing of muscles in a position of strain."

A walking program designed to upgrade your overall physical condition while it aids your relaxation, will help eliminate or relieve backaches as a byproduct benefit. So far as your back is concerned, would a jogging program be as beneficial as or more beneficial than a walking program? Probably not, especially if you have back problems now, because of the repeated shock impact each time you come down hard on your heels. Again, however, in matters of this kind, making general rules is rarely advisable; what would not work for nine people might turn out well for the tenth. Walking or running, if you already suffer from the aching back syndrome, chiropractor Dr. Jerome Abrams counsels against doing it on sand—a favored spot for beach walkers and runners—because you are thrown off balance with every step that you take, a procedure which can only aggravate back problems.

TRIMMING DOWN

Poor eating habits contribute significantly to the number of heart attacks each year. The American Heart Association spells it out in clear and blunt terms:

- Men in their middle years who are significantly overweight have about three times the risk of a fatal heart attack as compared with those of normal weight.
- Obesity also heightens the possibility of high blood pressure or diabetes.
- Since most people reach their normal adult weight between the ages of 21 and 25, fewer calories are needed after that to maintain normal weight.

Experience proves, however, that most people past thirty eat as much as they did in their 20s. Such people are often destined to become fatter when they burn up less energy as the result of a more sedentary life.

The food you eat is potential energy that will either be burned up as energy or stored as fat by your body.

The key to effective weight control lies in keeping the amount of food you eat and your amount of physical activity in balance. When the calories you consume equal the calories your body needs to fulfill its functions, your weight remains more or less stable. When you eat more than you need, the excess is stored and you "put on weight."

Most Americans are too fat because they either disregard the problem or rely on sporadic bursts of inspiration often triggered by somebody's new miracle diet. New miracle diets constitute one of this country's fastest growing and most profitable industries. Many imaginative and enterprising "experts" have become overnight millionaires as a result of it.

You must have seen it yourself. A variety of diet fads spring up each year with the regularity of tulips in springtime. Some crash diets achieve significant weight loss in relatively short periods, often due largely to the loss of body water. Such loss, unhappily, is all too quickly restored when normal food and liquid intake are resumed. Dieters who fail to realize that fat is lost very slowly become discouraged and abandon the effort, only to become reinspired when the next diet craze commences.

All of this tends to be self-defeating because trimming down and staying trimmed down is not a sometime or once-in-a-while proposition, but must become a way of life.

What Makes More Sense. The fact is that weight depends not only on how many calories you take in when you eat, but also on how many you use up being active. The overweight person who merely cuts down on his intake will make very slow progress in trimming his waistline.

The ideal way to lose weight is the sensible way, without resorting to extremes that are a great problem and sacrifice to maintain. A simple rationing program which combines a moderate cutback of sweet, fatty, high calorie food input with a moderate stepup of physical activity cannot but help you to trim down if you're overweight. Recent studies indicate, according to the President's Council On Physical Fitness and Sports, that lack of exercise is more often responsible for overweight than is overeating. These studies have compared the food intake and activity patterns of obese persons with those of normal weight. Several age levels—teen-agers, adults, and older persons—have been included in the studies. In each instance, the findings showed that the obese people did not consume any more calories than their normal-weighted age peers, but that they were very much less active.

In one experiment, a group of university students increased their daily food intake from 3,000 to 6,000 calories without gaining weight. This was accomplished merely by stepping up the amount of exercise they did each day. This is not cited as encouragement to go out and gorge yourself, merely to illustrate the importance of exercise.

The President's Council notes that two basic fallacies are widely held with respect to exercise and weight control. The first is that a great deal of time and effort is required to use up enough calories to affect weight materially. The second is that exercise increases the appetite and will therefore increase, not decrease, weight. Scientific experiments on animals and man have demonstrated the fallacy of both these assumptions.

How many inches would you like to trim from your waistline? How many pounds would you like to shed? You can easily, relatively effortlessly and, after a short time habitually, *as a way of life,* accomplish your goal by spending more time on your feet.

The truth of the matter is that the simplest, most natural, and most logical way to shed pounds is by *walking them off.*

Even if you maintain your same eating habits and pace walk for an hour each day, you will lose about three pounds per month, about 36 pounds in a year. If your goal is more ambitious than that, cut down moderately on your calorie intake and you will get rid of more excess fat. If it is less ambitious, walking just one extra mile each day at a good brisk pace will take off about a pound every month.

Keep in mind too, that as New York's Life Extension Institute points out, trim is not necessarily slim. "It is possible to be slim but not trim. To be trim requires muscle tone which is gained through exercise. Try to do some exercise each day. It should be one you enjoy—a sport, for example, or a brisk daily walk. Walking can do wonders for your health and your figure. It doesn't require special clothes or equipment and can be easily adapted to your lifestyle."

And as you will see as you read on in this book, it can be the best kind of fun.

NATURAL TRANQUILIZER

Untold millions of prescriptions are filled in the U.S. each year and more millions of heavily advertised tranquilizers are sold in the hope that the pills produced in torrents by this billion dollar industry will help the restless and sleepless to get some relief. But the truth of the matter is that even if the pill seems to help temporarily, it doesn't get to the basic cause of the problem.

So far as sleep is concerned, most of us have been led to believe that we must have at least eight hours each night to live and work at our peak. The fact is that as a general rule, the younger we are, the more sleep we require. In the early weeks of their life, babies need as much as 20 or 22 hours of sleep a day. As we grow older, the need steadily declines. Napoleon contended that "Men need six hours of sleep, women seven and blockheads eight." What category he fit into when he was caught napping at Waterloo isn't quite clear.

In any case, recent studies have shown that many people over fifty do not require more than four to five hours' sleep to function efficiently. Yet thousands who can sleep no more than this convince themselves they are undermining their health, become anxious about it, and turn to pills for relief that they don't really need.

"The trouble with sleeping pills," notes the Strang Clinic's Dr. Daniel G. Miller, "is that users develop a tolerance for them which requires taking more and more until side effects occur. The most common cause of sleeplessness in adults is depression. Fitful sleep and waking at four or five in the morning is a very common symptom of depression. Since most people do not like to admit they are depressed, they focus on the insomnia as their problem and treat it with sleeping pills. A University of Wisconsin psychiatrist has found that for this type of depression, an antidote as good as psychotherapy—and certainly better than pills—is to enroll the patients in a group physical fitness program."

Dr. Arnold Sykes, a Dallas physician, agrees. "Many people have trouble sleeping," he notes, "because they're too inactive by day. Exercise is sleep's favorite sidekick."

As increasing evidence shows, stress, strain, and tortured nights of sleeplessness can be counteracted and even elmininated by Nature's Tranquilizer, walking. Walking, more than any other exercise, activates all the muscles of your body so essential to the smooth and efficient functioning of your entire central nervous system.

MORE

Daily vigorous walking might be useful for the prevention or relief of literally dozens of physical ailments. One example is osteoarthritis, the type of arthritis most commonly associated with the aging process. Approximately 50 percent of the over-65 population—over 31 million Americans—suffer from this disease in varying degrees. This represents a 32 percent increase in the past several years.

One explanation for the rise is the growing population of older persons. But Dr. Daniel G. Miller notes another important factor as well: the increasing number of overweight and sedentary citizens. Thus the inactivity encouraged by the prominent roles which automobiles and television play in our lives must assume a significant part of the blame. Unused joints and muscles age and atrophy more rapidly. In contrast, Dr. Miller points out, dancers rarely develop arthritis. They usually remain supple and limber well into advanced age, as evidenced by dynamic one-man shows put on by such performers as Fred Astaire, when well into their seventies.

Even people with rheumatoid arthritis, a disease which may strike at any age, have in some cases found relief through programs that trained them how to increase the performance capacity and fitness of muscles. Bjorn Ekblom, M.D., a Swedish doctor who conducted programs in which muscle training, walking and cycling were featured, reported a good deal of success. Seven men and women recovered sufficiently well to return to previous jobs with complaints of pain significantly decreased and general psychological outlook improved.

Even symptoms of diabetes can be reduced or eliminated by walking, according to *Executive Health Report,* especially where light to moderate cases are developed in middle age. Dr. F.J. Buys of Potchefstroom University, Transvaal, South Africa, exercised eight diabetic patients for four 30-minute sessions per day for eight months. The goal was to attain cardiovascular fitness. A daily record of food intake was maintained, and tests for glucose tolerance and insulin response were performed monthly.

After eight months of regular walking, all but one of the patients had lost *all* symptoms of diabetes. Glucose tolerance tests were normal in seven of the participants. Two patients who had been taking phenformin, a drug used in diabetes treatment, were able to discontinue its use and still retain normal glucose tolerance. Dr. Buys was able to report a pleasant byproduct benefit as well: All the patients lost weight!

What it all seems to add up to is that the good health of your organs, arteries, muscles, and other physical components are as interdependent and interrelated as the parts of your automobile. When one breaks down it throws other parts out of kilter. When your heart and lungs function more efficiently, it provides a lift and a boost for the rest of your body just as a well-functioning carburetor is beneficial to your car's engine in general.

As increasing medical evidence bears out, a daily walking program aids digestion, increases oxygen intake, fosters more restful sleep, improves muscle tone and circulation, reduces anxiety and stress, and makes day-to-day living a joy instead of an ordeal to get through.

4

HEALTH IS JUST FOR STARTERS

> **"Unhappy businessmen, I am convinced, would increase their happiness more by walking six miles every day than by any conceivable change of philosophy."**
>
> *Bertrand Russell*

Nineteen years ago Bill Jenkins, a metal products salesman who covers a suburban territory outside of Cleveland, won a sales contest sponsored by his company. First prize was a vacation in Hawaii for himself and his wife, and they enjoyed every minute of it. Only 28 at the time, this was his hour of glory, the crowning achievement of an already impressive career. He was justifiably proud—number one in a sales organization where more than half the reps had three times his experience.

In those days Jenkins played a lot of handball and tennis. He had been on his college track team. He felt—and looked—trim. He had energy to spare, and had proved beyond all doubt that, from a career point of view, he had what it takes to succeed.

In recent years, unfortunately, Bill Jenkins had fallen on hard times. A good earner most of his life, he took to easy living and a year or so ago he tipped the scale at 210 pounds, up 40 pounds from the 170 he had weighed when he had graduated college. His fat buildup followed the all too classic pattern of indulgent eating and drinking coupled with inadequate exercise. Many salespeople put in a fair amount of walking as part of their job. Not Jenkins. His customers and prospects are dispersed throughout a twenty-five or thirty-mile area, and he was entirely dependent on wheels. In fact, wheels were a way of life for him. If he had to run an errand a block or two from his home for a pack of cigarettes or container of milk, it would never have occurred to him not to hop into his car.

Whatever walking he was forced to do from his car to a customer's office, he did slowly, dragging himself most of the way, instead of moving briskly. He did this mainly from habit because he felt tired most of the time, and found himself gasping for breath if he had to climb a flight or two of steps.

During the past ten years or so, Jenkins' sales performance followed a steady and gradual downhill curve. A year ago he ranked close to the bottom of the roster along with novices who, only a year or two on the job, weren't even established. When his sliding performance nagged at his mind, he tried to rationalize it out of his thoughts by telling himself:

"You're pushing fifty; you don't have the energy you once had."

"This new flock of youngsters are all gung ho and fired with ambition; you can't hope to keep up with them."

"You have a good cushion of reserves in the bank, and you're still making a living; that's good enough for you."

That's what he told himself. But he didn't really believe it. Still, he did nothing about it. Maybe one of these days . . . .

Then about ten months ago, the thunderbolt struck. His boss gave it to him straight from the hip.

"Bill, I've been putting off talking to you about this because of our personal friendship and your long service with the company. . . ."

Jenkins put on a good show of looking startled, but knew deep down that he wasn't startled at all. The gist of his boss's complaint was that he was assigned one of the company's preferred territories and it was yielding no more than a fraction of its business potential. Unless he built up his sales, he would have no choice but to let him go.

Although the bottom fell out when he heard it, Jenkins today admits that it's actually the best thing that could have happened to him, for it compelled him to take stock of himself. In his heart of hearts, Jenkins knew he had been permitting himself to go to pot for years.

One of his first moves was to talk to his doctor. This professional's response was, "Hurray! I've been telling you that for years. What did it take to wake you up?"

Jenkins told him. His blunt response: "I'm not surprised."

"Doc, what do you think I should do? Join a health spa?"

"You could. But it's not really necessary. All you have to do is cut out some of that junk food you've been eating and walk three or four miles per day. And I mean *walk*, not stroll."

Jenkins bought himself a pedometer to clock his distance. His goal is a minimum of four brisk miles daily. To cover the distance he sometimes parks a couple of blocks from a customer. If he doesn't cover it during the course of the day, he takes a long walk after dinner. A joyful eater, he doesn't eat substantially less, but he does his best to eliminate fats, starches, and sweets, relaxing his vigil somewhat only on weekends. Today, if he has to go a few blocks on an errand, it never even occurs to him to drive.

The results are more than gratifying. In his most recent visit to his doctor's office, he weighed in at 182, down from the 210 of ten months ago. His cholesterol count dropped from 310 to 200. His triglycerides fell from 390 to 130. His blood pressure now reads 135/80; ten months ago it was 190/120.

Jenkins feels better and looks better than he has in years. There's a new spring to his step. He opened three new accounts in as many months, and his sales curve is steadily rising. Today he shakes his head in disgust at the thought that he ever could have let himself go so thoroughly to seed.

YOUR CAREER MAY BE AT STAKE

Bill Jenkins is by no means an isolated case. Most major corporations and an increasing number of smaller firms sponsor physical fitness programs for their employees. Many deck out and maintain elaborately equipped gymnasiums and health clubs which some complete with professional instructors, or encourage executives to join clubs of their own by footing all or part of the tab. Some companies extend this expensive fringe benefit to include rank-and-file employees.

On their own, thousands of businesspeople and executives have been flocking to the hundreds of health spas, gyms, and athletic clubs which in recent years have been burgeoning throughout the U.S. Highly publicized emporiums like Dr. Kenneth H. Cooper's Clinic in Dallas are booked months in advance. Membership in chapters of the YMCA, America's Sunday school for physical fitness, has been reaching and exceeding capacity. The health equipment industry—muscle building machines and devices, treadmills, stationary bicycles, and the like, not to mention athletic gear—has been bursting its seams in the past decade or so.

Nationwide, hotel ads now feature swimming pools, health clubs, tennis courts, and well equipped gyms along with good food, fine service, and other attractions. Boston hotels advertise the Boston Common and Charles River banks as ideal for jogging and walking. Philadelphia's Marriott Motor Hotel publicizes the fact that it is ideally situated for access to the Fairmont Park and Benjamin Franklin Parkway walkways for walkers or Rittenhouse Square for "pre-rush-hour jogs." San Francisco innkeepers tout Golden Gate Park as ideal for a climbing walk to the top of Telegraph Hill.

Nor is the new awareness and concern over fitness always motivated by hoped for health benefits of and for themselves. Corporate executives and their employers alike, impressed by a growing number of studies, are increasingly coming to realize that physical well-being and good job performance are closely linked. Westport, Connecticut public relations agency head Richard R. Conarroe states the case in a nutshell: "In today's highly competitive marketplace, a manager needs his wits about him at all times to operate at peak efficiency. He has to stay physically fit to keep mentally awake. The principle of a 'sound mind in a sound body,' never had greater significance than it does today."

Werner F. Tersago, vice-president of Agfa-Gevaert Inc.'s U.S. division, who admits he is regarded as "something of a health nut," agrees. The unfit individual, he says, often feels fatigued and can't perform well. But the fatigue is mental, not physical, so that he even has trouble sleeping. Such problems, he implies, are more pronounced among Americans than Europeans.

"The European executive," he reasons, "doesn't feel the tension as much as an American would. Frequently, the European who becomes an executive is assured of having a job for life." He makes the added point that in Belgium, an executive who has been with the company 15 years cannot be legally fired.

Ben Proctor, a Chicago insurance executive, explains that the greater your responsibility and work load, the more efficiently you need to do the job effectively. Driving into work from a suburb, Proctor parks his car at a supermarket lot two miles from the office, and briskly walks the rest of the way. The four miles back and forth, plus elimination of the daily bun at coffee break time, helped him trim 34 pounds in the past two years. In his late fifties, he declares that he never felt better, and recently beat out two younger competitors for an important promotion. Hundreds of similar stories could be related. Borden, Inc. top executive Eugene J. Sullivan lost 10 pounds in a year simply by walking the 20 blocks to his office each day. Arnold De Witt, an Atlanta advertising man, gained eight pounds when a broken ankle interrupted his walking program for almost six months. "I was too weak-willed to cut back on the food correspondingly," he admits. "As a result I became sluggish and dull, a different man on the job."

THE CHEATERS

Michigan cardiologist Dr. Joseph Bertucci refers to the hilly golf course in his area as "Coronary Row." Executives flock there on Sundays to play a round of golf, he declares, and delude themselves that they're getting exercise. For those badly out of condition, trudging those hills is apt to do more harm than good, especially if they are among the small minority who lug their clubs along.

Most golfers, of course, ride the nation's fairways in golf carts, often equipped with holders for drinks. Even if they wait for the '19th hole' for refreshments, they could be winding up with a negative balance from the golfing experience.

"I enjoy the game of golf as much as anyone," says Howard Shapiro, a New York City physician, "but anyone who thinks a weekly round of golf is going to keep him in shape is only kidding himself."

If walking is so beneficial, what's wrong with golf? Even if you ride a cart you do a certain amount of walking. True. But the kind of strolling and waiting most golfers do during a game, isn't the kind of walking that does you any good physically. The walking isn't brisk enough or sustained long enough to accelerate your heart rate significantly, and the repeated resting usually negates any small benefit that might have accrued.

Dr. Kenneth Cooper, who uses the point system to rate various exercises, gives a round of golf a meager three points. Thus the executive who relies on his golf to stay physically fit would have to make the game his full time occupation.

If you enjoy golf and it relaxes you, by all means continue playing. But face the fact when you do that it is no substitute for walking.

THE WALKING WOMAN

A regular diet of walking benefits everyone and anyone in

dozens of exciting ways. But it has a whole set of unique and special plusses for women to think about.

The Way You Look. Few activities can beat walking for enhancing the way you look. Walking outdoors will put a healthy pink glow on your cheeks when the weather is cool. When you walk in the not-too-hot summer sun, it will give your face a flattering color without inflicting the burn and too-deep penetration so many women give themselves through prolonged stretched-out baking, the kind of exposure many doctors advise against. On top of that, it adds toning and supple firmness to your legs and thighs, as opposed to the lumpiness that sets in when one remains inactive too long.

Ellen Chernoff, a New Jersey woman in her thirties whose doctor persuaded her to get into the walking habit in an effort to get rid of a persistent feeling of fatigue, not only accomplished this purpose in a matter of weeks, but wound up with a byproduct plus that delighted her. "As a result of the walking," she says, "within a year's time I was able to size down from a 16 dress to a 12. My husband crows that getting rid of those old dresses is one of the most enjoyable extravagances he ever indulged in."

A Milwaukee woman remarked, "Walking 45 minutes a day does more for my figure, my looks and my posture— not to mention my morale—than anything I ever tried. I can't think of a beauty treatment or cosmetic to match it. On top of that it's free and it's natural."

Observant males are quick to echo these sentiments. The figure you want, it has been said, is inside the figure you have. Serious walking builds the calves on skinny legs, reduces hips, flattens the abdomen and redistributes the weight as Nature intended. The walking woman who takes care of her body is one of earth's more delectable sights. Hips and posterior undulating, pelvis moving, the woman in good shape looks her best when she walks, possessing a natural form and style that few males could match.

Pace walking is particularly beneficial for women with executive, clerical, or administrative jobs who spend most of the day sitting. The muscle action and movement helps to undo the hippiness and posterior spread that tends to develop as a result of too much time bound to a chair.

Continued walking, notes Herman Klein, a New York psychologist, will make any woman look better and will endow her with the grace and poise that are byproducts of practiced and efficient movement. It helps her psychologically as well; in fact, the way you look and feel go together. The poise and bearing you acquire through walking puts you more at ease in social situations, all of which works to enhance your appearance.

The Way You Feel. For the mothers of young children in particular, "getting out of the house" can be a renewing experience. However, in the midst of the hustle and bustle of too many chores and endless household responsibilities that never seem to get done—preparing the meals, keeping the house clean, washing the clothes, seeing to the childrens' needs, running all kinds of errands—this isn't always apparent. In fact, the young mother's eternal lament seems to go, "If I only had a minute or two to sit down and relax."

Important as sitting-down minutes and occasional coffee breaks may be, "getting-out-of-the-house minutes" can be just as important. For one thing, getting out of the house means getting away from it all, for a brief respite if nothing more. It gives you a change of scenery, a chance to recharge your batteries and view things through a freshened perspective. Getting out for a walk gives you a chance to think, not as a mother, or housewife, or maid, but as a person.

The problem is, who has the time? Hopefully *you,* if you only *make* the time. Ann Halpern, a Hackensack, New Jersey woman still in her twenties, with two pre-schoolers 2 and 4, hires a neighbor's teen-age daughter for an hour or so two or three days a week, and goes out for "a nice long walk that makes me feel like a new woman." One afternoon a week she has a cleaning girl in to help and invariably uses an hour of this time for walking, usually with some errand destination so that the walk does double duty. "The main thing," she says, "is that I avoid using the car whenever I can."

Other women with less opportunity than Alice to get off by themselves walk with the baby or small child in the carriage. This may not be as good as that occasional solo, but as one woman puts it, "I found that you can walk almost as briskly pushing a carriage as unencumbered, and you get the feeling that it's doing you some good personally, that you're doing something for yourself for a change. A byproduct benefit is that you save time in the process."

During Pregnancy. Walking had been described by French writer Laurence Pernoud as *"the* sport of the pregnant woman."* Never dangerous, he points out that it improves the circulation, especially in the legs, makes breathing easier, and helps the functioning of the digestive system which tends to grow lazy in pregnancy.

A host of physical problems and discomforts from heartburn and stomach ache to edema and varicose veins plague women in pregnancy. Many expectant mothers also become short of breath, particularly during the second half of the pregnancy. A walking program of a half hour to an hour each day, wearing good shoes with sensible heels and socks not too tight—started at the beginning of pregnancy—will alleviate these problems later on.

The pregnant woman can walk right up to the last day of pregnancy, Dr. Paul Ruegsegger notes. And Pernoud adds that walking every day in a quiet and airy place will enable a woman to absorb more easily the extra 25 percent of oxygen she will need for herself and her child. Overall, he concludes, it will make you feel better, and improve your chance of an easy delivery.

After Childbirth. Alma Davis, a Denver woman and the mother of two children, tells of her experience with walking in the month or two following delivery. After the birth of her first child, she immediately and conscientiously embarked on a walking program of about 45 minutes daily. Although she'd had a relatively difficult delivery running almost seven hours, her recovery was easy and rapid. She felt good within two to three weeks, the tiredness left her, and she was elated at the speed with which she regained her figure and general sense of well-being.

Her experience with her second child was another story entirely. "The birth itself was much easier than the first time," she recalls. "And perhaps for that reason I became lazy after the delivery. This time my feeling of tiredness persisted at least a month, even though my mother stayed with us at the time so that taking care of Jamie (her first child) was off my shoulders entirely. I continued suffering from stomach cramps which hadn't bothered me the first time, and had the feeling I would never stop looking like a burlap bag filled with potatoes."

Mrs. Davis assures me she is certain it was her failure to start any serious walking until about three weeks after the birth of her second child that accounted for the difference, and most doctors would agree she is right. As experience following childbirth seems to bear out time and again, new mothers who take brisk walks for at least a half hour a day after giving birth as well as before, are usually rewarded by regaining both their figures and stamina that much sooner.

Menstrual Periods. For some women, getting through menstruation constitutes a tougher siege than having a baby. A New Jersey woman complained to her gynecologist that she suffered severe stomach cramps during this period, was plagued by throbbing headaches, and was generally so miserable and irritable it was impossible to live with her.

"Is there anything I can take for relief?"

The doctor wrote her out a prescription. "But first try walking," he suggested. "You may not need the prescription."

At the beginning she decided to try both. After filling the prescription, she initiated a daily walking program consisting of two twenty minute segments. The cramps disappeared almost entirely. She still gets headaches, but they're less severe. When she stopped taking the medication, there was no discernible difference.

"Walking didn't eliminate the problem," she concedes, "but at least now it is one I can live with."

Medical studies prove that women who exercise regularly—walking, bike riding, aerobic exercises, etc.—suffer less menstrual pain and discomfort than women who are largely inactive. Athletes in particular complain less about *dysmenorrhea,* the medical term for menstrual pain, than women who hold down clerical or executive jobs.

"ANTI-AGE ANTIBIOTIC"

About a year ago John Sparkman, a 65 year old chemist I know, asked my advice about getting started on a walking program. The request surprised me because the most strenuous physical activity I had ever seen John indulge in was walking from his car to his house.

"Physical problem?" I asked.

"Not really." He explained that he had just come from a physical examination and his doctor had pronounced him in good shape for a man of his age. "But you won't be in good shape for long if you don't get more exercise."

When John asked for suggestions, the doctor recommended swimming, walking, and bicycle riding.

"Swimming's inconvenient," my friend told me. "I haven't been on a bike in thirty years and find stationary bike riding dull. If I must exercise, I think walking appeals to me most."

I got him started on a program. When I met him for lunch one day a couple of months ago, he confessed that he felt better than he had in years. "What astonishes me most about walking," he added, "is that I actually enjoy it. I never thought that could be possible."

Many others report similar reactions. Doctors define walking as "nature's own amazing anti-age antibiotic." Walking won't stop the aging process, but it can most certainly slow it down.

A caption in italics appearing under a *Prevention* magazine article titled, "You're Never Too Old To Grow Young," reads: "Would you believe a 50-year-old, starting from scratch, could get into better condition than most people are in at 30? It's true!"

The fact is that a person's physical well-being more often relates to his conditioning than his age. I know people in their seventies who feel—and in a few cases, even *look*—

better than many people in their forties and fifties. Progressive physicians stress the youth-sustaining and youth-restoring values of staying active more today than ever before. But there are still some doctors, unfortunately, who are conditioned to the rocking chair culture prevalent for too long in this country. For these practitioners the automatic prescription for scores of ailments is medication and plenty of rest.

This often heightens problems instead of relieving them. The notion that getting older means slowing down to inactivity is a misconception that does more harm than most other myths. Once you are past fifty, in fact, regular sensible exercise becomes more important than ever.

That muscle doesn't age was pointed out by Jana Parizkova, M.D., D. Sc., Charles University, Prague, Czechoslovakia. What is most important, she adds, is to maintain muscle mass (which, if the body does not get exercise, will decline with age). In her experience, unchanging muscle mass and body composition was a characteristic of men in their 70's and 80's exposed to proper conditioning.

The same thing holds true for cardiovascular disease. Heart trouble isn't "normal" in older people and, according to the National Heart, Lung and Blood Institute's Dr. Jeffrey S. Borer, "Aging itself does not appear to cause cardiovascular disease," but is related more to our modern lifestyle which encourages inactivity and lazy behavior.

Nor does age necessarily destroy exercise capacity, Swedish researcher Per-Olaf Astrand, M.D. points out. Dr. Astrand believes it is possible by means of a good training program to move one's capacity back 15 to 25 years toward birth.

However, for the person past forty or fifty who has been sedentary for many years, strenuous exercise such as running or tennis should not be initiated without a doctor's green light, so that for many older people the choices narrow down to walking, swimming and bike riding, all of which get excellent ratings by doctors.

THAT TIRED FEELING

It's a physiological fact of life that the less active we are, the more tired we tend to become. If you're fatigued from either inactivity or drudgery, there's nothing like a good snappy walk to make you feel alert and alive again.

Some people deliberately walk with this purpose in mind. Ann Gerstle, a Connecticut housewife and mother of four small children says, "I can't wait for my oldest to come home from school a little past three. By that hour of the day I feel dragged out and bedraggled. Ellie is a godsend. She minds the little ones for me while I get out for a quick twenty minute walk around the block. It gives me the second wind that I need."

An insurance company clerical employee who used to spend her entire lunch hour sitting and gabbing with coworkers now spends at least half of it walking. "Sitting at a desk for hours at a time tires me out more than anything," she says. "But when I get back to the office after walking, I feel like a new person. It's like a shot of adrenalin."

A psychologist would probably tell this woman she gets tired more from boredom than sitting. But since mental fatigue can be even more draining than physical fatigue, she's ahead of the game either way.

A professional basketball player in his late twenties once told me he could play an entire game without being taken out of the lineup once, and has done so, without getting tired. "But plop me in front of the TV for three hours, and I've had it."

I know personally that television has a more soporific effect on me than sleeping pills. Another thought to take with you is that people who feel exhausted all the time without a medical reason need exercise more than people who never get tired.

BARGAIN RATES

Whether you turn to exercise for health reasons, to improve your figure and general appearance, to keep yourself sharp on the job, or for some other reason, walking will be more considerate of your bank account than any other activity you could select.

If you go in for tennis, you probably own at least two tennis rackets you have restrung from time to time, a tennis bag, a half dozen sets of shorts and shirts, and a couple of warmup outfits. Golfers who delude themselves that golfing is exercise, usually pay even more to support their delusion. In his article for a medical publication, "The Jogging Snob," author James Coyle describes the Groupie who can recite the names and times of Boston Marathon winners for the past decade, can quote from the lead article in the current *Runners World,* sports a sticker, I'D RATHER BE JOGGING on her car's bumper, and owns seven jogging outfits—with Adidas to match. Should you decide to join up to shape up, a spa or health club membership will run you anything from about $300 per year to a thousand or more. If your taste runs to the more exclusive athletic club, you could be tagged for $2,000.

Or you may want to diet in style and in company with others. In that case you can sign up for a "fat farm" that will cost you from about $300 to $600 per week, and there are some that run higher than that. Health clinics and exercise centers which cater largely, but by no means exclusively to executives, charge stiff fees for short programs and the use of equipment and facilities. In fact, the main reason they're attractive to executives is because corporations usually pick up the tab.

Swimming and bike riding are relatively inexpensive exercises, and running doesn't have to cost much if you don't want it to. But no exercise is as much of a bargain as walking. Apart from a good sturdy pair of shoes which you should own in any case for the sake of your feet, it is easy and free, and requires no special training or coaching. It's probably the only way you can trim down your figure without trimming down your bankroll in the process.

INTERESTING PLACES, PEOPLE AND THINGS

A friend of mine, Herb Chesnik, whose main exercise for many years has been shuffling cards, informed me a few months back that he had resolved to get back into shape. When I asked what he had in mind, he informed me he had joined the Y. His plan wasn't to work out in the gym or play paddleball, a sport he once had enjoyed but wisely felt would be too strenuous to start again at age 50 after years of inactivity. He intended instead to swim at least three times a week and gradually build up his fitness until he could do fifty laps.

"A noble objective," I replied, and wished him well.

Later I ran into him and asked how he was progressing. His rather sheepish but laudably frank answer was, "I'm not."

"What happened?"

"Nothing happened; that's the trouble. Do you know that swimming can be boring as hell!"

The same complaint has been lodged against running and bicycle riding. In fact, one of the chief reasons many people don't exercise, or stop exercising, is because they don't *feel* like exercising, and the reason they don't feel like exercising is because most exercises bore them.

I have yet to hear anyone complain that walking is boring, despite the fact that it *can* be boring if you permit it to be. But generally, walkers find walking more interesting than most other exercises with the exception of competitive sports. If you train yourself to stay aware and observant, you will see all kinds of interesting people, places and things. Walkers are a friendly lot. If you like interesting company, there's no better time to be companionable than while walking. If you are a friendly walker, people will be friendly in response. Friendly runners and bicyclists simply don't have the time to be friendly. And have you ever tried to talk while you're swimming?

IT'S GOOD FOR SOCIETY

The Walking Association, Arlington, Virginia, is the first organization of its kind. It describes itself as having been formed for "those who already walk as an avocation or occupation or for recreation, recuperation, self-preservation, and transportation. It is even more for those who have yet to learn that feet evolved after millions of years not merely to depress a clutch or step on a gas accelerator."

The Association's executive director is an affable psychologist named Robert B. Sleight. One of his organization's chief aims, he declares, is to encourage walking as a means of transportation as well as a pleasurable outdoor experience. Many of the trips we take are short, he points out, under two miles, and very easy to walk.

"Think of the benefit to society!" he adds. "Think of the savings! There would be less air pollution, less need for gas and oil, less wear and tear on the car."

Just think how significant a contribution to America's energy problem could be made if everyone who drove a mile or two on an errand or visit were to use their feet instead.

5

GETTING READY

**"The greatest discovery of my
generation is that human beings
can alter their lives by altering
their attitudes of mind."**

William James

Do you really want to walk, that is, with a purpose in mind?

In "The Magic of Walking," Aaron Sussman and Ruth Goode note that walking is an acquired taste, an adult and sophisticated taste, like a taste for oysters, caviar, and wines. "Children," they add, "prefer hamburger and Coke. They have to grow up to the refined pleasures."

To acquire a worthwhile taste usually requires determination and persistence along with consideration and thought. It isn't enough to be momentarily motivated to start a walking program because a friend walks, or you read an article about walking, or you know that doctors recommend it, or it happens to be the easiest exercise you could undertake, or because you read about its benefits in a book. Impulsive commitments are impulsively broken. You should want to walk because you are *driven* to walk.

Our attitudes govern our actions. To start walking and continue walking in a way that will yield maximum value for you, the idea is to go about it positively in the right state of mind. This is rarely easy to achieve when your objective involves a change of established life patterns. But you can multiply your chance of success if you set a meaningful goal for yourself, a goal you care deeply about.

Start by asking yourself a few questions: Why did you decide to read this book? What is it about walking that captured your interest? What do you have in the back of your mind? Are you genuinely concerned about your health? Does it aggravate you that you're too heavy? Are you ambitious enough to climb in your job, to take the steps needed to charge yourself with the energy reserves success in business demands? Are you worried that your sleep is restless and you rarely seem able to relax?

Most people fail to get what they want out of life because they don't want it badly enough, or *consciously* enough, to take the action needed to fulfill their objectives. Creatures of habit, we fall back into accustomed life patterns unless we take steps to avoid it. Some people substitute action with promises they make to themselves.

Too often, "maybe some day" fades into never.

The trick is to pin down your desires and needs. Tell yourself as specifically as possible what you really want out of life. Then translate your desire into a simply spelled out goal and use every strategy and device at your command to commit yourself to this goal. That's the way to get moving.

A 45-year-old Washington, D.C. dentist was a chronic smoker, led a sedentary life, felt fatigued most of the time, and had a hacking cough that was very bad for business. The goal he set for himself was to stop smoking and get back into shape. He tore an artist's drawing of a clogged up cardiovascular system out of a medical magazine and tacked this grim reminder to his office wall where it stared him in the face all day long. Thus he never lost sight of his goal.

A woman of 35 who had gone to fat panicked when she realized her husband was losing interest in her sexually. The goal she set was to get back the slim and trim figure he once had admired and loved. With this aim in mind she made enlargements of two photographs of herself, one taken recently and one taken ten years before. She taped the pictures to the inside of her closet door so that she was forced to look at them every time she took out a dress, skirt, or slacks. The contrast was dramatic and made an unforgettable impression on her.

Another woman awoke one day to the realization that she had become her local pharmacy's favorite customer. Her goal was to substitute natural living for the drugged existence that had become for her a way of life. She had her husband install a small set of shelves in the bathroom. She then accumulated the collection of sixty-odd jars, tins, bottles and vials containing the medications and pills she had purchased in an effort to sleep better and stop feeling so tired, tensed up and irritable so much of the time, and kept the drugs on display on the shelves.

All these people planned and launched ambitious walking programs and have been following them conscientiously and enjoyably ever since. And all are successfully achieving their goals.

Are you serious about walking? Do you regard your inclination to walk as something more than an impulse or whim? If so, spell out what you hope to get out of walking and take some action if you can to keep your personal goal and prize in sight on a day-to-day basis. Otherwise, like my friend's swimming program, you're liable to give it up before you give it a chance.

Commit yourself to your goal. Announce it publicly to people you care about and who care about you. Get others to help if you need it. Join a group. Find a serious friend or loved one with a goal similar to your own. Take whatever steps you can to overcome the temptation to fall back into more familiar patterns of living after initiating your program. If you can set a goal for yourself that means enough to you, before you know it walking will become the acquired taste that riding in automobiles has already become for millions of tense, tired and under-exercised Americans.

STEP ONE: CHECK YOUR CONDITION

The first question to answer in initiating a vigorous walking program is: How vigorous? This becomes significant if your objective is to improve your health, or if you contemplate long walks with another goal in mind. For any activity to rate as a true exercise, it should make your heart and lungs work harder than usual. How strenuous a walking program you set up for yourself, and whether or not you will expand this program later on to include running or some other exercise, will depend mainly on your physical condition and secondarily on your age. If you're in good condition, many doctors will agree that age isn't much of a factor, but being a realist about your capabilities is.

In any case, if you are over 35, the recommended way to start your walking program is with a walk to your doctor. While it might be argued that a comprehensive physical examination is less critical for a beginning walker than a beginning runner, it makes sense nonetheless. As podiatrist and sports doctor Louis C. Galli states the case, preventive medicine is the direction in which progressive doctors are headed today. As is the case with any machine, you can't know what possible trouble spots to keep an eye on and keep under control until you give your body a checkup.

First Line of Defense. The periodic physical examination has been categorized as the "first line of defense" against crippling illness. One reason is that the big killers like heart disease often offer few warning signs in advance of striking. If a problem exists, you may not find it unless you look for it. If you do find it, the disease is postponable.

According to Dr. Morris Collen, who conducted a study comparing individuals who take physical examinations with those who do not, "If one has a checkup every year or two at age 35 and thereafter, directed at postponable disease, the mortality rate from these diseases after seven years is approximately 50% of what it would have been without exams."

Since the human body functions like a machine with its various tubes, valves, pump and other moving parts, it makes sense to give it at least the attention you would give your car, or a piece of household or office equipment. Yet many people seem to treat their cars with more care than their bodies. They put off being examined with the excuse that they haven't the time, that the cost is too high, for emotional reasons, or because they lack a true understanding of how the complete physical works, what it accomplishes, and the possible consequences of trusting to luck.

Before exercising or exerting yourself more than you are accustomed to, you might want to consider the advisability of taking an exercise stress test, especially if you're past 35. It is fairly expensive, usually running between $50 and $100 plus for this test alone, independent of the rest of the physical, but a good investment nonetheless. What it does is measure the maximum amount of oxygen your body can consume under stress. The test may be given on a treadmill with the angle of incline gradually raised, or pedaling a stationary bike with the tension gradually tightened. Analysis takes place while you exercise with your pulse rate, blood pressure, oxygen consumption and electrocardiogram (EKG) checked.

Dr. Kenneth H. Cooper, one of the earliest and most vehement advocates of the virtues of treadmill stress testing and a champion of jogging, claims that the two common tests for heart disease—the inactive EKG and the Masters two-step EKG—are inadequate. The resting EKG spots single-vessel coronary disease only about 15 percent of the time, he says. The more sophisticated Masters two-step test, in which a person is monitored while taking a step up and a step back, will pick up single-vessel coronary disease 35 percent of the time. Studies of stress tests such as the one given at Cooper Clinic, he adds, pick up single-vessel problems as much as 93 percent of the time.

Dr. Cooper's conditioning program is based on the body's efficiency in using oxygen. His clinic's treadmill is set at 3.3 mph. Of 5,000 persons who have undergone this test in a three-year period, only 8 percent were able to surpass the 22-minute mark on the moving incline, placing them among the elite of good health. If an individual is unable to endure at least 15 minutes on the treadmill, his coronary assessment is poor even if no EKG warning blips appear.

Stress testing of this type represents the ultimate in preventive health maintenance. Some doctors discount its value because they lack the proper testing equipment; others eschew it because it's a costly and time-consuming procedure which can take an hour or more. It is thus most prevalent at clinics and health examination organizations.

But even the stress test, like many others, notes the Strang Clinic's Dr. Daniel G. Miller, "is not 100 percent reliable. Some people with abnormal results have had studies of their coronary arteries which show them to be perfectly normal. Thus, an abnormal test result is a caution only, and does not mean heart disease or a bleak future. On the other hand, some middle-aged men and women, after a normal test, feel that the sky is the limit on physical exertion and have suffered a myocardial infarction. So although the test is useful and advisable, common sense and moderation—particularly for middle-aged converts to physical fitness—are even more useful."

When it comes to physical fitness, moderation and walking are synonymous.

Other Tests. If you have other medical problems or physical symptoms, the safest course is to consult your doctor about them before starting on any physical fitness program, even a moderate one. If you ever suffered any knee, ankle or leg injuries, for example, your best bet would be to check them out with an orthopedist. After a knee injury heals, even though you no longer have pain, your upper leg muscle may remain weak. With the balance of force between this and the hamstring muscle disrupted, the stress of pace walking could produce undue strain on the hamstring as your speed increases, a problem that can be corrected with the proper exercises prescribed by an expert.

Other exercises may be in order if you have back problems or nerve damage which would be determined by a neurological examination. This would test the muscle power of the thighs, legs and feet, as well as the reflexes of the knee and ankle.

Finally, notes orthopedist Dr. Vincent Giudice, it's a good idea to get yourself checked out by a podiatrist or orthopedic physician if you have any symptoms or discomfiture in walking. It may be nothing more than a simple foot problem, correctible with the right shoes or a built-in support. Bearing up under pain or discomfort may seem courageous at the time, but can only aggravate and worsen any condition that might exist.

Sufficient rest and nourishment are as important to good health as proper exercise. This is especially true for pregnant women and new mothers. Even if your main goal is to lose weight, combining a program of vigorous exercise with a rigorous diet could be harmful. The new mother who gets into the habit of napping daily to restore her energies, will find herself raring to go when her walking time comes. But for the first few weeks at least after giving birth, it's a good idea to touch base with your doctor to make sure he approves of the eating, exercising and rest schedules you set up for yourself.

EASY DOES IT

For an exercise program to yield the best results, it must be started gradually and practiced daily. Periodic inspirational bursts of over-exertion won't make up for lost time, and could add up to problems. Conscientious adherence to the pace walking principle will automatically prevent this from happening.

Don't get carried away by your eagerness to get back into shape. It's unrealistic to expect that you will be transformed into a topnotch physical specimen overnight. Overdoing a program at the start will result in strain and pain you wouldn't otherwise experience, and could make you wonder if the whole business is worth it.

Your body is built for walking, which makes it the most natural and ideal body-building exercise. Since "doing what comes naturally" is a God-given pleasure to enjoy, pushing yourself to the point where you turn it into an unpleasant chore could defeat your own purpose by turning you off and discouraging you. Avoid the kind of heat that drenches you in perspiration and bitter cold that makes you shiver. Don't walk so fast or so far that you wind up gasping for breath. Remember—pace yourself. If you take it easy you will work up to the beneficial exercise speed naturally and have fun while you're doing it.

Sensible pacing at the outset will give your body the time it needs to adjust to the extra demands you will be making on it. Attempting to out-walk your physical capabilities is simply asking for trouble.

How can you tell if you're maintaining a sensible pace or trying to outstrip yourself? Your body is your own best barometer. If you're overdoing it you'll get back protest signals quickly enough—persistent pain, or aches that are something more than just annoying. The more closely you heed your body's early warning signals, the more safely and surely your reserves will build up.

Another sign you should heed is fatigue. Ordinary tiredness is a byproduct of a good fitness program. Chuckles Dr. Arthur Greenspan, "If you are nervous and tired, brisk walking will make you relaxed and tired." When you first start walking especially, you will probably ache a bit and feel tired from the unaccustomed regimen and introduction to action of muscles long out of use. These symptoms will be mild compared with the aches and pains many runners experience, and will lessen as you get into shape. But a good healthy tiredness is a natural offshoot of an efficient exercise program and will make the subsequent rest all the more enjoyable. Exhaustion is another matter entirely. When you feel so tired your steps become sloppy and your feet start to drag, it is time to stop walking and sit down for a rest.

No matter what exercise you engage in, it should be increased on a gradual basis and when your body hurts, stopped. In walking as in jogging, notes C. Carson Conrad, "you follow a series of stress-recovery-stress-recovery periods. That means walk as briskly as you comfortably can, then stop, look around, enjoy your surroundings, before walking briskly again."

For the middle-aged person who's been chair-bound for years, his first week of serious walking might alternate five minutes of walking at a lively pace with three minutes of rest. Use the same recipe the following week, but walk a little faster. The third week make it eight minutes of walking to three minutes of rest. Increase your rate gradually until you're able to cover a mile in fifteen to twenty minutes. Continue this on a day-to-day basis, and you will be getting the benefits of good exercise without any of the problems.

THE TRAINING EFFECT

Good exercise implies a buildup of your body movement and pulse rate to the point where you get what Phoenix, Arizona's Institute of Preventive Medicine and Physical Fitness' Dr. Arthur J. Mollen calls the "training effect." To figure out what this is, he suggests that:

1. You subtract your age from 220.

2. Take 70% of this figure to arrive at your training pulse.

If you are 40, subtracting this from 220 leaves 180. Seventy percent of 180 is 126, your training pulse. At age 50 your training pulse would be about 119. Taking your pulse while walking is fairly easy to do if you have a watch with a sweep second hand.

Don't forget when you walk, that distance is more important than speed. Good exercise means exerting yourself, but it doesn't mean knocking yourself out. If you run hard for half an hour you won't burn up many more calories than you would walking at a lively pace. Thirty minutes of brisk walking will do your body more good than running fast for 20 minutes. And for any exercise to condition your cardiovascular system, it must be done on a regular basis.

Ideally, walking briskly for an hour a day is all you need to produce a marked improvement in the way your body functions and feels, and will help tone your muscles and slim down your figure if you have been leading a sedentary life. You should be able to reach this goal in about ten to twelve weeks—that is, progressing from relative inactivity to action —if your program includes at least five or six days of walking each week. A walking rate of under 3 miles per hour is slow and will do you little good as an exercise unless your age is truly advanced. Three miles per hour is considered leisurely. A good brisk rate starts at about 3½ miles per hour which is roughly equivalent to the standard Army pace of 120 steps to the minute. There is a greater difference than you might imagine between walking 3 miles per hour and 3½ miles per hour, and this difference is what makes up the extra energy quotient so beneficial to your heart and lungs. Using the sweep second hand of your watch and counting your steps, it is easy to establish your approximate rate while you walk.

I am in my fifties. I cover about 3½ miles in fifty minutes each day, missing Sundays more often than not, and cut my walking time in half on days I play tennis or swim.

RHYTHM

Rhythm is regarded by many veteran walkers as the single most important factor in building strength and endurance. The trick is to find the *natural* rhythm and stride you can maintain comfortably and get into the swing of it. Avoid the jerky uncoordinated movements that are hard on your legs. Strive for the longest step you can easily take.

Consciously lengthening your stride to its comfortable maximum may seem a bit awkward at first, but will soon feel easy and natural, because it *is* easy and natural. Let your arms swing out freely in tandem with the movement of your legs. Pace walking will get you accustomed to the *feel* of the step and make this kind of walking a habit whether you're deliberately engaging in exercise, shopping, or simply walking to get from one place to another.

You can usually spot an experienced walker by his smooth and coordinated gift. He permits Nature to take over and govern his movements, whereas the overanxious beginner too often tears off erratically. If both the novice and vet start on a long walk together each in his own style, the beginner usually pulls head at the outset but soon finds himself puffing and dragging while the expert plods along contentedly, going further and getting there faster.

The American Medical Association points out that the number of Americans who say they partake in some form of exercise daily has nearly doubled from 24 percent to 47 percent within the past 16 years. It adds that the evidence keeps piling up that regular physical activity may be a significant factor in preventing coronary heart disease, the nation's number one killer, and cites a recent study of San Francisco longshoremen as a good case in point. According to the survey, those longshoremen whose jobs required heavy physical activity had 46 percent fewer deaths due to coronary disease than their counterparts assigned to lighter duties.

The AMA concludes with a word of advice. Exercise, yes. But take it easy. You're not a longshoreman.

BEFORE YOU WALK

It's a beautiful spring day and you're in just the right frame of mind for a lively enjoyable walk. Well and good. But the truth of the matter is that, although you may be raring to go psychologically, you're probably not ready physically. Making the transition from an inactive state to the lively motion you contemplate will take some preparation.

While walking rates tops or near the top as a body conditioning exercise, depending on who does the rating, it ranks poorly as a flexibility exercise because the same motions are performed repeatedly. Thus, without taking steps to prevent it, certain leg muscles (those in back of your legs, in particular) may tighten up, producing an imbalance which could result in soreness or injury. In short, muscles and joints must be prepared for movement through a full range of motion. No one understands the importance of this warm-up procedure better than athletes.

If you ever watched a professional baseball or football team work out, you probably observed that before a ball is passed or a bat swung, it went through several minutes of muscle-stretching or flexibility exercises. It's a good example to follow regardless of what physical activity you engage in, walking and running in particular.

Orthopedists agree it is a good idea to stretch and loosen muscles before brisk walking or jogging, especially those of the lower extremities, and with particular attention paid to the achilles tendon.

Sprains and aches are most commonly caused by stretching muscles and ligaments beyond their capacity. Warming up, as the term applies, produces a slight rise in the body temperature which permits the built-in elasticity of muscles and sinews to accommodate the added stretch capability the exercises produce on the one hand, and increased respiration on the other.

Serious runners and walkers are conscientious when it comes to warming up and equally conscientious about warming down, which permits the blood to flow back to your heart more readily from your body's extremities, and eases your body's return to a resting state, preventing soreness and aches in the process. A good idea in making the transition from a brisk walk to a state of rest is to walk more slowly for two or three minutes, then spend five minutes or more on the warming down exercises.

The thing about warm-up in particular is that it's hard to appreciate its value until you have done it. Max Kahn, age 38, a New York salesman in excellent health who participated in a treadmill study conducted by a firm specializing in health and fitness examinations, stepped on a fastmoving treadmill without any previous warm-up. The result was an abnormal electrocardiogram despite his good health. He returned the following day and went through the same procedure, this time after a three-minute warm-up. The result was that all EKG warning signs disappeared. The same results held true in almost all of the test cases where healthy individuals were double-tested, first without warm-up, then with. When they were tested the second time, EKG warning signals either disappeared entirely or decreased.

Warm-ups and warm-downs can be overdone, however, just like the sport or exercise itself. The idea is to begin with five to ten minutes of *light* stretching exercises. (See Appendix E) Stretch, but don't overstretch. Overstretching can strain muscles during warm-ups just as it can during the activity for which you're warming up.

Staying in shape is something we would all like to do, and an objective a great many people periodically resolve to fulfill. But your chances of sticking to a healthful walking program will be greatly enhanced if you go to the trouble of getting a physical checkup and then planning your program.

It is worth repeating that the key to staying in shape,

or returning to fitness, rests not simply in exercise, but in *regular exercise* sustained on a day-to-day basis. As former Supreme Court Justice and walking afficionado William O. Douglas counseled, "Regular hiking is necessary if sore muscles are to be avoided." Most injuries and aches result from the delusion that an occasional few hours of sport are an adequate substitute for an exercise program. One of the beauties of walking is that it is the exercise you can most easily pursue with regularity. As Dr. Paul Ruegsegger states the case, "Anybody can walk twice a day for a half hour or so."

You don't have the time? Ridiculous! As you will see in Chapter 11, this isn't a valid excuse. You can *make* the time if your will is sufficiently strong, and there are dozens of ways you can do it.

6

TROUBLE AFOOT

> **"The feet take more punishment than any other part of the body."**
>
> *Floyd Gilmore, Alden Shoe Co.*

If you decide brisk walking, long walks, nature hiking or even walkathons are for you, what you will need most of all is the cooperation of your feet. Should you at some point decide to combine walking with running, this will hold doubly true.

Our feet endure all kinds of abuse. We keep them smothered for hours on end, burden them with top-heavy weight, and make them take the repeated shock of pounding on concrete and other hard surfaces. We pinch, twist and bend them in unnatural ways, subject them to the stress and strain of heavy lifting, and force them to conform to the whims of fashion-motivated shoe manufacturers.

Yet despite the handicaps they must stand up to, these miracles of engineering design are incredibly rugged. They are capable on the average of transporting us on foot about 65,000 miles during a lifetime, nearly the equivalent of three circumnavigations of the earth.

Like fingerprints, no two pair of feet are identical and no two feet are created equal. Thus, considering the workload we place on our feet and the functional flexibility we expect of them, some experts feel buying shoes from a retailer's shelf and hoping to get a perfect fit might be compared to purchasing a set of false teeth through the mail, or selecting a pair of eyeglasses from a rack.

THE MAIN PARTS

The human foot, containing 26 bones, 19 muscles, about 120 ligaments and innumerable blood vessels and nerves, is one of the most intricate parts of the body. Its functional efficiency depends on maintaining a fine balance of all its various parts, a balance that may be disrupted by poor walking habits, improper shoes, or inadequate foot care. The following rundown of major components will give you some idea of how they all work together.

Bones. Bones are linked together at the joints, and it is here that the movement occurs.

Arches. The foot's bones form three arches, two running lengthwise and one running across the instep. The main arch, called the *plantar* or *long medial,* extends from the heel to the ball of the foot. It presses down on the ground only at these two points, thus softening jolts which could shock the spinal column.

Ligaments. Ligaments, along with muscles, support the arches of the foot. They are strong, flexible, stress-resistant tissues that resemble strapping bands or cords. Forming the foot's first line of stability, they also check movement when the normal limit is reached, thus preventing undue stress and strain.

Tendons. These cord-like bands join the bones with the muscles. Their stabilizing function is aided when the muscles are strengthened. The much-abused achilles tendon which gives joggers so much trouble, runs up the back of the leg tying the calf muscles to the heel bone.

Ankle. The foot has seven *tarsals* or ankle bones dovetailing into the metatarsus. These join together to form the metatarsal arch, which helps give the foot its flexibility and resilience. The ankle, operating somewhat like a door hinge, does the same thing for the foot that the wrist does for the hand.

Tibia. This is the large leg bone which, together with the *fibula,* joins the ankle bone to the knee. It can take stresses up to an estimated 1,500 pounds.

Heel. The heel bone *(calcaneus),* supports an

estimated 25 percent of the body's weight, absorbing the shock of each step, and transmitting shock waves up through the leg.

Toes. The toe bones, or *phalanges,* help maintain balance. The big toe has two bones; the other toes, three each. Nine of the foot's 19 muscles are used to move the big toe alone.

GET ACQUAINTED WITH YOUR FEET

The foot has many functions, notes Dr. Louis C. Galli, podiatrist, but only two main responsibilities. "When the foot hits the ground," he says, "it is a loose bag of bones which must be flexible enough to adapt to the hard, soft, or irregular surface. Then as the leg passes over it must become rigid and act as a lever."

In the properly functioning foot the impact of the body's weight is transmitted upward when the heel strikes the ground. As the rest of the foot touches down, the *subtalar* joint bends, rolling the foot to the inside.

A great many feet, unfortunately, do not conform to this pattern. The three most common types of nonconformists are the high-arch, the bunion and the flat foot. (See Exhibit I.)

ALL FEET ARE NOT CREATED EQUAL

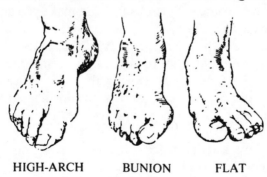

HIGH-ARCH   BUNION   FLAT

Exhibit I. Problem Feet

In the abnormal foot, the roll inside is excessive so that the subtalar joint doesn't lock back into place properly. This puts too much pressure on the inside of the foot which in time, unless corrected, collapses the arch. Because the toes tend to grab when this happens, trying to cling to the surface, bunions and hammer toes are apt to develop.

Of course the chance of your getting a good fit when you buy shoes multiplies appreciably if you have normal feet to begin with, that is feet that are neither flattened by a broken arch, or impaired by an arch that is too high.

How many of us fall into this so-called 'normal category'? Not very many, according to writer James C.G. Conniff, who researched the subject exhaustively. He says, "Only four length-width combinations account for the foot-fit needs of 25 percent of both men and women. The 75 percent whose needs take them outside that range, should probably consider getting custom-made shoes. It could be a cheaper way out of trouble than podiatry or even orthotics (prosthetic inserts, usually of durable plastic, which are placed inside the shoe and average around $300 each)."

FOOT KINETICS

Do your feet ache after brisk walking? Does it ever seem you lack the strength to pedal your bike up a slight incline? Do your legs feel wobbly after you run for a bus? Learning the basics of foot kinetics may help you understand why and suggest ways to alleviate the problem. It can make you a more efficient walker as well.

Kinetics is the scientific study of the forces which produce motion. Foot kinetics focuses on understanding the feet and their main function of moving the body efficiently. As you walk, your feet work in tandem in coordinated heel and toe action that creates a satisfying forward thrust movement and invigorating rhythm.

"Every activity places different stress on feet and legs," notes University of Wisconsin Professor Maurita Robarge, a kinesiologist who serves as consultant to Scholl, Inc. "That means there's a right and wrong way to move.

When you make the right moves, all exercises become easier and more fun.''

Unlike a machine, the body improves with movement. The idea is to find out which movements are useful and which ones to avoid.

Some Fundamental Guidelines. Professor Robarge spells out two basic principles of foot kinetics that can help guide your exercise and athletic movements and in this way maintain the desired balance among components of the legs and feet.

1. Know the limitations of feet and lower legs. When you initiate an exercise program, go slowly until your feet find the pace. Sudden repeated pressure on any part of the body can create stress and eventual injury.

2. Every activity requires a different movement. Learn to use your legs and feet efficiently.

This means thinking about the way you move. The more you move, the more aware you become of your body's capabilities. But to see health-aiding results, you must push muscles to new exertion. Doing the same 25 leg kicks every day, for example, is like marking time in a parade—you won't make much progress. In your movement stay alert for a slight stretching pull. This indicates that a muscle is being tested, extended, and conditioned. A quick, sharp, uncomfortable twinge is a stop alarm. It means you're exerting too much pressure, or that you may be trying an exercise or movement for which you are not yet ready.

THE FOOTSORE MAJORITY

According to the United States Health Service, about 87 percent of the population—approximately 190 million of us—suffer from some kind of foot problem, ranging from corns and bunions to fractures and sprains.

Apart from the batallion of general practitioners and orthopedists who treat some of these ills are some 7,500 podiatrists who, unlike the chiropodist of days past who operated out of the local barbershop, must undergo tough medical training and measure up to stiff licensing requirements. These doctors handle more than 35 million visits a year from patients with one or more of 300-odd foot ailments. On top of this, the nation's limping footsore majority part with an estimated $200 million annually for over-the-counter foot medications and gadgets, many of which provide little if any relief, and some of which do more harm than good.

A Department of Health, Education and Welfare study estimates that as many as 20 Americans in 2,000 suffer from foot disorders serious enough to disable them. Overall, there are probably less minor foot problems per capita today than 15 or 20 years ago because of trends to lower heels, and better and broad-toed shoes. But a substantial number of the corns, blisters and bunions we avoid with better shoes are made up for in large measure by millions of exercise-conscious Americans who plunge into athletic programs without proper forethought and care.

The thing to remember is that if physical fitness, or even simple walking pleasure is your goal, all it takes is a single chafed toe to cloud up an otherwise sunny day.

Foot Friction: The Pesky Culprit. According to Scholl, Inc., which is sponsoring an extensive public education program, "of 500 known foot ailments, approximately 95 percent can be traced to two causes: ill-fitting shoes and/or stockings, and improper care."

Major foot friction producers are narrow-toed and high heel shoes, shoes that are too tight or too loose, and cheaply made shoes that lack proper balance and support. A good shoe contains a rigid shank or arch support. Otherwise, notes podiatrist Dr. Richard O. Schuster, it's like parking a heavy weight on a plank spanning a ditch. The plank will sink into the ditch. So may the unprotected arch. The result: flat feet.

However, the term "flat feet" can be deceptive. Instead of flatness, it sometimes describes a weakening of the arch that occurs when ligaments holding the bones in their natural arched positions lose their tone or become strained.

With feet that are really flat, Dr. Galli explains, the feet are *too* flexible, causing the muscles to absorb too much of the shock of the foot coming down, which produces fatigue, swelling and pain. Flat feet require special support, whereas a too high arch places excessive weight on the ball of the foot.

Friction is responsible for a host of foot problems whether you exercise or not. The most vulnerable points are the tops and sides of toes, between toes, the sides of the forefoot, the ball of the foot, and the heel. The location of those tender pink tip-off spots will depend on the type of shoe misfit you are stuck with, the activities in which you engage, and the foot problems you already have.

Keep in mind that since no two feet are identical, a good shoe fit implies friction-free comfort for both shoes of the pair. Too often, while one shoe may fit reasonably well, the other may be too tight or too loose.

Ms. Limpy. Until recently, notes Professor Robarge, "Women have rarely tried or been able to realize their full physical potential. They're just beginning to flex new muscles, and we're seeing the first generation of 'bionic' woman, so to speak."

The best starting point for this new active life, she adds, is right down at the bottom with the feet and legs. Typically, in 'getting off on the right foot,' Ms. Determined-to-be-Active American has three hurdles to overcome. One is her conditioning, which more often than not has in the past been toward a sedentary life. The obvious solution here is to get started modestly and sensibly with a brisk walking program.

The second hurdle involves the biological reality of life that men and women are put together somewhat differently. It is rare for women to equal men's physical prowess. The answer here is to face up to this fact realistically. Hurdle number three is the easiest to overcome if you muster enough anger and indignation for this purpose. Rebel against high heel shoe fashions! The alternative could ruin your feet, by thrusting weight forward onto the ball of the foot, disrupting balance and creating toe and sole friction. High heels are as bad for your feet as cigarettes are for your lungs. They are fashionable only because they are touted and *promoted* as fashionable. Refuse to buy them and they will fall out of fashion in no time.

GIVE YOUR FEET A HELPING HAND

The Golden Rule applies as much to the relationship between you and your feet as it does to the relationship between you and other people. Treat your feet well and they will do well by you in return. Preventive maintenance is as important to keeping your feet healthy and avoiding foot problems as it is in safeguarding the general health of your body.

Clearly nothing is more vital to the well-being of your feet than the shoes in which you enclose them on a day-to-day basis. So critical is this to foot health in general and proper walking in particular, that I feel the subject warrants a complete chapter in this book and will very shortly be dealt with in detail. (Next chapter.) In the meantime, suffice it to say that the first and most important requirement of foot care is to buy shoes that fit, not after a week or more of break-in, but from the day that you get them. This won't be hard to achieve, most podiatrists believe, once you learn how and where to get properly fitted and follow the procedure religiously.

Although shoes should fit right from day one, they will require some break-in. The best way is to do this a little bit at a time before taking long walks or hikes with them.

It is also a good idea to switch footgear every day or, if this isn't practical, two or three times each week. I spoke with several people whose occupation and livelihood depend largely on walking, predominantly mail carriers and cops on the beat. If these people abuse their feet, they're in trouble. Two points many of them emphasized—beyond buying well constructed shoes that fit properly—are: 1. Switching footgear frequently helps relax foot muscles and permit feet to "breathe" easier. 2. Wearing light, color-fast socks is healthier for the feet. In fact, many mail carriers I talked with wear only white socks on the job.

An important no-no involves shoes with broken shanks or run-down heels. Both work against foot balance and are clear signs of neglected feet.

Feet that ache or hurt need special attention. Feet that are tired after a hard day of working, walking or exercise, are to be expected as normal, but deserve your care and attention as well. One way to baby and nurse tired feet is by massaging them. You can use an electric foot massager for this purpose, do the job with your fingers, or recruit a family member or friend for this chore. Whatever your preference, start massaging at the ball of the foot, kneading with your fingertips. Work along the sole up to the heel, then back again to the toes. Use your fingers to push each toe back and forth gently, to relax and relieve muscle tension. Knead in a foot cream if you feel that this helps.

If the weather is especially hot, or if you plan to do a good deal of walking or hiking, use rubbing alcohol on your feet in the morning and before you retire at night.

Finally, respect the little aches and friction signals you receive from your feet. If you can't walk with comfort, you probably shouldn't be walking. Stubbornly continuing to plod on in the face of discomfort is usually more foolhardy than heroic. Most serious foot injuries start as minor strain, rubbing or pain.

The Japanese, who seem to revere the feet more than most other cultures, long have indulged in the practice of putting them up on a pillow at night. Apart from a sign of respect for two members that serve you so well, this is excellent therapy, according to many podiatrists. Raising the level of your feet higher than the rest of your body every once in a while is a good way to keep them healthy and strong.

CARING FOR THE PROBLEM FOOT

Most foot problems are minor ones you can prevent, cure or relieve by yourself. More complicated problems produced by foot malformations or chronic conditions developed over the years by shoes that didn't fit properly fall into another category. These can usually be eliminated or solved to the point where you can live and walk comfortably with them, with the aid of custom-made shoes, devices or cushioning built into the shoes or, in extreme cases, with surgery.

What follows is a rundown of the simpler foot problems that represent the overwhelming majority, and some steps you can take in response.

THE PROBLEMS

Chafed Spots and Blisters. A blister, which results when chafing is ignored, is a thin, rounded swelling of the skin, containing watery matter. It is caused by irritation or burning.

Corns and Callouses. If the first signs of soreness are ignored, they rise up as Nature's way of protecting sensitive areas. Neither has "roots." They are simply layers of hard, dead skin. However, the pressure of this hard mass on sensitive nerves in the feet can be painful.

Bunions. This is an inflammation of the big toe, caused when it is squeezed against the second toe.

Hammer Toe. A toe caused to bend downward by repeated contraction.

STEPS TO TAKE

At the early sign of a chafed spot, take action. The first and most obvious move is to eliminate the source of the irritation which, other than an ill-fitting shoe, could be a stone fragment or wrinkled sock. Then cover the pink place with a moleskin patch, bandaid, or piece of surgical tape available in most drug stores and consisting of a piece of material with thin white felt on one side and adhesive on the other.

In planning long walks or hikes, take with you a supply of moleskin which you can cut to size, and a variety of sizes and shapes of corn and callous pads.

If you've passed the pink danger point, you can still do something about it. To relieve that smarting sensation on the bottom of the foot, for example, pad the area with a shock-absorbing foam cushion that fits the ball of the foot smoothly, and secure with the help of a toe loop.

Athlete's Foot. So named because it is easily picked up by going barefoot in locker rooms, athlete's foot is a fungus which thrives in a warm and damp atmosphere. The symptoms of itching and peeling skin start with the toes as a rule and spread rapidly.

Special preparations in spray, liquid, ointment or powder form are on the market that kill the fungi and help relieve the irritation. An extra precaution is to spray shoes with a deodorizer fungicide. And wearing thongs in locker and shower rooms could help avoid the problem in the first place.

For added protection, bathe your feet regularly; keep them clean and dry; sprinkle foot powder in socks. You will need only a fraction of the powder you would otherwise use if you apply it this way, and will find the application much more efficient.

Heel Spur. This is a bone projection on either the bottom or back of the heel. Sometimes extremely painful, and sometimes hardly noticeable, it is usually caused by an excessive pull of tendons or muscles attached to the bone.

Sponge rubber cut-outs or plastic heel cups can be designed to take the pressure off the heel, and thus relieve the pain. In extreme cases, surgery may be the best solution. Whatever the case, if you suspect that you have a heel spur that is causing you pain, your best bet and the safest course of action, is to consult a podiatrist or orthopedist to make sure, first, that it is properly identified, and second, that it is prescribed for professionally.

A Standing Invitation. Prolonged standing, especially if it is repeated often, can cause a whole rash of problems by placing special demands on the feet. To minimize this problem, Dr. Robarge suggests, when standing in a long counter line, for example, shift weight onto the left foot. Then isometrically "tighten" the muscles of the right leg, and repeat the procedure with your other foot. Doing this from time to time will relax both feet.

On the job or at home, after a long day on your feet, lift one foot onto a 12-inch elevation (a pile of books will do). This action will rest foot muscles and help to relieve lower back fatigue. (See Exhibit II.)

Exhibit II. Standing

"For an extremely abnormal foot that can't be fit by normal shoes," notes science writer Perry Garfinkel, "podiatrists cast a mold of the foot and then make a corrective device out of plastic. This fits into the shoe and corrects what is called *forefoot varus,* a deformity in which the first metatarsal head is at a sharper angle to the ground than the second, and the second higher than the third, forcing the foot to walk at an inclined plane."

In conclusion, any time you feel off stride, or rubbed the wrong way, take a few minutes to put your feet up on the couch and take a good look at your toes, heels, and soles. If you see or feel something amiss, chances are there will be a simple remedy to resolve it. Where chronic aches or foot pain exist, your best bet is to seek medical guidance. Your doctor will check for structural problems, such as fallen arches, or improper leg alignment. And if you have back problems, a good place to look to is your feet. "Backache and foot problems," Dr. Galli notes, "are often linked together."

HOW TO MAKE YOUR FEET SERVE YOU BETTER

Many foot problems can be avoided, podiatrists tell us, by a regular program of foot care that includes special exercises to strengthen foot muscles and increase flexibility.

Strength and flexibility are the two demands made on any muscle of the human body, and the most effective foot exercises are those designed with these objectives in mind. For it is these qualities that help prevent minor, as well as serious, injury that could occur when feet and legs are strained beyond their normal capabilities.

A variety of exercises exist for strengthening foot and leg muscles. Among the most effective and easiest to do are *isometric* exercises that produce muscle contraction without movement. These build muscle strength very quickly. Another way to strengthen muscles is through *isotonic* exercises that produce both contraction and movement.

Special exercises also exist to improve muscle flexibility. This can be achieved by giving foot and ankle joints a daily workout, moving feet in all directions to get the greatest range of movement—and by wearing comfortable, well-fitting shoes that don't cramp and inhibit the feet.

Why exercise feet and legs when you keep them hopping all day with dozens of errands and chores? Cooped up for hours on end, chores or not, they require regular limbering just as your whole body does. What follows is a checklist of simple foot and leg exercises especially beneficial to body building in general and foot health in particular. You won't have time to do them all, so select the ones you like best and spend ten minutes or so every day to make them part of your regular foot care program.

- Sit on the floor with your feet stretched out and pointing straight ahead. Curl your toes under and, with heels on the floor, turn your feet inward. Hold for a count of two, then relax. Repeat ten times.
- Walk around tiptoe in bare feet and stretch upward. This is a good exercise to repeat every day.
- Again in bare feet, try picking up marbles or a pencil with your toes. This also helps to limber your arches.

- Walk alternately on the inner and outer edges of your feet, keeping soles off the floor as much as possible.
- After bathing or showering, stand on the end of a towel and try to "rake" in the rest of it with your toes.
- While sitting, push down on the bottom of your shoes with a toe-curling action until you feel your arches rise. Repeat ten to twelve times.
- Dip toes into sand, or curl toes under while standing on the carpet, keeping heels on the floor. This will help strengthen the foot's natural shock-absorber, the arch, and improve flexibility as well.
- Sit on the floor with legs extended straight out, feet touching, toes pointed upward. Force your head toward your knees to stretch hamstrings and achilles tendon.
- While seated on a chair, point your toes downward, touching the floor. "Walk" them in tiny steps away from you for as far as they'll go. Then point toes upward with heels touching the floor and "walk" back.
- For better foot flexibility, sit on the floor, keep your legs straight, and grasp the toes of your feet with both hands. Pull your feet toward you until you feel the stretch in the back of the lower legs. Release, then repeat a dozen or so times.
- Try the "jock walk." As you walk, rise up on the toes of one foot before transferring your body's weight to the other foot.
- After shower or bath, take 30 seconds to bend as if trying to touch your toes with your fingertips. Then, holding steady, let your upper body hang until you feel the stretch on the back of your legs. This exercise is most beneficial after shower or bath when your muscles are warm and relaxed.

In addition, try exercise sandals. (See Exhibit III.) They approximate natural walking conditions, allow the feet to "breathe" and flex freely.

"Just walking in a well designed sandal is an exercise all by itself," notes Professor Robarge. Wearing them around the house, backyard and beach club will help you limber up feet and lower legs, as well as cooling down hot feet after brisk walking or athletic activity.

Chicago's Dr. James Ahstrom, Jr., Clinical Associate Professor of Orthopedic Surgery, Abraham Lincoln School of Medicine, University of Illinois, agrees. Says he, "The sandal requires increased use of the intrinsic muscles of the foot as well as the short toe flexors. In itself, this action is beneficial since it encourages exercise of those muscles which get only a minimal amount in ordinary shoes. Also, the anterior tibial and long toe extensors (muscles) are exercised to a greater degree than in conventional footgear. As a result," he adds, "wearing the sandal tends to strengthen muscles of the foot—which can be helpful to a leg-exercise program."

Exhibit III. Kinetic Sandals (Courtesy of Scholl, Inc.)

Considering the soaring prices of footgear these days, an exercise that's considered outstanding for your feet is good for your pocketbook as well. That's simply walking around barefoot, especially on soft earth or sand, regarded by running's high priest Dr. George Sheehan as one of the best exercises your feet could get.

Kinetic Plan for Toe-To-Total Body Fitness

If you have just five minutes a day to spend on an exercise-fitness routine, here is a plan that will make you kinetically ready for an active life.

Starting Position	Action
	1. Grasping a chairback, swing leg forward with knee bent and toe pointed forcefully. Swing leg back and outward at a 45° angle with ankle joint forcefully flexed.
	2. Stand with feet a shoulder span apart. Raise and hold arms slightly forward. Shift weight onto right foot; kick left leg up to touch outstretched left hand. Lower leg. Shift weight to left foot. Repeat with right leg.
	3. Clasping hands behind head, round lower back against the floor, and forcefully contract abdominal muscles. Begin a rocking motion.

Exhibit IV. Kinetic Plan For Toe-To-Total Body Fitness

Duration	Conditioning Benefits	Reducing Benefits
Repeat 12 times, each leg. Forcefully changing and holding the foot position described is important to obtain lower leg benefits.	Strengthens: 1. anterior, lower leg muscles. 2. posterior abdominal muscles.	Reduces: hips
Do 10 kicks for each leg.	Strengthens: posterior leg muscles.	Reduces: hips
Continue until you feel fatigue stress in lower back area. Repeat daily.	Strengthens: 1. lower back 2 .abdominal muscles.	Reduces: waist; abdomen area.

Courtesy of Scholl, Inc.

Many podiatrists and orthopedists agree. They favor going without shoes and socks as much as possible on rugs, grass, earth and other soft surfaces. This gives the foot's musculature a chance to strengthen and flex in a natural way. Walking barefoot on hard surfaces, however, such as city sidewalks and streets, is definitely not recommended. This is bad for the bones of the feet. (See Exhibit IV).

7

IF THE SHOE
FITS, WEAR IT

**"Shoes do not cause foot
problems, they aggravate them.
Foot problems are hereditary."**
Dr. Lewis C. Galli, Podiatrist

"Hurl after me a shoe, and I'll be merry whatever I do."

The English dramatist Ben Jonson penned this line about three-and-a-half centuries ago. Shoes were good luck symbols in ancient Ireland and Scotland. Even in America, tying old shoes to the back of cars occupied by newlyweds stands as an expression of wished-for good luck and happiness.

But in most cases, the shoes we wear today bring anything but good luck. According to shoe expert Floyd Gilmore, nine out of ten Americans buy and wear misfitted footgear, producing more misery than joy.

In olden days shoes were made of pieces of hide or braided grass secured to the feet by leather cords to protect them against rough stones, hot sand, and the cold. (Such shoes are still in existence in many underdeveloped parts of the world.) As shoes developed, more attention was paid to the decorative aspects of footwear than to shaping them properly to the contours and size of the foot. The ancient Greeks, Romans and Egyptians displayed their rank by the type of shoes they wore. Prominent and moneyed citizens could be identified by long, pointed shoes; the higher the rank, the fancier the footgear.

Shoe making today is big business, with billions of dollars worth of shoes manufactured and imported each year. More than 200 operations are often involved in the production of a single shoe. Still, with some notable exceptions, more attention is paid to shoe fashion than foot health, largely because many buyers pay more attention to the way shoes look than to the way they fit.

There is only one practical and sensible way to buy shoes—that is, to protect and support the feet, which doesn't mean they cannot also be good-looking and fashionable. However, for the sake of good health, the first requirement for shoes is that they should be fitted to the shape of the foot and consist of materials that stand up strong and firm under rough use and the abuses of weather. Thus, obtaining the right shoe size is no guarantee that the shoes will wear well or fit properly.

GOOD FIT, BETTER MILEAGE

It is difficult to walk properly or engage efficiently in any kind of athletic activity in footgear that rubs, squeezes or bites. Millions of Americans who buy poor-fitting shoes pay for them more dearly than in money in terms of blisters, corns, callouses, curled toes, and in more severe cases damaged cartilage and arthritic toes (hallux rigidus).

What should you look for when you go out to buy shoes? "The most important aspect of shoe fitting is proper length," Johnston & Murphy, a division of Genesco, notes in its instructions to salespeople. "This is determined by the length of the foot from ball to heel, not from toe to heel."

A shoe of the proper length will:

1. Provide support underneath the arch of the foot;

2. Permit the vamps (part of the shoe covering the instep) to crease properly when worn;

3. Allow the uppers (part of the shoe above the sole) to maintain their original shape, as they fit the feet the same

way they fit the last, or form, on which the shoes were built; and

4. Provide the greatest degree of comfort as well as a pleasing appearance.

The proper width, which is also important, is relatively easy to determine once the right length has been calculated. When slip-on shoes are fitted, variations of instep heights must also be reckoned with since some insteps are too high for certain slip-on patterns.

The Last Comes First. One of the main considerations in the production of quality footwear is the precision construction of the "last," or hardwood "mold" that is formed to match the shape of the foot. Operating under the basic premise that no two pair of feet are exactly the same, most manufacturers use several lasts in a variety of shapes. In shopping for shoes, your best bet is to keep trying different shapes until you find the one that feels most comfortable and fits your particular type of foot.

To fit a wide range of feet and to accommodate prescriptions for individual problems and needs, shoe expert Floyd Gilmore identifies three distinct types of last that are most generally used: Truflare, Trubalance, and Modified. (See Exhibit V.)

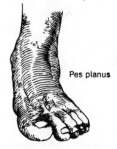

Pes planus

Truflare Last. For normal to extremely pronated, everted pes planus foot. Backpart gives firm heel and ankle fit even in extreme cases.

Pronounced angulation of ball tread fits everted foot, also accommodates tailor's bunion.

Trubalance Last. For normal to extremely pronated heavy foot with square fore-foot or splay foot. Wide ball tread, straight inner border, wide outer border with ample lateral displacement from the fifth joint back to the heel.

Accommodates more complex prescribed corrections, particularly full plantor inserts.

Hallux valgus and eversion of forefoot.

Exhibit V. Truflare, Trubalance, & Modified Lasts

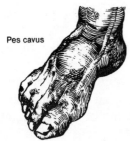

Pes cavus

Modified Last. Recommended for pes cavus foot shape, also for flexible pronated straight line foot. Long forepart and high broad toe with straight inner border line.

Short back part holds foot firmly while forefoot is unrestricted.

It's a good idea to have your feet measured on every shoe-buying trip, since foot size can change and lengthen with exercise or even weather conditions. One mail carrier told me, for example, that he experiences no foot problems most of the year. But when seasonal weather changes take place, his feet ache and grow tired so that he needs more rest than usual. Changes may even occur within the same day, especially under temperature conditions when it is cool in the morning and hot in the afternoon. The afternoon, incidentally, is the best time to try on shoes, according to most experts, since the feet expand slightly during this time of day. They also advise to try on both shoes and give them a good walking test in the store.

ANATOMY OF A GOOD SHOE

The shoe that fits properly, notes a spokesman for Scholl, Inc., will be a half-inch longer than your foot, with room at the front for toe movement. It will have a sole as wide as your foot, with the widest part at the second joint of the big toe, fit snugly at the heel and instep, and have a soft, supple upper made of fine leather or fabric.

Approximately 20 percent of athletic injuries could be prevented by proper shoes and prescreening for tight joints or other abnormalities, according to Dr. Dinesh Patel, co-director of Massachusetts General Hospital's Sports Medicine Clinic. This becomes understandable in light of the fact that millions of feet structured by nature to accommodate one type of last get squeezed, twisted and pushed into shoes modeled on a distinctly different type of last.

For any kind of exercise or athletic activity to be efficient a good walking shoe is a must. For miles and many hours of comfort, pick a style with a flat heel and broad, rounded toe. The well-fitted shoe will give the toes wiggle space on the one hand, but grip the back of the foot to keep the heel from sliding out and rubbing at each step. Good shoes are also designed to flex and bend in conjunction with the foot's "hinge"—located between the first and fifth toes.

From the higher grade manufacturer's point of view, shoes of superior quality are:

- Made of fine leather, usually plump, mellow calfskin or luxuriously soft kid that is naturally porous and lets the foot breathe. There is no substitute for leather. Unlike plastic and synthetics, it lasts longer and looks better as well.
- Carefully sewn, thus assuring that the seams will lie smoothly and that the finished shoe will not warp.
- Expertly *lasted*. Lasting is of prime importance in shoe-making, for it shapes the leather for the life of the shoe. First the upper is pulled firmly and smoothly over the toe last and temporarily fastened. Then the side laster smooths the upper over the last on each side and fastens it to the insole.
- Equipped with a strong firm welt. This is a strip of leather or other material stitched into the shoe between the sole and the upper. The welt holds the upper and insole leathers together.
- Fitted with steel shanks. Located at the underside of the shoe, the shanks are rolled under great pressure to insure a firm fit and lasting support under the insole.

Shoe manufacturer Johnston & Murphy adds: "The cavity between the insole and the outer sole is then filled with a mixture of ground cork and an adhesive. This mixture never really hardens, thus providing a comfortable, elastic surface for the foot as long as the shoe is worn.

"The outer of the shoe is roughed out of leather, which is then sewn to the shoe through the welting. The heels are attached with nails and glue, then both soles and heels are trimmed to closely conform to the shape of the shoe. The edges of the soles are coated with a wax-based ink and heat-treated to assure penetration. This treatment improves both the appearance and the durability of the sole edge. Finally, the soles are stained to compliment the color of the finished shoe, and sanded and buffed to a smooth finish. At this point, the last (the block or form shaped like the foot) is carefully pulled from the shoe, and the finished product is closely inspected.''

CAUTION: DON'T PUT YOUR FEET IN THE HANDS OF A SHOE CLERK

One day a woman limped into a New York shoe store and asked for Irving Russin, a shoe and foot "maven" with over thirty years in the business selling shoes and managing shoe stores. She was shopping for shoes and had been referred to Russin by a friend. She wondered if he could help her as he had once helped the friend.

Russin, a small, graying, affable man, replied, "I can try. What's the problem?"

As it developed, the woman had a fallen metatarsal which caused a variety of ills from foot cramps to burning and pain. For a long time she was convinced she could never be fitted, once had had a pair of shoes custom built at great expense, but it hadn't worked out. Russin examined and measured her feet and selected a pair of shoes properly suited to the shape of her foot. He inserted a metatarsal pad and went to the back of the store and made other adjustments, all of which took pressure off the metatarsal and off the ball of the foot. As a result, he relieved a condition that had been plaguing the woman for years.

The salesman, who has an impressive bag of such tricks, can recount dozens of similar stories. Most involve situations where, by ingeniously designing and locating a variety of special wedges, pads, foam rubber inserts and cutouts, he had helped customers solve all kinds of minor foot problems, and sometimes back problems as well since the two are sometimes closely related. More often than not the solution is simply to remove pressure from sensitive areas where the pain is being produced. But it must be noted that Russin is a rare exception among shoe store personnel. As he himself sadly admits, "Most shoe salesmen know very little about feet and about how to fit shoes."

Floyd Gilmore and other experts agree. If the shopper depends on the sales clerk, his chance of being properly fitted is slight. On top of this, even if a particular salesperson did happen to be well qualified for his job, it probably, from his way of thinking at least, wouldn't be in his best interest to do the job that's required. The problem is that proper fitting takes time, and even in the "better stores," most shoe clerks work on salary and commission. Thus the more shoes they sell, the more commissions they earn, so that fast turnover is the name of the shoe selling game. This is not true of most "comfort stores," (stores that specialize in custom fitting people who have special foot problems), according to Gilmore. Salespeople in these outlets usually work only on salary.

Of course, the really good salesperson understands like any other sales professional, that if he gives the customer a proper fit and good service, he will win the customer's loyalty and build up a following which over the long pull will stand him in good stead. In dealing with problem feet, however, even the pro who knows his business must know where to draw the line. "If my simple solutions don't help," Russin says, "I don't fool around. I send the customer to an orthopedist or podiatrist."

"That's the proper outlook to take," Gilmore notes. "A salesman's main obligation is to fit the shoe to the shape of the foot. When it comes to correcting the foot's balance, it's a specialist's job. The salesperson shouldn't try to play doctor."

Picking the Pros from the Schmoes. Unfortunately, the chief contribution made by too many shoe clerks, particularly in selling fashion shoes to female clientele, is the oft-repeated observation, "They look stunning on you."

How can you differentiate between the well qualified salesperson who actually helps in the selection and fitting of shoes and the clerk who functions as a fifth wheel in what is often a virtual self-service operation? One tipoff is the volume-oriented salesperson's strong focus on how the shoes look and his apparent disinterest in how they feel.

"A good shoe salesman," says Gilmore, "knows the foot's anatomy. He knows what goes into shoe construction. And he's experienced enough to spot when a problem exists."

On top of that, he'll check your feet when you are standing, not seated. Also while you are standing, he will measure *each* foot for length and width individually, keeping the likelihood of foot variations in mind and, assuming your shoes are not custom made, he will fit you to the longer foot. He will lace the shoe himself, and encourage you to test-walk the pair, questioning you when you do so to ascertain that there is no heel slippage or side gapping, no pinch or rub, and that the ball of the foot fits snugly where the arch meets the sole.

When was the last time you got this kind of service? Sometimes, in fact, the main difference between the "better store" where you're apt to pay $60 or more for a pair of shoes, and the mass volume store where shoes start at about $15 or $18, is that in the higher priced store the salesperson will remove the shoes you are wearing and lace up the pairs you try on, whereas the volume store sales clerk, waiting on three or four customers at a time, will let you do it yourself.

In essence, the salesperson who takes pride in the service he gives will provide you with the shoe that most closely fits the shape of your foot, which is always the number one consideration. If you find a pro who does this to the satisfaction of both you and your feet, he will be deserving of your loyalty. Finally, as Russin points out, if the conscientious salesperson sees a problem beyond his training and expertise, he will suggest that you visit an orthopedist or podiatrist. And as an added criterion, if you observe a particular salesperson being asked for by name by customers who come into the store, you can be pretty sure he has good service to offer.

DO YOU NEED SPECIALLY PRESCRIBED SHOES?

Where special foot problems requiring prescription footwear exist, and they do exist in a good many cases, lasts must be scientifically engineered and modified with three objectives in mind. To:

1. Fit each different foot shape with hindfoot control and forefoot freedom.

2. Accommodate prescribed corrections without losing the fitting requirements.

3. Hold its shape as a stable foundation to correct or rebalance the foot.

To be ideally fitted, the Alden Shoe Co., prescription footwear manufacturers, pinpoint 6 distinct foot types to which lasts must be tailored:

1. *Low Arch/Outflare:* A flat foot with marked angulation and forefoot eversion (evert meaning to turn inside out or outward). The last must accommodate enlarged great toe joint and Tailor's bunion.

2. *Low Arch/Straight:* A flat foot with straight inside flare and moderate angulation.

3. *Low Arch/Flexible:* A flat foot which is flexible and responds well to hind foot elevation. Usually not an extreme foot shape.

4. *Low Arch/Heavy:* A flat foot which is not only heavy but usually rigid as well. Sometimes having a lateral spread which must be accommodated for proper fitting.

5. *Moderate Arch/Straight:* For the straight, moderately weak foot which responds to elevation with inside correction. Moderate angulation (sharper than usual angle between the first and fifth toes) of ball tread.

6. *High Arch/Straight:* Usually a contracted high arch and high instep foot with straight inside line and little angulation of ball tread. Can have tight heel cords and contracted or even hammer toes.

If you have a relatively normal type foot, detailed information about the different foot types and last categories may be of interest to you, but not essential to the good health of your feet. If you're lucky enough to have bypassed the serious foot problems, your main concern should be to get a good fit and thus preserve the foot health you already enjoy.

But if you do have problem feet, or find it extremely difficult to get fitted, it may be worth your while to give the alternative of prescription footwear some serious thought. Needless to say, custom-built shoes are more expensive than shoes you buy off the shelf just like anything else that is tailored to your particular need. But—and this could be a big 'but' for you—if specially prescribed shoes relieve or prevent troublesome foot problems, they could save you over the long run, apart from the pain and physical limitations incurred, a bundle of money as well. This is especially true if, as a result of having your shoes made to order, you will avoid being treated by a doctor whose fees will probably be higher than either the custom fitted shoes themselves or any orthotic device (a custom-made shoe insert usually prescribed by a doctor) you may need.

SHOE CARE

Treat your shoes right and they'll be kind to your feet in return. Your footgear will give you better service, last longer, look better, and hold its shape well if you take proper care of it. Here are some guidelines to follow to get the most effective use out of the shoes you wear:

Cleanliness. Floyd Gilmore points out that the shoe is the only article of clothing that isn't washed. This needn't be so, he maintains. A shoe smells because of the presence of bacteria. One way to destroy the bacteria and thus eliminate the odor is to let the shoes dry out for 24 hours. Also, notes Gilmore, bleach will kill the bacteria. He suggests cleaning the inside of the shoe with a cloth lightly dipped into bleach.

Switching. Shoe experts agree that shoes will hold up better and maintain their attractive appearance if not worn every day. Ideally, you should have at least three pair of shoes to rotate. This isn't a luxury either, since it should take three times as long to wear out three pair of shoes as it would take to run down a single pair. Shoes need time to "recover" from being worn. The leather will reshape itself and the effects of perspiration will be diminished if the shoe is permitted to rest between wearings.

Leather Maintenance. Fine leather needs continued attention to retain its good texture and natural qualities. Dryness harms leather. Its natural oils and those absorbed in tanning must be replenished regularly. You can accomplish this by using three basic "nutriments"—saddle soap, shoe cream, and wax polish. Saddle soap removes stains and dirt from the surface. Shoe cream penetrates the leather and keeps it soft and supple. Wax polish restores the lustrous look of the leather, nourishes it, and protects the shoe surface from scuffing.

New Shoes. In the factory's finishing room, shoes are cleaned, polished and often sprayed to preserve the finish. But the polish tends to dry out by the time you start wearing the shoes. It's a good idea to apply a wax polish before your first wear to prevent scratches. After this, shoes should be periodically conditioned by applying saddle soap and letting it dry; working shoe cream into the leather, and buffing with a soft cloth; then applying wax polish to bring out a high gloss.

Weather. Rain, snow, and slush damage leather especially if shoes aren't treated immediately. If your shoes get soaked in a storm, insert shoe trees as soon as you get home and let them dry at room temperature, away from direct heat which tends to warp and twist the leather. When shoes are dry, apply wax polish. If you have a particularly warm place in your heart for your shoes, treat them to an application of mink oil, using around the seams and stitching and in more exposed areas.

Spots. After walking through snow and slush, notes Allen-Edmonds Shoe Co., white spots may appear on the shoe. This is due to salt and other ice-melting chemicals spread on sidewalks and streets. Unless these stains are treated immediately, the leather fibers can weaken and separate. First, let the shoes dry with shoe trees inserted. Then remove the deposits with saddle soap. If the leather is seriously discolored, touch up the affected area with a matching alcohol-based dye. Finally, recondition the leather with shoe cream, and then wax polish.

Never use any type of cleaner that contains an acid or detergent. Both damage fine leather and will age the shoe. If shoes become heavily soiled, try a mild application of Ivory soap on a damp cloth, wipe off, and allow to dry. Then apply paste wax or shoe cream.

Shoe Trees. Floyd Gilmore stresses the importance of inserting shoe trees after each wearing to maintain the proper shape of the shoes. Wooden shoe trees are usually better than metal since they absorb moisture while metal tends to corrode in time.

Shoe Horns. You should use one, made of metal or plastic, anytime you put on a pair of shoes. This keeps the back of the shoe intact and prevents it from being abused, an important factor in maintaining the shape.

WHAT ABOUT SNEAKERS?

"I love them," one custom shoe manufacturer told me. "They throw the body out of balance and bring us dozens of customers."

They also figure in the story of Bud Philips, a young New Jersey attorney, now a walking afficionado, who relates how he had gotten off to a terrible start. For one thing, together with a friend, John Gerstenberg, who had joined him in a mutual physical fitness pledge, he launched their program by taking a long (10 mile) hike before they were properly conditioned. On top of that, Philips recalls, "John and I wore thin-soled sneakers through which we could feel every stone on the path. And the synthetic rubber made our feet perspire heavily on the sunbeaten tarred roads as well."

Actually, the notion that sneakers are bad for your feet isn't a new one, or one that originated as a byproduct of the running/jogging craze. I can remember my own mother periodically admonishing me not to wear sneakers all day. ("You'll get flat feet!")

Well, I did wear sneakers on too many days and my feet never got flat. The subject is a somewhat controversial one today. Some foot doctors counsel against wearing sneakers; others don't. Podiatrist Rob McGregor, in fact, is convinced that the idea of sneakers ruining your feet is propaganda. Kids don't get tired or footsore from wearing sneakers, he maintains. "But that fat, indolent hypertensive adult who runs around in his sneakers on weekends is going to have a lot of problems. That's mainly because he *is* fat and indolent and hypertensive and he has a lousy musculoskeletel system. I don't think we should blame the sneaker."

Be that as it may. I don't expect to settle the controversy here. But one thing is for certain: There are sneakers, and there are sneakers. The old worry about sneakers being bad for the feet, promulgated by thousands of mothers along with my own, alluded undoubtedly to the cheap flimsily constructed footwear that in pre-inflation days sold for anywhere from about $1.50 a pair to $3.00 or $4.00 per pair for the better grades. Some of these sneaker types still sell for well under $10.00.

But in the main, as writer Perry Garfinkel tells us, even the word "sneaker" itself is passé. The correct term, he says, is "athletic footwear," if you please. Like the shoe industry, athletic footwear is big business today with no less than 26 companies turning it out, and not only the image, but the quality, has been substantially upgraded in recent years. So far as running in particular is concerned, cognizant that a great many foot and knee problems are caused by poor-fitting footwear, athletic shoe manufacturers have made significant design innovations with better foot health in mind.

How can you tell a "sneaker" from an "athletic shoe?" By its design and construction, for one thing; by its price for another. The better athletic shoes are well made—well padded, well cushioned, with elevated heel, and thick sole that is firm and strong, light weight but heavy duty. One glance at this shoe alongside the flimsy old-fashioned sneaker would instantly highlight the differences. The higher quality athletic shoes are usually priced at about $30 and upward a pair, with a slightly better price if you catch a good sale.

As the caption to Garfinkel's *Science Digest* article titled, "Anatomy of a Sneaker . . . er, Athletic Shoe," states: "Science has transformed the once lowly sneaker from an ugly slab of rubber and hunk of canvas into an extremely sophisticated and exotic piece of footwear.''

A WORD ABOUT SOCKS

The best socks for hard walking, hiking, exercise and athletic activity are those made of natural fabrics, most commonly cotton or wool. Nylon prevents the foot from breathing and causes it to perspire more freely, which fosters athlete's foot and produces friction as well.

However, some nylon reinforcement at heel and toe, usually 10 to 30 percent, increases the sock's durability without detracting appreciably from its other qualities. Are you better off with thick or thin socks? The thicker, tennis-weight variety is generally preferred for hard physical exercise for the resilience, sweat absorption and general comfort they offer. Wool is a good insulator too and keeps you warm in cold weather. But if you engage in brisk walking during warm summer months, you may find thin cotton socks cooler and more comfortable. Comfort, after all, is what it's all about— the main deciding factor in what to purchase and wear.

Some walkers and runners find that two pair of socks, with the thinner ones worn on the inside, helps reduce friction between feet and shoes. The best advice I can offer is to experiment on your own and pick the sock, or combination of socks, that gives you the most comfort and wear.

IN CONCLUSION: A FEW FOOTNOTES

- If you plan to do some rugged hiking or back-packing, you'll probably need a good pair of strong sturdy boots. Here especially, there's no substitute for leather. The better boots have smooth leather uppers, and a thin leather lining that adds warmth while it cuts down friction. For general use, a sole thickness of a half inch is about right. Of course, extreme terrains—mountains, desert, snow belts, etc. —will require boots that are made for the purpose.

- What about those fashionable boots for the ladies? Another matter entirely. Doctors advise against wearing them too many hours at a stretch. They are too binding and restrictive of the entire foot and leg structure from toe to knee. The synthetics, which cut off natural breathing from the knee down, are worst of all. If you must wear them because they're chic and in, at least zip them down or, better still, slip out of them from time to time when you visit or sit.
- Whether you shop for shoes or boots, run your fingers over the inside right down to the toes to spot for stitching or other protrusions that could chafe and irritate the foot.
- Even the way you lace your shoes could have an effect on foot comfort. If your shoes are too tightly laced the pressure may cause cramping or other foot pain. You can eliminate uncomfortable pressure down the lacing strip by easing up on the tightness, or inserting a tongue pad properly snipped to comfort convenience. And sometimes lacing your shoes from side to side instead of diagonally will help relieve instep pressure.
- Nothing is quite so invigorating as a brisk walk to work in the morning if you don't live too far away, or can drive or take public transportation part of the way. Podiatrist Dr. Paul Ruegsegger suggests to women who work that they keep a pair of extra fashionable shoes in the office or plant, so they can walk to work in lower heeled, broader toed comfortable shoes and change when they reach their destination.

8

STRAIGHTEN UP AND WALK RIGHT

"In our entrancement with the
motorcar, we have forgotten how
much more efficient and how much
more flexible the footwalker is."

Lewis Mumford

Let us assume your feet are in good shape and your
shoes fit right for the shape they are in. All right, now you're
ready to walk.

You would like to start a pace walking program to
slim down, shape up, or feel better—or for the sheer joy of
walking. Okay, what's the first step? Before getting seriously
involved, you probably have a few questions, such as: How
far? How fast? How to? Is there a right and wrong way to
walk?

Basically, the answers depend on your age, physical
capabilities, and limitations (if you have any). If you're not
elderly and if you are in relatively good shape—no serious
heart, lung or foot ailments—the answer may depend on your
goal. Why do you want to try serious walking? What do you
hope to get out of it?

An old Greek proverb tells us: "Before you can score
you must first have a goal."

Constancy to purpose, the British statesman Benjamin Disraeli agrees, is the secret of success.

In studies conducted at the University of California, a group of women were told to eat whatever they wanted to, but to get out and walk. They did, with determination and gusto, for up to 2 or 3 hours a day. At the end of a year, they lost an average of 22 pounds. "It is often said," Dr. Grant Gwinup comments, "that you can't actually lose weight by exercise alone. We found this was simply not true."

If you are convinced that the man or woman of your dreams will be yours if you take off 35 pounds and that brisk, energetic walking is the best way to do it, several hours a day might not seem an unreasonable amount of time to devote to this activity. What you hope and expect to get out of walking will help govern not only how much you walk, but your rate of speed as well.

HOW TO

What's the best way to walk? Is there a recommended style? Apart from adhering to the pace walking concept, these are tough questions to answer.

Next time you're seated on a park bench, standing on a street corner, or looking out of a window, take a few moments to observe the way people walk. You'll notice that just as no two pair of feet are exactly alike, no two people walk in just the same way. The way you walk is a highly personal matter. Posture, stride and gait vary from individual to individual. One person's stride is long and graceful; another uses short jerky steps. Some walkers swing their arms back and forth; others move hardly at all. One person's head bobs from side to side as he walks; another's remains still and erect.

If you are a close and perceptive observer, you can learn things about people from the way they walk. Studying a person's style and gait may tell you whether or not he takes pride in himself and has good self esteem. You can judge if an individual is self-confident from the way he or she walks, or if he or she is self-conscious and shy. Snobbishness is

Straighten Up And Walk Right   107

sometimes revealed as well, along with conceit and pomposity. Style of walking will give you clues as to whether a person is friendly and sociable, indrawn and meek, or has an authoritarian manner. Walking labels an individual as easygoing and tranquil, or rigid and tense.

Salespeople are counseled to walk into a prospect's office looking businesslike and alert, with shoulders back and head held high. Actresses and models are taught to walk erect holding a book on their heads. The way a person walks into a room causes him to be noticed or not. An accomplished leader usually walks with a natural dignity and poise; the braggard walks with a swagger. The way you walk plays an important part in shaping your image. Body language is a way of expressing yourself.

Walking adds to your beauty and grace, or decreases your appeal and attractiveness.

Some people walk unconventionally with long reaching steps in the manner of Abraham Lincoln. Others walk with a waddle in the manner of Alfred Hitchcock. Such styles may not be particularly graceful, but may make the person look more interesting.

The size and shape of your body and the length of your legs will help determine your walking style and gait. So will your mental outlook and general philosophy of life.

Improving Your Style. Can you improve the way you walk? Sure. You can improve almost anything you do if you work at it. But how hard you should work at developing an appealing walking style is another question only you can answer, referring again to your personal goals. My advice is not to be overly concerned about the way you look when you walk for the sake of appearance alone. For walking to be effective and enjoyable, it should be natural and comfortable. If you work too hard at correcting minor characteristics in a search for the ultimate in grace, walking may become too much of a chore and you'll be defeating your purpose. On the other hand—er, foot—if you developed habits over the years that make your walking less effective as an exercise, or impair your endurance or enjoyment of walking, it will be worth your while to work hard at eliminating them.

Take the duck walk, for example; toes turned out when you walk. Or the pigeon-toed walk, with feet turned in at each step. Such walking is undesirable, not only from an appearance standpoint, but for walking efficiency as well. The duck walk, in particular, tends to break down your arches and throw your leg and foot system—along with other parts of the body—out of alignment and balance. It also tires you faster and makes a brisk healthful pace more difficult. Pointing your toes straight out ahead of you in the direction you're walking will eventually get you out of these habits. A good daily exercise is to practice walking along a straight line in the manner of a tightrope walker. If he ever used the duck or pigeon-toed walk, he'd be in trouble.

Pay Attention To Your Posture. Good posture is as important to good walking as it is to general health. "Walk like you're wearing a crown," author Thomas Stonebeck advises.

"Bad posture *can* be corrected," notes Dr. Raymond Harris, who wrote *Guide To Fitness After Fifty.* "And it's *never* too late to start."

The fact is, Stonebeck adds, "It's not easy to face the world with poor posture. When you're slumped forward, it shifts your body weight backward from the vertebrae of the spine to the muscles and ligaments of the lower back—which leads to fatigue, disfiguration such as swayback (the medical term is lordosis) and pain."

Medical and fitness writer Magda Rosenberg counsels: "When you walk, stand straight, and pull in your stomach and buttocks. Straighten out your shoulders and hold your head up, but don't tilt it back. Make believe that there is a line up your spine straight through your head. For a longer and more graceful stride, swing your legs from the hip as you take each step, and let the motion of your hips propel you. Don't walk from the knees; the knee joints are most vulnerable to injury. As you walk, swing your arms freely. Put a bounce in your step."

The key to posture improvement is constant awareness. Think straight often enough, and you'll walk straight eventually, even if you formerly walked with a slouch. Stretching and straightening exercises also help. Like anything else, breaking a bad habit is mainly a matter of repetition and practice. Repeat the good straight walking habit on a day-to-day basis and it will supersede the bad one quickly enough.

STEPPING OUT ON THE TOWN

John Edwards, a man of 40 I know, who has been sedentary for at least 15 years, told me recently he had decided to do something about it. I asked him what he had in mind. Knowing me as an enthusiastic walker, he wanted to know if I thought walking could help him.

"It can help anyone," I replied, "who goes about it in the right way."

"I'm 25 pounds overweight," Edwards said, "and I get winded too easily. What do you think I should do?"

I advised him to map out a walking program, starting with relatively modest objectives, and gradually working himself, at his own pace, up to a daily regimen of three or four miles per hour. I also advised him to check first with his doctor, and assuming he got the go-ahead, to make sure he owned a comfortable pair of well made shoes.

After helping him work out the details, I said, "Don't expect dramatic changes overnight. Don't forget—it took you 15 years to get yourself out of shape. You won't reverse the tide in a week."

A few weeks later I ran into Edwards and asked how he was doing with his walking program. His reply was half irritated, half apologetic. "That isn't for me. I got aches and pains where I never had them before, and felt more tired than ever. I'm planning to join up at the Spa."

Further questioning revealed he had tried to accomplish too much in too little time, became discouraged when he saw no results, and quit in less than a week.

I pulled no punches in telling him, "John, on that basis you're right. Walking isn't for you."

He gave me a look, then grumbled, "You may have a point. Maybe I'll try it again."

Maybe he will; maybe he won't.

A fact of life well worth facing is that longstanding habits aren't easy to break. We tend to become set in our ways. Periodically struck by inspiration, anxiety, or short-lived bursts of resolution, we impulsively decide to take action.

It usually takes more than that, which brings us back to the subject of goals. Oliver Wendell Holmes once said, "The great thing in this world is not so much where we stand as in what direction we are moving."

My friend John Edwards knew well enough where he stood, but lacked the motivation to keep moving ahead toward his goal. Another man I know is a walking afficionado today because he had the right motivation. He started his program shortly after his annual physical checkup. As he put it, "My doctor scared the hell out of me."

A woman I read about in a national magazine had the right motivation when she discovered her husband was losing interest in her because she had become flabby and lethargic. Another woman initiated a successful walking program when she went on record as resolving to lose 15 pounds in six months, and backed up her commitment by betting a friend fifty dollars she would do it. She won the bet and has remained slim ever since.

A doctor told me just the other day, "I'd bet millions of people would become brisk walkers in a hurry if they really knew how much was at stake." ·

Cliché or not, it is one of life's great truisms: You will succeed if you have the will to succeed.

Thomas Carlyle wrote: "A man (this was before the women's movement) with a half-volition goes backwards and forwards, and makes no way on the smoothest road; a man with a whole volition advances on the roughest and will reach his purpose, if there be even a little wisdom in it."

If you've been physically inactive for years and are truly determined to do something about it, start your program with short walks of up to ten minutes at a time. Gradually increase the distance and pace on a day-to-day basis. Dr. Robert B. Sleight, executive director of The Walking Association in Arlington, Virginia, states, "For most people, walking should begin at a comfortable speed. Gradually increase speed to one mile in 20 minutes, then up to three miles in an hour. Finally, for many people, a reasonable goal is three miles in 45 minutes."

No one knows better than you how you feel. Monitor your system closely any time you take exercise. Pay heed to the signals you get back from your body. If you can breeze through that allotted 10 minutes with no problem, you're ready to step up your regimen.

In testing yourself, however, The President's Council on Physical Fitness and Sports offers a word of caution: "If during these tests you experience nausea, trembling, extreme breathlessness, pounding in the head, or pain in the chest, stop immediately. If the symptoms persist beyond the point of temporary discomfort, check with your physician.

"The symptoms described are signs that you have reached the limits of your present exercise tolerance. The point at which they occur will indicate where you should begin in the exercise program."

Pay close attention to your feet and knees as well. If you experience anything more than a minor problem you can remedy with a corn pad or moleskin patch, check it out with your doctor before going on with the program.

DO IT DAILY

I've touched on this point in an earlier chapter, but it bears repetition: Exercise daily whether you walk, swim, ride a bicycle, or run. Keep in mind the woes of the "weekend jock." Especially as you get past age 35, occasional spurts of energy can do you more harm than good.

Exercise needs vary from one person to the next, but under ordinary conditions most doctors recommend 40 to 60 minutes every day as a minimum. And they stress the need for regularity. The notion that one can achieve an acceptable level of strength, endurance, and flexibility by working out in a spa once or twice a week or with that once or twice a week tennis game is little more than wishful thinking despite the weight loss experienced (which is probably due more to sweated-out water than anything else). Studies and surveys prove that daily bouts of exercise produce the best results.

A spokesman for Manhattan's Executive Health Examiners sums it up in a nutshell: "It's the daily routine that works best, and 15 minutes a day is better than two hours twice a week."

SPEED AND DISTANCE OBJECTIVES

I'll never forget how pleasantly surprised I was once I learned how to walk properly, that I could increase my rate of speed 30 percent or so and find the faster pace less tiring than the way I formerly walked. It was a revelation to me and I have since heard this statement echoed by dozens of serious walkers. I had always taken it for granted as most people probably do that the faster you move, the more energy you expend, the more tired you get. It's not so.

Actually, I had been walking for years before I really started to pace walk. Let me explain what I mean by this seeming contradiction. Getting back to the start of my walking experience, it would be hard to imagine a more sedentary occupation than that of a writer. Other than when I visit an editor or travel somewhere to do research, I am seated at my typewriter. You may recall my mentioning earlier that it was this prolonged sitting without any physical activity that led to a back problem some years ago. The solution to the back problem was exercise. Since finding this out the hard way, I interrupt my stint at the typewriter every hour or so with two or three minutes of moving around, and twice a day go outside for walks.

I had been doing this for 12 years or so on the premise that walking was good for my health in general and my back in particular. But not until recently had I given any thought to how fast I was walking. Nor had it occurred to me that 'walking' might mean anything other than moving one foot after the other at my habitual rate. It was only when I started doing research for this book that a host of new facts started revealing themselves.

The walking I had done before this time had apparently helped my back since it was functioning well with the help of occasional chiropractic 'adjustments'. But in my conversations with doctors, most notably cardiologists, I learned that for walking to be most beneficial it must be sufficiently vigorous to produce a "tonic effect." As one doctor pointed out, "It should make you work hard enough to breathe heavily and even perspire a little."

That's when I started to step up my pace, in part by moving a bit faster, but mostly by lengthening my stride. Two benefits quickly resulted. First I could walk more and tire less. Second, after about six weeks of this my average weight dropped as if by magic from 178 pounds to 175, just about what it should be for my height and build.

Dr. Alan Levy, who is the physician for the (football) Giants and the (basketball) Nets, put it to me tersely enough: "Walking at a good brisk pace for more than 20 minutes at a time, raises the pulse rate to 70 percent of maximum. It is just as good as running."

Doing What Comes Naturally. Some doctors advise patients to walk at their natural pace. But they often fail to point out that their natural pace is not necessarily their habitual pace, or the pace they have become accustomed to using. Most people walk slower than their natural pace for a variety of reasons: restrictions created by clothing or ill-fitting shoes, the simple habit of not moving briskly, or the habit of taking short steps. The solution, of course, is to smoothly *pace* your walking.

As the pace walker knows from experience, merely by stepping a bit livelier and increasing the length of your step to your body's normal capacity (which depends on your age, physical condition, and the length of your legs) you fall into the natural rhythm and momentum that carries you freely and easily from one stride to the next. In the process your walking rate is boosted from slow to moderate to brisk. You keep a giant step ahead of fatigue; you burn more fat-producing calories; and you do the most good for your cardiovascular system.

What is *your* natural pace? The main determining factor is your height and the length of your legs. The way to find out is simply to lengthen your stride and walk energetically. However, sometimes doing what comes naturally can lead to unnatural problems. Jack and Mary, a couple I know, decided to enter a walking program together in order to lose pounds and gain health. When they asked me how fast they should walk, I advised them to try what I stated above: "Step lively and lengthen your stride." They decided to take my advice.

Jack and Mary both leave for work at 8:15 in the morning. Part of their exercise plan, they confided, was to rise a half hour earlier each day and take a brisk walk together. If that's not "togetherness," I don't know what is.

"That sounds great," I replied.

A week later they were back with a beef. They had followed my advice to the letter. "The trouble is," Jack explained, "my comfortable natural stride is about 125 steps per minute, according to my watch; Mary's is just a little bit over 100." He is six feet four inches tall; Mary is five feet three-and-a-half.

"We can't exercise together," Jack groused. "We each have to walk alone."

I had no answer for that.

THE AGE LIMITATION

The U.S. Army's standard for a brisk walking pace is 120 steps per minute. This may be easy for one person, hard for another. A 17-year-old, athletically active youth could probably walk 5 miles at this rate without breathing hard. A 70-year-old might be taxed to the extreme.

Supreme Court Justice and hiking afficionado William O. Douglas wrote about a three-day backpacking trip along the Olympic Beach in the State of Washington he once took with a group of about 160 people. Of these, 26 were over 60, four were over 70 years old, and four under 10 Douglas himself was 66 at the time.

"Though the teen-ager can walk competitively," Douglas notes, "the oldster must set his own pace. That is why hiking outlasts tennis, squash, touch football and other sports. At the age of 66, I cannot keep up with the 26-year-old hiker. It would be foolish to try. But I can finish the 30 miles before dark—if I set my own pace. A stroll is not a hike. Strolling indeed is tiring. Why, I am not sure. But a bracing hike is invigorating, and while one comes in weary, a 30-mile hike will give his body a good tone for several days.

If you are 60 or over, taking for granted how much tone you can endure safely and comfortably may not be a very good idea. That 30-mile hike Justice Douglas talks about could be a bit much even for youngsters of 40 and 50.

"Fortunately," states a booklet prepared jointly by The President's Council on Physical Fitness and Sports and the Administration on Aging, "even if you have let too many years slip by when good intentions of keeping fit were sacrificed to other demands of life, you still can pick up at *some level of physical performance* and work yourself up several notches."

How many notches will depend on the shape you are in, best determined after a chat with your doctor, and the amount of energy you are willing and able to expend.

The best indication of how much and how strenuous exercise you can take will be your own body's responses. Notes Dr. Louis C. Galli, head of the Medical Committee for the New York Marathon, "If you walk until you are tired or breathless, or get cramps in your legs, especially the back of the legs, it will give you an idea of your capabilities."

Cardiologist Dr. George Sheehan, who is the author of "Running and Being," states, "Cardiac stress tests and other analytical techniques will be no help if you don't listen to your body."

This applies at age 30, as well as age 80.

ON HILLY TERRAIN

The longest mile I ever walked was in hilly San Francisco from my daughter's apartment to the Mark Hopkins Hotel. It was uphill most of the way and I was bushed before I reached my destination.

The definition of a mile is precise: It measures 5,280 feet, in cold weather or hot, on a sunny day in Miami or a rainy day in Pittsburgh. But a mile can seem interminably long if you walk it in extremely hot weather, in ill-fitting shoes, or on particularly rough or hilly terrain. If you are badly out of shape, exercise up and down hills may be too taxing for your system, and in extreme cases, dangerous.

One mark of the skilled and experienced walker is that he or she walks with an easy, natural rhythm and stride. This is simple to maintain and in time will become habitual on level ground. Walking hills is another matter entirely, due to the change in the relationship between your body and the angle that is formed by the hill which shifts the center of gravity. Thus walking up and down hills, you will have to develop a completely different style. Climbing uphill, try to find a new kind of rhythm arrived at by shortening your step and leaning slightly forward from the ankles. Make sure your forward tilt is not from the hips since continually leaning forward from the hips will strain your lower back muscles, resulting in back fatigue (and more serious problems if repeated too often).

Walking downhill, the idea is to reduce your speed and stride until you attain maximum comfort, thus avoiding excessive pressure and strain on your knees, ankles and feet. Actually, three different rhythms are involved in uphill, downhill and ground level walking. Time and experience will help you find the ideal style and rhythm for you. In the meantime, the important thing to remember is that if you are timing yourself when you walk, or trying to establish your most efficient and productive pace, it should be done on level ground.

WALKING TOGS AND ACCOUTREMENTS

Following an interview with Dan Green, an associate publisher of Simon and Schuster, which put out "Running and Being," regarded by running cultists as a metaphysical treatise, *Newsday* columnist Leslie Hanscom predicted that the torrent of books on the joy of running would soon be superseded by an avalanche of walking books. Should his forecast come true, and here at least is one piece of evidence, America may soon be swamped by a rash of walkathons (walking events), walkarenas (places where walkers can walk), and walkemporiums (marts where walkers can purchase all kinds of walking togs and accoutrements from W Shirts and warmup suits to gold-knobbed walking sticks and jeweled pedometers).

Actually, the fact of the matter is if there is one exercise or athletic activity—depending on how you prefer to think of it—where no special equipment or facilities are needed, it is walking. Running ranks a close second. So unless you decide to adopt walking as a cult requiring special outfitting and emblems, please feel free to do it in your everyday clothes and at the time and place of your choice.

That doesn't mean you shouldn't pay attention to what you wear when you walk. You should, at least to the extent that clothing, and most certainly footgear, plays a major role in the comfort index you achieve. Thus in all kinds of weather, when it comes to how you dress, apart from any personal concern you may have about your appearance, comfort is the main factor to consider in selecting your walkrobe.

Basically, the objective in cold weather is to keep warm. And the most comfortable garments are the kind that insulate you best against the wind and chill and at the same time aren't too heavy. Some of the light weight ski jackets on the market are ideal for this purpose. I picked one up at a sale for the amazing believe-it-or-not price of $16.99.

It is also important in cold weather to keep the extremities covered. A confirmed sissy, when the temperature hovers around 25 to 30 degrees, for example, I go out walking garbed in my superbargain of a ski jacket with a wool sweater on underneath it. Tennis socks warm my feet; a wool scarf protects my neck against the chill; one of those fake black Persian lamb hats with the ear flaps turned down keep my head and ears warm; a pair of lined leather gloves take care of my hands. I may look like a man from outer space, but the winter chill doesn't cause me to shiver.

If the weather is under 25 degrees, or if it's a blustery 32, I don't go out walking at all. I walk in my house making the circuit through living room, kitchen, and dining room.

Keeping comfortably cool in warm weather is less of a problem. If the temperature range is from the middle sixties to the mid-eighties, light slacks and a sport shirt will serve you just fine. I like to wear an undershirt under the sport shirt to absorb the perspiration. If the weather is hot rather than warm, I find a shady place to walk, although there are times when the temperature is in the high sixties or seventies when it feels delightful to walk with the sun beating down on you. A pair of good quality sunglasses will remedy any sun glare problem. When the thermometer soars into the nineties, I prefer to do the old reliable living room-kitchen-dining room circuit with the air conditioner going full blast.

Do You Need a Pedometer? Actually, you can walk efficiently and effectively without one, although you may find it a handy gadget to own. They're not very expensive. You can pick up a good one in a department or sporting goods store for about twelve dollars or so. A pedometer, adjusted to the length of your stride (a simple adjustment to make) will tell you how far you've walked. Thus, if your objective is to go two, three or four miles, you won't undershoot or overshoot your target. Dividing the number of minutes you walk by the amount of distance you cover will, of course, give you your walking rate, a good figure to know.

Personally, I'm more concerned about the amount of time I spend walking than the distance I cover, so I find a wristwatch essential. As long as you own a stopwatch or standard watch with a second hand, you don't really need a pedometer. But you may want one regardless. One thing it can do is add a bit of fun and interest to your walking program.

Walkers In The Night. If you decide to become a night walker, and live in an area where you can do this without getting mugged, what you wear can be a safety as well as a comfort factor, especially if you plan to walk on roads where cars travel. In that case, it's a good idea to wear light clothes that will make you more visible to motorists. As an added precaution, you have the options of a reflective vest, reflective wrist band, or strips of reflective tape on your shoes.

Walking Sticks. Here's a no-charge prediction: Walking sticks will come back into vogue as walking comes into its own. Cane producers report that sales already are up sharply over previous years.

Is a cane a useful walking accessory to own? Could be, especially if you plan to walk on trails or along rough terrain. But regardless of where you walk, walking sticklers praise the cane's value as a rhythm aid and abetter. The repeated swing of the stick acts as a kind of metronome for walkers, helping to create a regular back and forth beat. On hilly or wooded paths the walking stick can be used as a kind of third leg when needed, a means of balance and support.

When the going gets rough, notes author Colin Fletcher, a good sturdy cane will convert you from an insecure biped to a confident triped, and serve as a balancing aid when you're crossing a creek in the bargain.

On top of better rhythm and balance, there are some who claim psychological benefits as a byproduct of carrying a walking stick. These include:

- The added security you get when walking alone down a dark city street.
- Protection should you be attacked by an unfriendly dog.
- Additional peace of mind if you have a solid brass or hardwood cane near at hand should your car break down in a deserted area.
- And swinging a walking stick while you walk can help give you a bouncy and jaunty gait that is exclusively yours.

9

THE THINKING PERSON'S EXERCISE

"Walking has the best value as
gymnastics of the mind."

Ralph Waldo Emerson

One of the most useful and, at the same time, most taken-for-granted benefits of walking is the therapeutic effect it can have on one's mind. This is especially significant today in light of the psycho-biological shock being inflicted on so many of us by the jolting impacts of rapid change coupled with growing uncertaintly regarding many vital aspects of our lives. Never in the history of mankind has any society been subjected to such dangerously high levels of tension, anger, fear and anxiety.

As a nation what are we doing in response? One thing we are most certainly doing is stuffing an unprecedented volume of medications and drugs down our gullets. The American consumer spends mind-boggling sums on tranquilizers, sleeping pills, elixirs and mechanical aids to induce relaxation. Each year increased millions are spent merely to advertise the newest crop of tablets, soporifics and drugs introduced on the marketplace. Despite innumerable warnings by medical experts that pill popping rarely reduces the underlying causes of tension and anxiety and can produce serious side effects in the bargain, the public continues buying and popping.

It becomes increasingly clear that unless steps are taken to deal more intelligently and effectively with anxiety and stress, conditions will inevitably worsen as pressures continue to mount and build in intensity. In the view of many psychiatrists and psychologists, what many Americans in the pressurized mainstream of life need most are psychological time outs to wind down and get back to normal.

It is here that mounting evidence underlines the therapeutic value of walking. As one doctor told me, "If millions of Americans could develop the habit of walking off their anxieties with the deliberation and regularity with which they pop tranquilizers and antidepressants, we'd enjoy a more peaceful and healthy society with such diseases as high blood pressure and ulcers greatly reduced."

SOMA & PSYCHE: GET THE TEAM WORKING TOGETHER

It's no secret that mental turmoil can produce a host of bodily ailments. Or that physical problems can throw your thoughts all out of kilter. As psychiatrist Dr. James Lawrence Evans, Jr. points out, "A close corollary exists between body and mind. A strong healthy body can do wonders for our mental outlook, and visa versa."

The mind and body interact continuously, sending signals back and forth on a regular basis. Your mental and physical well-being depend in large measure on the amount of effective teamwork you can foster between them. Human beings function in a sense like computers. A monitoring and control system—the proprioceptive nerve network—operates much like a central core unit, the part of the computer that processes information and instructions. Actually, prioceptors are sensory receptors, chiefly in muscles, tendons and joints. They respond to stimuli arising within the organism, thus keeping tabs on your bodily functions and informing your master control unit, the brain, how everything is going.

Messages travel both ways. If we get a worrisome thought, muscles tighten in response. If we sense a pain in the stomach or chest, nerve ends relay the news to the brain, resulting in a wave of anxiety.

As any doctor could confirm, when people are stricken with certain physical illnesses they tend to function irrationally. Conditions that affect us physiologically—heat, humidity, oxygen level, air impurity—can have a profound effect on our minds. At times when we are hardly aware of it, the body may be exercising powerful control over our thoughts. Control may be positive or negative depending on the kind of messages being transmitted.

It is where the message exchange is continuously and overwhelmingly detrimental that we get into trouble. A kind of pattern develops and the danger is getting caught up in a damaging cycle, or "loop." The psyche, in such a situation, sends out SOS's stemming from anxiety, anger and fear. The physiological responses—aches, pains, tremors, nausea—are quickly relayed back. Clearly the process undermines both the mind and the body, and it usually takes more than pills or medication for the cycle to be broken.

"Anxiety isn't a natural state; we talk ourselves into it," explains Joseph N. Paquette, Ph. D, a psychologist with Fair Lawn, New Jersey's Counseling and Psychotherapy Center. "The most extreme manifestation of anxiety is panic." He calls the specter of a drowning person to mind. He is drowning because he is not thinking clearly. His emotions are in control; they dictate his bodily movement and a visceral reaction takes place.

To function normally and healthfully, Dr. Paquette maintains, "A person must bring his thinking and actions into balance. In a state of anxiety, one or the other gets out of hand and takes over control."

He uses the Ballantine three ring logo as an analogy, except that here the rings represent thinking, feeling and action. For normalcy to prevail, all three must be in balance and smoothly coordinated. In the over-anxious or hyper individual the balance is upset, thus depriving him of the ability to exercise logic.

"Introducing a physical activity," states Dr. Paquette, "is an acceptable method of dissipating anxiety. In the absence of movement," he explains, "anxiety manifests itself viscerally: the stomach muscles contract, other muscles tighten, breathing becomes labored; our normal stress tolerance is exceeded.''

You can see how this works for yourself, he suggests. Deliberately tighten your stomach muscles. Then try to breathe. You will soon get the picture.

"Walking," Dr. Paquette adds, "enables you to release your anxiety in an easy and natural way. Your stomach muscles relax. You can breathe easily again.''

It is a medically valid means of introducing positive input into the system already battered by too heavy and continuous a barrage of negative proprioceptive messages. The rhythmic action of walking forces muscles to function in harmonious and coordinated fashion. This can have a remarkably soothing and smoothing effect on the whole nervous system. It creates a genuine and natural tranquility caused by the easing of muscle tension and the dissipation of anxieties, far more healthful and beneficial than the *semblance* of tranquility artificially induced by drugs and pills which numb, dull and slow the brain.

Executive Health Report describes the beneficial effect of walking on the nervous system as "vastly important." The value of psychosomatic physiology and medicine, it states, has not been adequately appreciated. It concludes further that a five mile walk "will do more good for an unhappy and otherwise healthy man than all the tranquilizers (today so much overused and abused) with none of these drugs' side-effects!"

Dr. Gabe Mirkin, nationally known sports medicine authority, echoes this opinion. Exercise later in life, he says, can increase longevity and have a more tranquilizing effect than the most commonly used tranquilizers.

A psychiatrist I interviewed called to mind a patient who, on one of her early visits, appeared more uptight and tense than he had ever seen her. She was so upset she even showed up more than an hour early for her session, having mistaken the time. When the doctor pointed this out, it seemed to make her more distraught than ever. Although the psychiatrist was expecting another patient within a few minutes a thought occurred to him. He took the woman's blood pressure and noted that it was dangerously close to the 200 mark.

"Do me a favor," he said. "It's a beautiful day. Instead of waiting all tensed up in the office, go outside and take a nice long walk. Blank your mind if you can. Let the sun beat down hard on your face. Do your best to relax."

The patient followed his counsel. When her session started an hour or so later, she was noticeably calmer and much more relaxed. The doctor took her blood pressure again and saw it had plummeted down to a more comfortable 165. It was evidence enough to convince this intelligent patient whose main diagnosis was "anxiety neurosis" to make walking part of her regular daily regimen from that day on.

At this point I must throw in a disclaimer. The foregoing explanation of how the anxiety cycle can be broken is necessarily oversimplified. Exercise in general and walking in particular most certainly can be of great value in situations that are not too far out of hand. Where deep and serious mental health problems exist, however, it takes more than exercise to restore the psyche to normal although, even in situations of deep anxiety or depression, exercise often is included as part of the recovery or rehabilitation program. Dr. Evans who, along with many other psychiatrists, rates walking as "the best exercise there is," strongly endorses it as a vital rehabilitation tool.

ESCAPE THERAPY

Quite literally, walking away from mental pressures and irritants can produce psychological magic. However as much as we may love our spouse and children, enjoy our friends, or appreciate our job, there are times when the strongest need we feel at the moment is to get off by ourselves. If you work aggressively to recognize and appreciate this need when you feel it, and identify it as normal and natural and no valid source of guilt feelings, you will be able to deal with it realistically and, hopefully, do something about it.

What I'm talking about is walking as a means of escape from harassing household or job situations when pressures start to build beyond acceptable limits. Sometimes you can, with a little advance planning and forethought, walk away from your problems. That doesn't imply the problems will solve themselves in your absence. But the odds are high they will seem a whole lot less formidable.

Walk away? Where? Destination isn't important. In fact, the most practical destination of all may be no destination at all. The idea is to wander off like a fast-moving gypsy.

Of course, many would-be escapees—housewives, in particular—may feel they can't afford this luxury. One woman told me quite bluntly, "Are you kidding? I don't have the soft life my husband has. Eight hours on the job and he knows he's finished. My work is never done."

This point of view might be hard to deny or refute, and doing so might take another book in itself. But one point can be made: Once we overcome mental turmoil, we function a great deal more efficiently.

I know a mother of three small children who has eight or ten teen-age "stringers" on tap. When she feels the need for escape therapy, she gets on the telephone and keeps calling until she finds one available for an hour. Then she takes off and just walks, often around a large park in the neighborhood.

"I think of this as strictly selfish me-time," she explains. "But actually it benefits the whole family, especially the kids. The walk gives me a chance to reaffirm my identity. It helps me put my life in perspective, and gives me a priceless solitude I couldn't begin to describe."

She walks as briskly as possible, because her mind and body seek a kind of coordination and rhythm only fast walking can bring. How fast? She doesn't know. She never timed herself and has no interest in doing so now. "But if I walked any faster," she says, "I think I'd be running."

She believes the walking is also good for her physical fitness and looks. ("I never come back feeling tired.") And all it costs is a dollar for the sitter. When she returns home she feels recharged and renewed, more loving and patient, a better mother than ever.

I asked her if she tried to blank her mind while she walked. She replied slowly, after pausing to ponder the question. "Not really. I think of all kinds of things. I suppose to some extent I even fantasize and dream." She grinned. "I think some of my thoughts would probably shock my husband. That's fine. It makes the time all the more private. The one thing I *don't* think about is household chores and obligations."

She told me that at one time she believed that getting away meant simply changing the scene. "If the household bit got to me or the kids were driving me up the wall, I'd get away to the supermarket if I could, or run Jim's suit over to the cleaner's. But it isn't the same. There's something about taking off on a long walk by yourself and *for* yourself. There's something about the physical movement involved, the rhythm of body and mind in synchronized harmony. That dollar outlay three or four times a week is the best investment I make."

It's an interesting thought. You are never more your own person than when you are off walking alone. It's one of the few and rare times when no one can make demands on you or influence your thinking. Nobody can invade your privacy against your will. You're in charge. You're the one in control.

CONTROLLING STRESS

Stress is as much a part of our day-to-day lives as polluted air and inflation. But unlike air pollution and inflation, stress doesn't have to be bad for you. It is what makes some people function effectively and get a kick out of life. Others, unfortunately, respond to stress with ulcers and heart attacks. Controlled, stress can provide the energy and incentive needed for outstanding performance. Uncontrolled, it can kill us.

We are concerned here primarily with uncontrolled stress and what we can do to control it. Specifically, this is the kind of stress that activates gastric juices when they are supposed to be still, eroding stomach linings and resulting in ulcers. It is the kind of stress that raises the blood pressure, causes indigestion and heart problems, creates breathing difficulties, strains marriage and other relationships, provokes temper outbursts and accidents, drives men and women to drink, and triggers the sale of billions of dollars worth of tranquilizers and drugs.

In the world of business, stress undermines productivity, boosts absenteeism, hikes insurance costs for hospitalization and premature death. The dollar loss to American industry attributed to stress ranges from $10 billion to $20 billion a year, depending on whose estimate you go by. It's no wonder more and more corporations are sponsoring exercise and other programs designed to help the stress-prone executive, and declaring that the investment makes good business sense.

What Causes Stress? Dr. Hans Selye, director of the International Institute of Stress at the University of Montreal, has been studying stress most of his life. He breaks down the physiological process (or "general adaptation syndrome" as he calls it) into three stages: alarm reaction, resistance and exhaustion. During the first stage, the body acknowledges the stressor (stress inducing factor), which might be the news of getting fired. The body's response is immediate. The pituitary-adrenal-cortical system produces arousal hormones necessary for either "flight or fight"—that is, either adapting to the stressor or resisting it. The pulse quickens and the lungs take in more oxygen to fuel the muscles, the blood sugar level goes up, the pupils dilate, digestion slows and perspiration increases.

In the resistance/adaptive stage, the body begins to repair the damage done by arousal, and the stress symptoms mostly vanish. But if the stressful situation continues, the body's adaptive energy will eventually run out and exhaustion will set in. During this stage, bodily functions will slow down and continued exposure to stress will result in disease. The weakest organs, determined by hereditary predisposition, diet and life style, will break down first.

An infinite variety of stressors bombard us from all directions at any and all hours of the day. Most are minor and momentary, but get enough of them working together and the cumulative effect can be significant. Someone cuts you off in busy traffic. The damned telephone doesn't stop ringing when you're trying to think. A competitor makes a move that gets an edge on you. Your boss reminds you about a past due report. The shoemaker soaks you $4.50 for a pair of heels, and after a week you can see they won't last more than a couple of months. You're late for work and the train doesn't arrive. Someone's operating a pneumatic drill just outside your office window.

Then there are the persistent and repetitive stressors, the ones you live with day in and day out. You hate your boss and can't keep it out of your mind. An employee working for you does a substandard job, and flauntingly couldn't care less; but you can't fire him because of his long seniority, and you can't transfer him because no one else wants him. You have marital problems that seem to get progressively worse; your sex life is lousy and you're constantly bickering. You're having trouble with the kids; they're rambunctious and refuse to obey you. Trying to communicate with them appears to be a hopeless affair.

This is just a very small sampling of some of the stresses attacking millions of Americans each day.

How Vulnerable Are You? Stress is inevitable. There's no way to escape it other than becoming a hermit. The question is: Who's in charge, you or the stress? Are you a *victim* of stress? Or managing to keep it fairly well under control? The following checklist will give you some indication. How many of the following signposts of stress ring a bell for you personally? Respond to the following questionnaire as objectively as you can. Then score yourself at the end.

1. Do you often gulp down your meals?
2. Are you angry and irritable much of the time?
3. Do you feel you can't keep up with the clock?
4. Do you sleep poorly at night or take sleep-inducing drugs?
5. Do you smoke too much?
6. Do you have frequent headaches?

7. Do you have very few enjoyable interests outside of your work?
8. Do you take more than two hard drinks at lunch or before dinner?
9. Do you rarely take a vacation?
10. Do you suffer from indigestion?
11. Do you often feel tense and unable to relax?
12. Are you bored much of the time?
13. Do you pop too many pills?
14. Do you feel insecure in your job?
15. Do you hate your boss?
16. Do you feel you're not getting the salary and recognition you deserve?
17. Do you have trouble getting along with your spouse?
18. Do you worry about the future?
19. Do you feel you receive more frustration than joy from your children?
20. Are you tired much of the time?

If you have three or less YES answers, you probably have stress pretty well under control. Four to 6 YES answers puts you in the average category. Seven or more mean you are probably under significant stress with corrective measures recommended as quickly as possible.

Drs. Robert L. Woolfolk and Frank C. Richardson, psychologists and co-authors of "Stress Sanity and Survival," call attention to what they describe as, misconceptions about stress. The No. 1 myth, they say, is that people always know when they're under stress. No so, they claim. Often people become so accustomed to stress that they become unaware of it. Or we may suffer the debilitating effects of stress without feeling tense.

Another misconception is that stress only affects people who live high-pressure lives. "Many ordinary individuals," say the psychologists, "experience the constant stress of worry, leading unfulfilled lives or of not being what they would like to be. Stress," they add, is not caused by events that happen to us, "but rather the views we take of events."

What Can You Do About It? To counter undesirable stress, become active. Many people under pressure forget that plain physical action will help dissipate stress if you do it consistently.

In a well publicized experiment, Dr. Hans Selye subjected ten sedentary laboratory rats to the repeated ordeal of blinding lights, deafening noise and electric shocks. Within a month all ten rats were dead.

He then selected ten other rats from the same lab group and forced them to run on a treadmill until they were in prime muscular condition. He then subjected them to the same stress impacts endured by the ten rats that had died. After a month of this torture the well exercised rats were still alive and well. Having been developed physically through an action program, they were equipped to survive the *psychological stresses* that had killed their sedentary counterparts.

Apparently the "strong mind in a strong body" concept applies to rats as well as to humans.

In combating stress as a human, however, the kind of action you take can have an important bearing on the results. Competitive sports in particular can sometimes do more harm than good depending on your personal temperament. I once observed a golfer become so frustrated and enraged at himself, he slammed his golf club against a nearby tree and broke it. From a stress reduction and health improvement point of view, engaging in the sport was not only self-defeating, it was self-destructive. He might as well have stayed home and had another fight with his wife.

In a similar state of frustration and rage, I once watched a tennis player fling his racket over the fence upon missing an easy slam shot ten feet from the net. This "athlete" is 61 years old, and refuses to admit to himself he no longer has the reflexes of a 20-year-old. He spends about $25 a week on lessons, plays every morning from seven to eight, every night from nine to eleven. He owns at least 14 tennis rackets, has a "tennis library" at home, purchases all kinds of tennis aids and appurtenances. And he's a mediocre player at best. His attitude and outlook are so grim, the game inflicts far more stress than it relieves. Yet he talks himself and others into believing that the main reason he invests so much of himself in tennis is for the exercise and relaxation value he gets out of it. He's only kidding himself. Tennis has become an obsession with him and obsessions have a way of heightening stress.

Which brings us back to walking. Walking may not be the *only* exercise you can engage in to help dissipate stress. Swimming, bike riding, and for some, running, may be just as effective. And if you relax playing tennis and are in condition to do so, this may help you as well. A man I know chops up logs for his fireplace when he feels the need to work off anger or stress, and rates this action as second to none.

But it would be hard to find an exercise more ideal for stress dissipation than walking, from the standpoints of *both* convenience and action. You can walk at a moment's notice any time you feel tense. Rarely is one more calm, rational and under control than when taking a walk. Where you walk, when you walk, how fast you walk, and for how long you walk are in your hands entirely.

You have control of your breathing as well. Deep breathing is an excellent antidote to stress. Under the grip of stress, you feel tight, tense and on edge. At this point a brisk invigorating walk, breathing deeply, would be the best favor you could do for yourself. It's almost impossible for your stomach to knot up while you're breathing deeply. Try it and see for yourself.

SPIRITS BOOSTER

Many people testify that walking bolsters their state of mind and morale when they need it most.

A college student, the son of a friend of mine, quit a summer clerical job after two weeks because he said "it was driving him up the wall." The work, as he described it, entailed posting figures from invoices to accounts receivable cards, doing the same thing over and over again ad infinitum eight hours a day. He could not tolerate the boredom. Once as a youth I had a similarly deadly boring job and know just how he felt.

He found a messenger boy job in its place. It involved carrying packages and messages to and from customers within a two or three mile radius of the home office. "This job required no more mental activity than the posting job," the young man explained. "But here I was physically active. I was keeping myself in condition and at the same time was free to let my thoughts take control while I walked. I didn't find it boring at all."

William P. Morgan, Ed. D., goes a step further. Exercise is good for your head, he maintains, and states that clinically depressed people improve with physical training.

One reason, explains psychologist Joseph N. Paquette, "is that physical activity can introduce a feeling of well-being. Walking helps you to function more efficiently. Also, you know you're doing something positive and constructive for yourself, and this makes you feel better."

Notes psychiatrist Dr. James Lawrence Evans, Jr., who treats several elderly people, "I advise all my patients suffering from depression to walk at least a half mile every day."

WALKING UNCHAINS THE MIND

For creative thought to be most effective, it must be free-ranging and unencumbered. Sustained physical action tends to dissipate those emotional intruders that restrain free thinking. This may take place on the conscious or unconscious level. As a writer I have experienced it often.

I can recall occasions, for example, when I had been wrestling with a particularly tough piece of writing. At such times I've kept writing and rewriting a specific segment, often consisting of no more than two or three paragraphs. Maybe I wanted to get a particular point across in a particular way, but my creative mind refused to cooperate. I tried first using one approach, then another. Finally, my conscious level of thought filled with the problem, I go out for a walk. While walking, I'm still reviewing those paragraphs, examining different alternatives. Gradually, almost magically it seems, the thought sequences and words fall into place. I pause briefly in my walk to jot down in the notebook I always carry what has been revealed through my thinking.

That's one kind of situation. Other times, in the midst of a writing project, with no special problem encountered, I get up from my typewriter for the walking break I take at least once a day. This time my conscious thoughts are on nothing in particular. But my subconscious is working away. Again, as if by magic, my mind starts getting bombarded by ideas, intriguing approaches, phrases that seem to come out of the blue, provocative avenues of thought to explore. Again, out comes the notebook and I find myself scribbling away, concerned lest the precious thoughts drift away on the breeze as ideas are so apt to do when you don't jot them down.

This too has happened to me time and again. Other writers I know confirm the experience. And though the process may seem almost uncanny, there's no magic involved. The fact is that the sustained physical action of walking enhances creative thinking on both the conscious and subconscious levels through its absorption and dissipation of those anti-think interlopers—anxieties, fears, irritations, pressures and strains—which seem to work so much harder and more effectively when we are physically inactive.

I know a brilliant public relations writer who has developed the ability to compose by talking into a tape recorder. This man is at his creative best when pacing back and forth across a room talking into a machine. He's absolutely convinced that he writes and thinks more efficiently walking than at any other time, partly because he falls into a rhythm that brings his mind and body into good synchronization.

I know just what he means. Brisk walking has a rhythm of its own. So do sustained thinking and writing. When I am getting along well with my typewriter, the thoughts and words seem to flow to a beat. Sometimes while walking I am able to coordinate the rhythm of thinking and walking. It is at such times that the ideas come spilling out in a most gratifying flow.

TAKE YOUR PROBLEM FOR A WALK

Next time you find yourself wrestling with a difficult decision or struggling with a tough problem, try exercising your way to a solution. Get up from your table or desk and take your problem for a walk. This approach will add a number of plusses. For one thing, there will be just the two of you alone, you and your problem. No ringing telephones or other outside intrusions. No one to influence your judgment or interfere with your thoughts.

For another thing, no matter how complex your problem, walking will help keep your mind clear. Straining too hard to arrange the elements of a complicated problem into logical order and priority, the tendency is to tighten up and grow stressful. Stress hampers rational thinking. Physical action, as we said, absorbs stress. That's all there is to it. "One of the best ways to reduce stress is by walking," says Dr. Joseph N. Paquette. "Your muscles are no longer tense. You can think more efficiently."

With problem-solving as with creative thinking, physical activity can be useful whatever mental level you are using to deal with the problem. Taking your problem for a walk in conscious quest of a solution can help you organize your thoughts more clearly for the reasons cited above. Walking is at least as beneficial, if not more so, when working with problems on the unconscious level.

Psychologists define *incubation* as a major phase in the solution of complicated problems. This takes place when the conscious mind isn't working on the problem. Incubation occurs most efficiently when the housewife is out of the kitchen, the executive is away from his desk, the writer is removed from his typewriter, the engineer from his drawing board. Separated from his accustomed work environment, the subject isn't even aware his mind is busy on the problem because the work is taking place at the unconscious level.

Supreme Court Justice William O. Douglas, a famed hiker and walker, describes this experience while off on a hike. "The mind is lost in a world far from office or professional routine. As a result, magical things happen. The subconscious carries a heavy burden of our worries, concerns and problems. On a long hike it functions free of additional tensions and pressures. And somehow or other it seems to unravel many a tangled skein of problems . . . .

"While writing a book or a lecture, I have come to a cul-de-sac, the next terminal being hidden from view. Or an argued case has projected difficult questions that loom so large that no opinion can be written until they are resolved. While my conscious processes are engaged in searching out the wild persimmon tree or a sassafras bush . . . the subconscious is solving my professional or personal problems . . . . Answers and solutions, previously bothersome, become clear as day."

I have heard a similar reaction from a computer programmer I know. There are times, he says, when his mind seems to get so boggled down by the mass of complicated data and instructions he must deal with, that the problem he is working on at the moment takes on the aspects of a maze which appears to have no exit. When it reaches the point where his thinking has become fuzzy, he says, he sets the problem aside and walks to a coffee shop a few blocks away. Often, when he returns to the job a half hour later, the problem that seemed unfathomable when he left, is suddenly solved as if by magic.

As psychiatrist Dr. Anna Burton explains the phenomenon, rhythmic activity without conscious thought induces lower levels of consciousness to become activated. Many hard problems, she adds, find solutions at lower levels of the mind.

10

IN GOOD COMPANY

**"Can two walk together,
except they be agreed?"**

Amos III, 3.

Today's serious walker is in good company indeed, past and present company included. In decades past, while the self-important indulged themselves in flaunting their affluence by riding in expensive and ornate coaches and carriages, the genuinely important walked for the sheer joy and satisfaction of walking. Walkers usually don't feel the need to prove their "success," to themselves or to others. Some of history's most outstanding scholars, statesmen, and creative and free-ranging intellectuals were almost as well known as for their walking habits as for accomplishments in their chosen fields.

The famed chemist and physicist Michael Faraday thought nothing of walking 20 miles in a day, and one day covered 45 miles, despite his worried wife's vehement protests.

The famous Greek philosophers—Socrates, Plato and Aristotle—all conducted teaching sessions afoot under the premise that the mind becomes clearer as the body warms up. Many of Socrates' famed dialogues took place on walks which caused not only spirits to mesh, but minds as well. Aristotle, one might speculate, was often too charged up and overloaded with energy to remain seated while he taught.

"Man's most formidable asset is curiosity," he wrote, "which is a truly explosive force. It makes us eternally restless, so that we seek and yearn and never stand still."

Almost 100 years ago, John Muir, the naturalist, conservationist and writer who founded the Sierra Club, walked the wilderness in then-unexplored far California which would one day be named Muir Woods in honor of him. On his unending walks in search of beauty in general and plant life in particular, he tramped through many parts of the United States, Europe, Asia, Africa, and even the Arctic. His explorations included six years in the Yosemite Valley, and it was largely through his efforts that President Theodore Roosevelt set aside 148,000,000 acres of forest reserves.

Another fervent searcher after beauty was Vachel Lindsay. In 1912, at age 33, he set out on a walking tour of the West. A rhymer by occupation (in other words, "no visible means of support"), he bypassed the cities, preached beauty and joy, and avoided manual labor. By his own account he met many strange and wonderful people. Some thought he was a crackpot; some wrote him off as a lazy good-for-nothing bum; still others secretly envied him. He slept in old box cars, haylofts and livery stables, and sometimes in style when he met up with a sympatico host. In time he became known as the "Vagabond Poet" because as he tramped through the West he recited poems in exchange for lodging and food. Out of Lindsay's walking experience emerged one of America's truly great poets, famous for his jazz-like rhythm and style.

If there's a father of walking, in America at least, it would have to be Henry David Thoreau. Commenting on his "A Winter Walk," Donald Zochert writes, "Here Thoreau captures the ultimate in walking: the mind and body are in step, the eye is clear, the ear alert and the skin alive, and the walker himself is indispensably a part of the path he walks."

Thoreau was a familiar sight around Concord more than a century ago, traipsing the countryside and exchanging ideas with Ralph Waldo Emerson and other young free thinkers of the day. Or he would roam the woods or the banks of Walden Pond by himself in search of the ever-new wonders of Nature he could never seem to get enough of. Emerson once said of walking that there the two ancient precepts—'Know thyself' and 'Study Nature'—are united at last. Thoreau was more cynical. No one really understands the art of walking, he said.

Thoreau attracted, and is continuing to attract, many followers and emulators. One of these was botanist Luther Burbank, who enjoyed nothing more than to take long walks in the California hills in search of unusual plants and seeds. Another Thoreau fan, author Henry Beston, moved into a weather-beaten Cape Cod shack when he was 39 years old and recorded his experience in "The Outermost House." Tramping the same paths traversed by his idol before him, Beston kept a lonely vigil, communicating with Nature, matching his knowledge and skills against the elements, and loving every minute of it.

Others among the famous combined walking with their professional or artistic interests. Naturalist-artist John James Audubon explored much of pioneer America afoot, sketching and painting wildlife and birds as he traveled. The renowned composer and pianist Johannes Brahms, together with a violinist friend named Remenyi, embarked on numerous walking tours of Germany, supporting themselves by playing "gigs" in Hamburg, Hanover and other towns along the way. Artist Vincent Van Gogh created some of his greatest masterpieces while wandering afoot among mining villages of Holland's Borinage, and in sun-drenched Arles in the south of France where so many of his stunning yellows found their way to his canvasses.

In some cases walking played a direct and crucial role in converting weak bodies to strength. Supreme Court Justice William O. Douglas suffered from infantile paralysis as a child. Like Teddy Roosevelt before him, he refused to give in to ill health or weakness and had no intention of permitting it to hamper his lust for life and the great outdoors. Douglas was a determined and adventuresome man who refused to take walking for granted. He hiked with a will and a purpose all over the world. He pitched his tent atop mountains, forded angry rivers and streams, experienced the feeling of power and joy that comes with walking 40 miles in a day with a pack on your back. Walking, he strongly believed, heals both your body and mind.

Equating "good company" with *great* company, the list could go on for pages. Many of the world's greatest poets, essayists and writers—Jonson, Keats, Shelley, Wordsworth, Coleridge, Emerson, Carlyle, Stevenson and Scott to name a small sampling—were known also to be enthusiastic and dedicated walkers. Jane Austen was a walker who made walkers of her heroines as well. President Dwight D. Eisenhower did most of his walking on golf courses, but both Truman and Johnson scheduled brisk daily walks and were famous for their walking interviews during which newsmen half their age had a hard time keeping up. By his own admission, Abraham Lincoln did some of his best thinking while walking alone.

What impels walkers to walk? A few do it to set or break records. Authors Aaron Sussman and Ruth Goode describe an early 19th century gentleman named Captain Robert Barclay who walked 1,000 miles in a thousand consecutive hours. And they tell about a Peruvian Boy Scout who walked 18,000 miles from Buenos Aires to New York in two years. Other stories outline the feats of record holders who walked backward, walked on their hands, or did their stints clad in weird and zany attire—to attract attention, or just for the hell of it.

But true walkers, note Sussman and Goode, "do not walk to make records or to win monuments. They walk for no reason but to enjoy the pleasure of walking. This may be the purely physical enjoyment of stretching muscles, expanding lungs, and the rhythmic relaxation from crown to toe in man's most natural exercise. Or it may be the psychological release of walking away from desk, telephone, automobile, errands, shopping lists, the sheer dailiness of everyday life, and enjoying the most available, least expensive of vacations, whether for an hour, an afternoon, or a weekend."

A FAMILY LOVE AFFAIR

Knowing that such world beaters as Aristotle and Thoreau, Jane Austen and Harry Truman were dedicated walkers before you, may give you a nice warm glow if you decide to hop on the bandwagon yourself. But the company that will give you the biggest lift of all is the company you'll be in if your whole family decides to walk together. I've run into several walking families and almost invariably I get the feeling there's something unique and special about them. It's not a thing you can pinpoint specifically. It's a kind of togetherness and sharing you sense.

Family walking or hiking offers an opportunity for shared interests and togetherness that would be difficult to duplicate. Actually, the opportunity exists for a short time only, because once youngsters grow into their teens, the activity becomes too tame for them. They are now ready for hiking or backpacking of a more rugged nature.

I talked with Jim Kempner, a quality control engineer who, together with his wife Ann, two boys and a girl, have been family hiking for about seven years. He takes the activity for granted as part of their lifestyle.

"To be truthful," he said, "we don't give it much thought. It's just something we do. Ann and I enjoyed walking together for as long as we can remember. It was only natural to get the kids into the act when they were old enough."

"What do you enjoy most about it?"

Jim shrugged. "Getting away from the house. The open spaces and fresh air. The trees, flowers, birds and, I don't know, it's just something good and wholesome we can all do together."

He added, "Today it's down to four of us. Our oldest boy prefers to go backpacking with his friends. But I think he'll always be a walker. I suppose it gets in your blood."

Most walking families I interviewed have, like the Kempners, been doing it together for years. And like the Kempners, they tend to take walking for granted. It's something they enjoy doing together. I have yet to encounter one walking family which engages in the activity with a psychological objective in mind such as "to improve communication" or "to develop better closeness and rapport," although there's little doubt that these ends are accomplished.

The fact of the matter is that sometimes the things people do spontaneously and without conscious planning—such as worshipping together, vacationing together, picnicking together, and sailing together—do more to strengthen the bonds of caring and love than therapeutic programs developed and set up for this purpose.

Every walking family I ever met let me know they enjoyed the activity for one reason or another. Naturally, otherwise they wouldn't be doing it. One family in particular seemed genuinely excited and enthusiastic about their walking experience. The reason: They had been doing it only 5 months. They'd started walking for health purposes and expanded the activity to include the children who were aged 7 and 9. The reason they were enthusiastic, the 32 year old mother in particular, was that family walking was still fresh and new to them and they were still experiencing the joys of discovery.

The mother waxed almost poetic in responding to my questions. "I think family walking has done something special in establishing a bond between us; we never felt so together before." As an afterthought, she added, "The way I view it, walking and camping together in scenic places is like a family love affair."

Kitty Florey describes in *Prevention* magazine how her family of "three blobs"—Papa Blob, Mama Blob and Baby Blob—turned to family walking and now—no longer blobs—look forward all week to those Saturday jaunts. On top of that, she says, once the walking bug bites, you get into the habit of walking and walk to places you either would have driven to or not visited in the past.

"On a sunny afternoon," she writes, "we'll find time to stroll around the neighborhood. We've discovered the fun of 'zig-zag walks'—you take a right, then a left, then a right, etc., indefinitely—which have led us to unexplored parts of our own community. If we're going out to eat, we walk to the restaurant—and find ourselves eating less than we used to when we get there. We walk to the library, to visit friends, to stores. All three of us are trimmer and more energetic."

Parent and Child—One-To-One. I suppose we all have certain memories that stand out in our lives as very special and precious. One of my own fondest memories dates back to when I was a boy of 8 or 9. I can still remember the joy and exhilaration I used to feel when, once or twice a week, my father would take me walking with him. He was a silent walker and a very fast walker, so fast that at times I had to half run to keep up with him. But mostly we walked hand in hand, and sometimes, although hardly a word was exchanged there was communication between us—and an abundance of love.

Years later similar memories were fashioned on walks I took with my daughter Madeleine, who today is an emancipated and independent young woman and an executive in the publishing industry. It is not an easy thing to bring across, but I believe there are never enough traded feelings between parents and children. Too often too much is assumed or taken for granted on both sides about what one or the other feels about important issues and events. In my experience, walking together presents a natural and matchless opportunity to express one's honest innermost feelings about life and life's values, aspirations and goals. Somehow I have found the home less conducive to this kind of expression. Walking together, it is easier to relax barriers and drop inhibitions. At least I have found it that way, and I have spoken to many people who seem to feel the same.

I remember one day in particular eight or nine years ago when Madeleine and I walked four hours through the streets of Fort Lauderdale, Florida, just walking and talking. I don't remember what we talked about, but I do remember the rhythm we shared, the joy we felt doing it, and most of all the love and warmth that flowed between us. Another walk that stands out in my mind is a full day hike Madeleine and I took along a physical fitness trail laid out by the government in the town of Kaprun, Austria, with the foothills of the Alps hovering over us. On that day, in addition to the beautiful intimacy of shared opinions and feelings, was the scenic glory of the environment which, in a very positive way, tends to cut mortals down to size.

In her own personal storehouse of memories, Madeleine confided recently, were the walks we used to take when she was six or seven years old. On those walks I would make up stories about dolls and stuffed animals in a department store that came to life during the night. Amazingly, to this day Madeleine can recite most of their adventures as if the walks we took had occurred only yesterday.

Then there is Alma, a woman I know in her mid-forties, who has a daughter of 22 named Lisa. Alma's background is quite proper and very conservative. Lisa is of the new breed of free-thinking and free-acting young women. She lives with a young man, but displays no interest in marriage, an attitude that causes her mother considerable heartache. Still, she loves her daughter and does not want to lose her. Understandably, given the diversity of their philosophies, it hasn't been easy for Alma and Lisa to communicate on any meaningful level—except under one set of circumstances.

Mother and daughter do have one strong interest in common. They are both extremely fashion conscious and are both chronic shoppers. On the precept that the family who walks together talks together, they often go shopping together traipsing from one end of the shopping mall to the other, back and forth, for hours and hours. Alma told me that the only time she and Lisa really get close to one another is during these shopping tours. To the maximum degree possible, Lisa lets down her reserves and honestly and openly reveals how she thinks and feels about the things that really count. "It's been a liberal education for me," Alma admitted. "It made me understand her point of view. It gave me insights and sensitivity I couldn't have acquired in any other way that I know. If not for these walks together—an activity we both look forward to—our relationship by now would probably be purely superficial."

Marital Booster Shot. No one in his right mind would suggest that walking is the key to marital bliss. In fact, I can recall a movie some years back where the husband enticed his wife to join him on a long walk in the country. His purpose as it turned out was to push her off a cliff.

Walking, of itself, cannot mend a broken marriage or shore up an ill-conceived relationship. But where the marriage, however rocky, has some good plusses going for it, walking together can help.

One element that can strengthen a marriage is common interests. The more common interests a couple share, the more activities they enjoy together, the better the chance that the union will survive. One psychiatrist I interviewed described a couple who once came to him for marital help. "Despite their problems and differences," he said, "they had a whole lot going for them, and underlying the frustration and bitterness were genuine feelings of love. They both wanted to save the marriage."

Typically, the husband was an executive, and the wife's chief complaint was the ancient one that he was married to his job. When he protested this wasn't so, she challenged him to name activities they engaged in together. Apart from standard social and family obligations, there was very little he could call to mind.

The psychiatrist suggested they bring in a list of activities they engaged in independently of the other during non-office hours. He listed jogging, tennis and golf. She named contract bridge, tennis, and semi-weekly visits to the spa. They then worked up a list of activities they might be able to engage in together. Walking headed the list after the psychiatrist convinced the husband he could get the same cardiovascular benefits out of walking that he got out of jogging. He continues a men's tennis game once a week, and she continues her women's tennis game; but in addition they play mixed doubles and sometimes substitute Saturday night tennis parties for more routine social engagements. Finally, he is now taking up contract bridge, and admits he enjoys it.

They still have a way to go, the therapist said, but now that they're sharing activities they both enjoy, things are much better between them.

Dr. Elias Savitsky, another psychiatrist, believes one

of the main benefits of walking from the marital point of view, lies in the common activity it provides for married people young and old.

Psychiatrist Dr. James Lawrence Evans, Jr. points out that one of the main problems that exists between husband and wife, and between parents and children is the lack of communication. He says, "Anything that tends to improve communication will be beneficial to the relationship. Walking," he adds, "can accomplish a great deal in this direction."

Psychologist Joseph N. Paquette notes that society unconsciously erects many barriers to communication. A prime example is the TV set. A group of people in the living room engaged in discussion about three different topics is another one. Time commitments, people always on the rush to get someplace or another, is a third. Often when two people need to communicate, the presence of a child or third person, is barrier enough to foster small talk or silence.

"The beauty of walking," Dr. Paquette says, "is that it breaks down all barriers to communication. It provides the most favorable and conducive conditions."

WALKING FOR COMPANIONSHIP

Many great walkers and hikers, Ernest Hemingway, Justice William O. Douglas, Johannes Brahms, to cite some good examples, sought companionship when they walked, not all of the time but some of the time.

Gene Slade of Leonia, New Jersey has been hiking and backpacking all of his life. His love and joy is the great out-of-doors. But, he says thoughtfully, a special kind of intimacy exists if you're out there with somebody else. "There's one feeling you get when you're off in the wilds by yourself and alone in communion with Nature. There's another kind of feeling when you share it with someone who is truly compatible. It's two different experiences."

Another veteran hiker told me quite bluntly, "If your friend's of the opposite sex, that's no handicap. Talk about the joys of hiking. That's the ultimate! I think it was Izaak Walton who said, 'Fishing isn't all fishing!' Well, hiking isn't all hiking!"

My idea of Utopia, he added, is to be off alone in the woods with a good-looking woman. *That's* companionship!

To many walkers walking is more than just walking. Except when Gene Slade joins his wife June on a group hike, he usually takes off with a set objective in mind. A highly skilled fly fisherman, his goal may be to fish a remote stream in the Adirondacks or Canada. Or, a sophisticated photographer, on another day his goal may be to film birdlife or the scenic beauties of Nature. Sometimes he'll set off alone, other times with a friend.

Another man I met through a shared musical interest —he plays the flute; I blow a saxophone—is now 38 and lives in the same New Jersey town he was born in. Last year he met a woman clarinetist who played in the high school band with him more than two decades ago. They got into a conversation and decided it would be nice to get a chamber group going. They succeeded in collecting three other ex-high school musicians and set up a rehearsal in one of their houses. The session showed promise, but there were accoustical problems.

Finally, somebody had a brainstorm. "Hey listen," he said, "I'm at least ten pounds overweight."

The others looked at him strangely. His idea wasn't strange at all. A wooded area was located about six miles away. "Sunday mornings," he said, "in the spring, summer and fall when the weather permits, why don't we meet on the main road with our instruments and hike up to the woods?"

It was an appealing idea and they seized on it. When they reach their destination they unpack their instruments, set up their music stands, and join the birds and insects in song. It would be difficult to find a concert hall or auditorium more conducive to the rondos and divertimentos of Mozart and Grieg than the little clearing where they play.

Social Walking. While in Florida last year, my wife and I met Mrs. Shirley Wagner, a recently widowed woman in her fifties who had relocated from Rhode Island to Fort Lauderdale. When she learned I was writing a book about walking, she exclaimed, "Oh, I can tell you all about walking."

A writer's dream. "Go ahead, I'm listening."

Mrs. Wagner had always hated cold weather, and when her husband died she decided to move to Florida. Her friends and relatives counseled against it. "Your family is here in Providence, and all your close friends. You'll be lonely in Florida; you won't know what to do with yourself."

Mrs. Wagner didn't see it that way. She wanted to make a new life for herself. She had one friend who had moved to Fort Lauderdale, and wrote her all about Holiday Park. This city-owned park presents a model the whole country could go by. It has almost anything anyone of any age could desire, from horseshoes and shuffleboard to soccer and baseball fields. It has a concert house and a theatre that offers top-grade entertainment, social halls for folk, square and ballroom dancing, studios for bridge. It has handball and paddleball courts, and a host of well kept tennis courts presided over by tennis pro Jim Evert (Chris's father and coach).

Holiday Park also features a long bicycle path and walking circuits that are pleasant and safe any time of the day, night or week.

Mrs. Wagner admits that when she first moved down there—wisely renting for starters, rather than buying—she was nervous. It was the biggest change she ever had made. But it was the spring of the year and the weather was glorious. She started walking around Holiday Park.

"From the very first day," she recalls, "I met all kinds of people: other widows like myself, interesting men, a schoolteacher who is trying to help me find a job. Walkers are the friendliest people in the world!"

Her days, evenings and weekends are filled with all kinds of activities like dancing and bridge and, at least two hours a day, walking.

"Since I've been down here," she adds, "I've shed eight unneeded pounds. As far as being lonely is concerned— I simply don't have the time."

Manhunts. Then you have the group hikes sponsored by hiking clubs all over the U.S. They're publicized in the club's newsletter, and anyone who wants to participate is welcome. One veteran hiker told me, "Serious hikers avoid these events."

He explained, "Group hikes often attract as many as fifty people or more, and you get all kinds of kooks, people under psychiatric treatment, people who go on the hikes because it gives them an opportunity to unload their problems on others."

I shrugged. "One person's 'kook' may be another person's pleasant companion."

"Maybe so, and if that's what you're looking for, okay. But I wouldn't recommend group hikes for really serious hikers."

A female hiker agrees with him in part. She said, "Many people join hiking clubs and participate in group hikes because they're lonely, and it's a good way to make friends. And a lot of women I know go on group hikes with one purpose in mind: to meet men.

"The trouble," she added, "is that nine times out of ten all they meet are a lot of other women."

She explained that hikes are often graded A, B and C by order of toughness, judged by distance and terrain. "The easiest ones are the C hikes, and on these you generally find a predominance of women in their fifties and sixties. The woman who signs up on a C hike in the hope of meeting a man won't have much of a chance. She'd be better off toughening up a bit, then signing up for an A hike where the ratio of women to men is usually less one-sided."

Senior Citizens. It isn't news to anyone that the retiree's number one problem is to keep interestingly and productively occupied. Another critical problem is to keep physically fit. Also ranking high on the list is the need for the retired man or woman to manage finances in such a way that money doesn't become a source of nagging anxiety.

Walking is an ideal way to help solve all of these problems:

- Many seniors join walking clubs, or form little groups of their own. They participate in organized tours—set up by the clubs, or, in some cases by city health or recreational agencies—or they plan day tours of their own, usually to points of interest in the area. Benefits derived include companionship, along with cultural and education values, plus an interesting and enjoyable way to spend one's time.

- Walking provides much-needed exercise designed to maintain good health in general and strengthen the cardiovascular system in particular.
- Walking tours are inexpensive, producing no excess drain on inflation-bombarded financial reserves.

WALKERS IN LOVE

The ultimate in walking is the walks that are shared by two people in love. The best company you could ever be in when walking—or at any other time, for that matter—is the company of your lover.

What makes walking with a loved one so special? Psychologist Joseph N. Paquette says that when two people walk together a privacy and intimacy result which, when combined with the physical contact of bodies touching and hands being held, makes the atmosphere conducive to emotional closeness.

When lovers walk together all their senses are sharpened and a heightened awareness is created. They see beauty in things they might otherwise overlook—the red and gold of leaves in the fall, a little bird's trilling song, a gull sweeping across the horizon, the blue-green swirl of angry waves, a child's sunny smile—because it's a time when beauty has an added significance. Love and beauty are bed mates.

In good country walking, the lungs fill up with fresh air, the blood circulates with more vigor and zest. Lovers feel a glorious sense of well-being enhanced by the come-alive rhythm of their synchronized steps, walking creates for them, as in dancing, the unity, joy and togetherness experienced by a well coordinated team.

Lovers possess the ability to take everyday things and ascribe to them unique depths and dimensions. They share the joy of discovery where ordinary mortals might see nothing out of the ordinary.

The 18th century Swiss philosopher and theologian John Caspar Lavater summed it up neatly when he wrote: "Love sees what no eye sees; love hears what no ear hears; and what never rose in the heart of man love prepares for its object."

When lovers walk, the bonds of love are strengthened. They observe and react as one person. In city walking, from a superior vantage point they co-editorialize on the follies and foibles of the human condition in whispered comments or wise knowing glances. It takes very little to delight them: A middle-aged woman dressed like a teen-ager; a fat man who walks funny; a platinum blonde bleachee with swiveling hips; a taxi driver hollering at a too-careful driver; a snooty looking woman walking a look-alike poodle. Everything has a special meaning for them. Everything has a uniqueness only they can pinpoint and appreciate.

To walkers in love, walking is a lovemaking experience.

11

WHERE AND WHEN

> "(Walking's) overwhelming advantage
> is that it can be done by anyone,
> anytime, anywhere—and it doesn't
> even look like exercise."
>
> *Dr. Kenneth H. Cooper*

It couldn't possibly be planned and organized, but sometimes you get the feeling that the modern world is conspiring to keep people from walking. If you have a short errand to do, to buy a quart of milk or drop something off at a friend's house, the car is always at hand. Virtually all modern business and apartment buildings have elevators which people mindlessly use even if waiting for the lift will take longer than walking up the two or three flights. Department stores have escalators to ease your journey from one floor to the next. Major airports feature electric walkways to transport you automatically to and from gates. Even golfers, theoretically out for the exercise, use electric golf carts more often than not. In short, any time you feel too lazy to walk you will get all the cooperation and encouragement you could possibly want.

But if you are determined to pace walk your way to good health despite the conspiracy, doing so will be no problem. No one can keep you from walking. Anyone and everyone with two healthy legs can walk, anywhere and everywhere, any time they have the time or make the time.

TOO BUSY TO EXERCISE

Warmup and warmdown are recommended for just about any exercise or athletic activity, including walking. But walking requires less preparation time and less warmdown attention than almost any other activity. Since you won't be stretching and straining muscles unnaturally, no extensive warmup is needed. Thus the most common alibi for not following through on good intentions—*I'm too busy to do it*—is denied to the great majority of Americans. Unlike most other exercises or sports, you can fulfill your daily walking quota in tailored-to-your-schedule segments.

The swimmer, bicyclist or paddle ball player who pleads he's too busy to pursue the sport on a continuing basis, might have a valid problem. It's inconvenient for most working people, if not downright impossible, to interrupt a business day to take a swim, go for a bike ride, or play a couple of games of paddle ball. The walker doesn't have this problem to worry about. If time pressures force him to, he can take his exercise in snatches four or five times a day.

In my own case, as I said earlier, I schedule two sessions each day which I allot to walking, unless I have an afternoon spa visit or tennis game scheduled. "For you that's no problem," you may reply. "You're self-employed. Your time is your own."

Agreed. Self-employed people and housewives (without small children) usually have maximum flexibility since they control their own time. But even if you're on a strict nine-to-five work schedule, you probably can fit in enough walking—ten minutes here, ten minutes there—to fulfill your exercise needs. As the 19th century clergyman-philosopher Caleb C. Colton once wrote: "Much may be done in those little shreds and patches of time, which every day produces, and which most men throw away."

Ideally, if you can manage to devote about an hour each day to brisk and energetic walking, it will probably increase your oxygen intake capacity and strengthen your cardiovascular system, not to mention a host of other physical and psychological benefits. If you can break down this hour into two half-hour segments, as most people can do if their determination is strong enough, well and good. But if this is impractical or inconvenient for you, you can break down the hour into three 20 minute or even four 15 minute periods, into manageable segments which you can tie easily and naturally into your normal day-to-day pattern. Here are some of the ways you can make those "little shreds and patches of time" work to your best personal advantage:

A Cleveland man lives three-quarters of a mile from the railroad station where he takes the train to go to work. In the past his wife drove him to the station, and picked him up after work. Today he rises about 15 minutes earlier, walks to the station in the morning, and walks home in the evening.

An Atlanta nurse, instead of driving to and from the hospital every day as she had been doing for years, now parks at a shopping center about a mile from the hospital and walks the rest of the way. After work, she says, the brisk walk back to her car at the shopping center helps to recharge her batteries.

The senior vice president of a large consumer products company, as a top level officer, enjoyed one of the plant's most highly preferred parking spots about 30 steps from the front entrance. Because he felt he wasn't getting enough exercise, he recently gave up his spot by the door, and parks a half mile away ("which forces me to walk whether I like it or not.").

A Philadelphia man lives on the eleventh floor of a high rise apartment building. Six months ago he started riding the elevator to the ninth floor and walking up the other two flights. A couple of months after that he began getting off at the eighth floor and walking the rest of the way. More recently he cut off another floor and now walks *four* flights to his apartment. Walking up flights of stairs can be good exercise if you are in proper condition and don't overdo it. Before walking up more than two flights on a regular basis, however, it would be wise to check it out with your doctor.

A man who works in a Wall Street brokerage office rides the subway to work and gets off the train a station ahead of the one that is closest to his office. He walks the rest of the way and walks back the same distance after work. This completes about one-third of the daily quota he has set for himself.

A food industry executive devotes more than an hour a day to reading and responding to screened correspondence. For years he performed this chore in the conventional manner, talking into a recording machine at his desk. He recently switched to both reading the letters and dictating his answers while briskly pacing his spacious office. He feels the rhythm of the pacing helps the idea and word flow as well. In the afternoon, when his secretary puts the typed correspondence on his desk, he reviews the letters while walking back and forth across his office, then sits down at his desk to sign them. This adds up to well over an hour of walking each day. Weekends he refuses to get into his car for any errand under a mile.

Make the Most of Your Lunch Hour. Your lunch hour can either enhance your health or undermine it, depending on whether you use it wisely and well or abuse it. Millions of Americans abuse their lunch hour by overeating and/or overdrinking. The worst abusers are those who have a relatively heavy lunch at midday, then sit down to a heavy meal when they get home in the evening, with little exercise in between.

Jim Temple, an assistant sales manager with an industrial products manufacturer, told me it's a pattern that becomes habitual and difficult to break. "You fall into a groove," he says. "Half the time I'd take customers to lunch; the other half I'd eat with sales supervisors or salespeople. The fact that you could often put in a chit makes it easier to do; ordering becomes even more of a habit when you don't have to pay for it. Typically, I'd have a main course, a side dish or two, coffee and desert—and at least two drinks."

One day 6 months ago Jim's doctor informed him he was 30 pounds overweight and that his heart was "acting up a little bit."

"I'm not a brave man," Temple said. "I asked him what I should do. His answer was simple enough: 'Eat less; exercise more'."

Today, Temple said, except in rare emergencies where special customer problems are involved, I lunch alone. He eats at the counter of a fast service coffee shoppe and he's done in 15 minutes.

The rest of his lunch hour he walks. He's given up fatty foods and rich deserts, and takes a brisk 30 minute walk after dinner at home. In the six months he has been following this regimen, he's lost 14 pounds, and says he hasn't felt so "full of pizzazz" in years.

Many people take advantage of their lunch hours to fit in walking stints it might be difficult or inconvenient to accomplish other times of the day. Two secretaries who work for an insurance company a little more than a mile away from the Neiman-Marcus Department Store in Dallas, wolf down sandwiches at their desks every day, then take off full steam ahead for the store. The walking comes to about 20 minutes each way. The 20 minutes of browsing in Neiman-Marcus, with an occasional purchase thrown in, serves as a reward for the exercise.

Do you work for your livelihood? Do you have a lunch hour that's yours to do with what you wish? If so, while wolfing down sandwiches isn't recommended, you should still have enough time to get in at least a half hour of walking. Too busy to walk? Nonsense!

AWAY FROM HOME

I don't believe in suggesting "good" places to walk and "bad" places to avoid because walking preferences, like friendship preferences, are a matter of personal and individual choice. As far as where *not* to walk is concerned, I would make only two broad recommendations: Especially if you are visiting in a strange city, don't go exploring too adventuresomely without first finding out where it's safe to walk and where it's not so safe. Obviously, you should be six times as careful before exploring at night. The other place I would suggest avoiding, whatever your walking preference, is in, or adjacent to, a high traffic area where the odds are high that all beauty and interest has been bulldozed out of existence to begin with. And if that doesn't bother you, you have the auto exhaust to contend with.

Where then is the best place to walk? That's a question only you are truly qualified to answer. Assuming you are fairly well acquainted with your own community and neighborhood, time and experience have probably already taught you where you most like to walk. Anyone else's suggestion would reflect his preference more than yours. When you're away from home, it's another matter entirely. Here a few suggestions might help whether you're visiting in a large metropolitan area, or spending time with friends or relatives in the suburbs.

CITY WALKING

Every city has a character of its own largely shaped by the size of the city; the way it's laid out; the size, shape and style of its buildings; and most of all by the way its people interact with other people. The definition of a tourist is "a person who is traveling for pleasure." So if you're off on a holiday to New York, San Francisco or Milwaukee, you are there as a tourist. If you're visiting your Aunt Minnie in Houston, you are there as a tourist. There's no better time or opportunity to get in some good enjoyable, educational and health conditioning walking than when you travel as a tourist.

My suggestion, if you're planning a trip, is to spend some time in the public library a couple of weeks in advance. Most people who presumably "plan" trips don't really plan. More often they don't really have a good fix on how they are going to spend their time until they get where they are going. Then they nervously spend precious holiday time to make last minute decisions—often poor ones—because they didn't take enough time to weigh the alternatives.

If you're going to visit a city, take three or four of the most recent books about the city out of the library. Then take the books home and sit down with your spouse, friend, lover or whomever else you may be going with if you're not going alone, and determine what points of interest you would most like to visit.

Every large city I've ever visited has something for everyone depending on personal likes and dislikes. Some people enjoy the excitement and hubbub of the downtown theatre, night club, business and shopping centers. Others prefer the gentler pleasures of friendly parks, lovely cathedrals and historical landmarks.

What's most important, and not always so easy, is to be honest with yourself. Most of us to one degree or other are victims of a conditioned society. Don't race off to Points of Interest A, B, and C because they're listed in all the tour guide books, or because the names are well known to you. Whenever I visit France, for example, I resolve *not* to visit the Eiffel Tower. That doesn't mean *you* should avoid visiting it. But you shouldn't visit it unless your desire to visit it extends beyond your being able to tell your friend or neighbor that you've seen it. A little white lie is preferrable to wasting half a vacation day doing something you don't really enjoy. In short, the only significant gauge of whether or not you should go here or there is your own personal interest.

I have a confession to make. I have seen so many cathedrals all over Europe, America, Canada and points north, south, east and west that I'm simply tired of looking at them. I'm no atheist, but cathedrals bore me. It has gotten to the point where they all look the same to me, even the different ones. I reached this conclusion—at least I recalled it *consciously*—a year or two ago. I only wish this light had come to me about eight years ago. Think of all the boring trips I might have avoided!

Please don't misunderstand the point I am making. This is a personal idiosyncrasy. I know people who have seen twice as many cathedrals as I have, and just can't get enough of them. It's unlikely they will ever reach a saturation point. On the other hand, I love to visit zoos and aquariums. I know people who hate them—cathedral lovers yet! Watching the monkeys or seals go into their acts makes them yawn. *I* could observe them for hours. As the ancient saw goes: "There's no accounting for taste." Well and good. The trick when you're a tourist is to define your tastes explicitly and make plans to accommodate them.

When you're a tourist, walking and looking are inter-dependent. The more you enjoy looking, the more you enjoy walking. A great walk is a walk where you really liked what you saw. All major cities tout their special places of interest. Unfortunately, not all "places of interest" are interesting. In fact, some are downright dull. The problem is to decide in advance if you can decide which "places of interest" are most likely to interest you.

Suppose you were going to spend two or three days in Chicago. Would you enjoy visiting the Board of Trade Building where you can see how the grain and commodity exchanges work? Would you like to see the Merchandise Mart, one of the world's largest commercial office buildings? What about the site of The O'Leary House and Barn where, according to legend, Mrs. O'Leary's cow kicked over the lantern that started the Chicago fire? These along with many other attractions are listed as "places of interest."

In San Francisco, one of my favorite cities, would you be intrigued by the Ruins of Mission San Juan Capistrano, now the summer home of the famous Capistrano swallows? Would you like to take a panoramic view of the city from the Top Of the Mark Hopkins Hotel? Would you enjoy walking the streets of San Francisco's fabulous Chinatown, or picturesque Japan Town? Or would you be fascinated by the city's striking architecture with its strong Spanish and Oriental influence?

In unique New York City, would you be entranced by its towering skyscrapers? Would you like to walk up and down Broadway from 42nd Street to 52nd Street? How would you like to see Rockefeller Center, the "city within a city" where, it has been said, a person could live self-sufficiently without ever having to leave? Would you enjoy visiting century-old St. Patrick's Cathedral, one of the world's best-known Roman Catholic churches? Would you get a thrill visiting Manhattan's Fraunces Tavern built in 1719, the inn where Washington said goodbye to his men? What would you think of walking through Manhattan's unsurpassable Metropolitan Museum of Art, Museum of Modern Art, American Museum of Natural History, Guggenheim Museum, and many others? How would you enjoy visiting the world-famous Bronx Zoo, a vast park land where one could walk in a state of enchantment for hours on end?

In New Orleans, can you picture yourself walking through the old French Quarter? Or up and down picturesque Royal Street with its captivating shops? Or along blarey, brassy Bourbon Street with its honkey tonks and jazzy night spots? How would you like to walk through some of the side streets featuring exciting French and Spanish architecture until you stumbled on Exposition Hall, rundown, decrepit-looking—and one of the world's great jazz emporiums?

Or, taking a quick flight to Los Angeles, would it interest you to walk up and down posh Beverly Hills streets with their neatly trimmed palms and million dollar homes of the stars? Would the city's buildings of many diverse architectural styles intrigue you, from its adobe missions to its French and English traditional dwellings? Would you like to visit the Farmer's Market, a grand bazaar covering 24 acres? Would it thrill you to walk down Hollywood and Vine, and stomp your feet where the stars stomped? How would you feel about visiting Knott's Berry Farm which, among other attractions, features a ghost town, a wagon camp, and a mile-long narrow gauge railroad?

These are just a few of the choices awaiting you in a handful of great American cities. At no time is walking more enjoyable than when you are on vacation or holiday. Deciding what you enjoy most in advance and planning your schedule accordingly—not to the minute, but on a general basis—can heighten the joy of walking and looking to the maximum.

GROUND RULES

A soft grass or dirt surface, if you can find a good flat stretch of terrain, is obviously easier on the feet than a hard concrete surface like your average sidewalk. Unfortunately, soft ground often has unsuspected irregularities which can cause a foot to trip or an ankle to twist. Ideal soft surfaces are hard to find. If you have to walk a soft surface tentatively, on the lookout for rocks, holes and bumps, walking briskly is difficult and establishing a good steady rhythm is well nigh impossible.

Beach walking has a special appeal for a great many people. For me most beaches have very little walking appeal, but a great deal of environmental appeal. The hard sand surface of Daytona Beach, Florida is a notable exception. This is a walker's mecca where even cars can drive on the surface without sinking in.

Nothing on earth could duplicate the feeling of the microscopic mortal on a lonely beach looking out at the ocean during the prelude to a gathering storm. To greet one's nostrils, the scent of the salt-sprayed air; to greet one's eyes, the sight of the roiling waves gathering anger and power for the Big Show later on; to greet one's ears, the alternating roar, whisper and bark of the sea combined with the elements as Act One gathers momentum. Standing alone on a beach before or during a storm—and at other times as well—can be a memorable physical and emotional experience.

But if you have walking for exercise or intellectual walking in mind, I would rate beach walking low. The surface is rarely level, or uniformly hard or soft. You will find stretches where you will sink in too deeply, making progress draggy and labored. Beach walking can be even more unpredictable than trail hiking. Here you will come across a patch strewn with rocks and sharp stones; there you will run into slippery or slimy ground covered with seaweed or glop washed up from the sea.

But where else do you have so perfect an opportunity to shed your footwear and walk free? A number of places. Walking barefoot can be therapeutic if you do it on a soft flat path, on grass, or on your living room carpet. However your average beach, which at first glance may seem fine for barefoot walking, usually offers an inhospitable surface which becomes even more inhospitable with the hot sun beating down on it.

Are there enough places in America designed for walkers specifically? Of course not! Even though you can walk any time, anywhere, and for as long as you wish, except for a handful of exceptions our nation's cities and communities weren't designed with the walker in mind. The Walking Association and other hiking/walking groups are working to promote more pedestrian paths in America (see Appendix G). The Association's director, Dr. Robert B. Sleight, believes sidewalks are not ideal places to walk as a rule. "They're not really scenic," he says. "Sidewalks are hard on the feet, and there's often traffic nearby."

He describes sidewalk walking as unpleasant. Of course, it all depends on the sidewalk and where it's located. I find many sidewalks on suburban tree-lined streets quite pleasant to walk. I enjoy looking at houses and especially in spring, summer and fall, find the flowers, trees and flowering shrubs very pretty to view. And some sidewalks running through parks are delightful. From my own personal experience, I see concrete surfaces as quite hazardous for runners, not much of a danger to walkers who wear sturdy, well-fitted and comfortable shoes.

AN INALIENABLE RIGHT! OR IS IT?

You can derive unexpected pleasures from walking. The story is told of a New Yorker who decided to walk the streets of Manhattan at 3 o'clock in the morning and found the experience stimulating. "People do the most peculiar things at that time!" he enthused. "Observing the city after midnight can be a pleasant and unusual experience."

It most certainly can. And it is precisely because of the "peculiar things" some people are likely to do in big cities after dark—things like muggings, holdups and rapes—that you wouldn't find many New Yorkers willing to venture outside their triple-locked doors.

Theoretically, no right I know of is as unassailable in America as a person's right to walk where he wishes and when he wishes so long as he doesn't trespass on private property from which he is barred. Still, in some neighborhoods, going for a walk isn't as easy as it sounds. In most big cities and metropolitan areas, muggings and purse snatchings are far from uncommon. And more often than not, the victim is an elderly person (although I know of teen-agers and young college students who have also been held up).

Some people, because of limitations linked to their occupations, find it impractical or inconvenient to walk even when they can do so safely and comfortably. A salesman I interviewed spends almost all of his lunch hours dining with prospects or customers. Giving up this important part of his business time to go walking wouldn't be economically feasible. He lives in Newark, New Jersey and would be apprehensive in Newark streets after dark. He can't see rising a half hour early to walk, finding his sleep too important. Another man I know operates a small stationery store where he is locked in from morning to dusk. His home is in a section of Cleveland where night walking is not recommended.

The problem isn't very widespread. But some people, whose work schedules or personal habits are restrictive, can't manage to work in enough time snatches during the day to fulfill their walking quota. If they genuinely wish to take advantage of this unsurpassed exercise and can't do so at night, they are faced with a problem. It's a problem Ben Hirsch, a 62-year-old Houston accountant, felt keenly indeed. It was summer time and he had just come from the doctor, who saw he was going to fat and prescribed a regimen of brisk walking as the ideal way to shed some weight and get back into shape.

Hirsch's problem was that the midday temperature was usually too hot for walking. He rises at 6:45 a.m. to get to work by 8:30 and wasn't about to get up any earlier. For him the ideal time to walk was after dinner, but the idea of walking around his neighborhood after dark was enough to give him a chill.

Discussing the situation with his wife, she suggested, "How about the mall?"

His initial response was to grumble. Edith had been plotting and striving to get him to take her shopping for as long as he could remember, usually not too successfully. But this was a thought.

It took only one sample walk to convince Ben Hirsch that the enclosed shopping mall is the serious walker's dream. Air conditioned in hot weather, the temperature is ideal. And the whole setup is designed to catch and hold the walker's attention. Hirsch says he can't think of a more interesting place to walk. When they arrive at the mall, Hirsch takes off on his own, which is just perfect with Edith; she couldn't keep up with him anyhow and has her mind on other things like shoes and sweaters, costume jewelry and dresses.

They usually spend an hour-and-a-half there, after which Hirsch picks Edith up by the fountain. He alternates the pace of his walks: 20 minutes of brisk Army walking during which he concentrates more on the exercise than observing, followed by ten minutes of leisurely walking, during which he takes in the sights (advertised sales in store windows, the antics of children, the dapper salesman demonstrating electric comfort chairs which do everything but give you a rubdown, the professional musician pounding out "Blue Skies" on a home organ complete with about 15 rhythm attachments). Then he's off again on another 20 minutes of serious walking.

"It's like a fairyland for walkers," he told me, "and my doctor couldn't be more pleased with the weight I've been losing." He chuckled. "You know, I get the feeling I'm putting one over on him. Mall walking isn't exercise—it's fun!"

BEATING THE WEATHER

The rain is pelting down, and it's time for your walk. What to do?

Walk indoors where it's as dry as a bone.

It's ninety-four degrees in the shade. Even if you wear short shorts or a bikini, brisk walking in this kind of heat will make you pretty uncomfortable at best, could result in heat prostration or worse should the heat prove to be more than you can bear. What to do?

Walk indoors where it's air conditioned and comfortable.

The thermometer reads 10° Fahrenheit; but with the wind-chill factor it feels more like twenty below. Walking, to be an effective exercise, must put a little strain on your heart. Brisk walking in sub-freezing temperature could put too much strain on your heart, not to mention the miserable discomfort you feel. What to do?

Walk indoors where it's heated and the environment is temperature-controlled.

"In days of temperature extremes," cautions Dr. H.C. Elkton, "you're better off not exercising at all if the alternative is to risk over-exerting your heart."

But there's no need to give up your walking if you can do it in your own apartment or home or, like Mr. Hirsch, in your friendly, temperature-controlled, neighborhood shopping mall.

Traipsing the living room/kitchen/dining room circuit, the only problem to conquer is boredom. I overcome this as I've said by turning on the radio to a news station and bringing myself up to date on what is going on in the world while I walk. Or you may prefer turning on some classical or popular music.

Ed Finley, a friend and walking associate, is studying Spanish because his son married a Mexican girl. On most weekends, whatever the weather, he does his walking indoors in time to his recorded Spanish lesson of the day: *Buenas dias, amigo, como esta. . .*

GET MORE FUN OUT OF WALKING

My daughter Madeleine can swim 50 laps in a 100 foot pool and enjoys every minute of it. I swim a couple of times a week because I think swimming is an excellent exercise. But, quite frankly, it bores me.

Feelings about walking vary as well. Some people jump at any opportunity they can get to walk; walking just makes them feel good. I enjoy walking most of the time, but every once in a while find it a chore. Some people appreciate the health, emotional and intellectual values of walking, but are easily bored by it.

If you genuinely enjoy the walking you do, and find it interesting, invigorating and rewarding, your best bet may be to leave well enough alone. If you are too often bored, and don't really look forward to your walking stints, you may find one or more of the following ideas applied by some people to make their walking more fun, helpful:

- Vary the route you cover from day to day; take off in one direction one day, the opposite direction the next day.
- Try carrying a radio with you. Listen to music or the news while you walk.
- Make friends along accustomed routes. I like to walk the same route again and again. One reason is that there are small children who look for me, and we've become good friends. I've also grown friendly with a few senior citizens; having someone to say "Hi" and a few words helps to brighten their day and mine as well.
- Walk alone sometimes; other times invite a walking companion to join you if you can find one available.
- Reward yourself for walking. Visit somebody you like. Chances are you will enjoy the walk there and the walk back almost as much as the visit. Walk to a store and make an interesting purchase such as a record or book. Walk to an interesting place or event, such as the public library, or a little league ball game.

You can enhance the fun and joy of walking by giving the wheres and whens of it more consideration and thought. Be creative!

12

HITTING THE TRAIL

"I like to walk about amidst the beautiful things that adorn the world."

George Santayana

You hear a lot of disparaging talk these days about our plasticized, computerized, automated society. But you don't see many of the gripers abandoning the comforts and conveniences of "civilized" living. Despite its obvious drawbacks, I'd be the last one to knock modern life. It offers too many advantages I wouldn't like living without, such as the much-maligned automobile.

If civilization as we know it today suddenly disappeared, a whole army would be at work trying to reinvent it. Consider the benefits. If you're hungry it's a simple matter to drop into the nearest eating place; if at home to raid the refrigerator, or put up something to cook on the automatic gas or electric range. If the weather's inclement, you can go indoors. If it's too cool indoors, you can turn up the thermostat. If you're tired, a comfortable bed is usually handy. Cold and hot water taps are nearby if you're thirsty, or want to wash. If you need a shower or bath, you step into a shower stall or tub. When you need to relieve yourself, a toilet is probably close by wherever you happen to be. If you're in the mood for amusement (or boredom), the flick of a switch will snap your TV to life. If transportation's your requirement, the car is parked nearby, and once inside your destination, you'll probably find an elevator or escalator to take you to the floor of your choice. Clearly, modern technology has been geared to minimizing human movement and effort to the lowest possible degree which, in one sense, is all to the good. We get things done faster and easier.

But life has a way of exacting payment for the conveniences it gives us. Inactivity and lack of exercise, the doctors agree, causes our bodies to deteriorate prematurely. Less obviously, city-bound existence tends to dull our senses and diminish our awareness of the beauties of both nature and the natural functions of the body and mind. Encapsulating ourselves in civilization's protective shell, we lose touch with many values and benefits hard to find in the concrete metropolis.

THE GETAWAY URGE

Feeling oppressed by city-induced deprivation, millions of urban dwellers, yearning to breathe the fresh country air and communicate with nature, hit the trail every chance they get. But along with the body-and-mind-renewing values of the great outdoors, they also find a lot of inconvenience and discomfort that makes many getaways wonder why in the name of common sense they are doing it.

It's a good question. What prompts hordes of people from ages nine to ninety to forsake the ease of civilized living to hit the trail with all its hardships and, in some cases, dangers? Is it a yearning to pit oneself against the elements? A longing for adventure and excitement? A desire to escape the complications and demands of an accelerated society? An attempt to wind down from the tension and stress of pressure cooker jobs or marital hassles? A desire to have some time alone to communicate with oneself?

For some the answer may lie with one or more of these things. Most hikers and backpackers I've spoken with found it hard to explain why they hiked and what they got out of it. But almost invariably what came through was an intense emotional feeling. They *love* hitting the trail. They *love* getting away. It fulfills a basic physical and psychological need.

Author Eric Meves puts it this way: "Intense experience is what backpacking is all about. It's not equipment, it's not maps, it's not the natural environment. It's what all these things instill in you, the individual backpacker, as part of the backpacking experience."

One hiker I interviewed scratched the back of his head and grinned. "I don't know, you swim bare-ass in a cool mountain lake. Where can you duplicate that?"

There's no question backpacking is a highly personal and individual business. You don't do it for the record. You're not competing against anyone, unless it be Nature.

Outdoors editor and journalist Andrew J. Carra asked a friend what he got out of backpacking. Writes Carra, "He enjoyed driving his body uphill and down, feeling his muscles exerting themselves, feeling the country air fill his lungs, feeling the feet, yards, and miles trail off behind him, knowing that everything he needed was strapped on his back. He didn't know what he was accomplishing, but he knew he was filled with a sense of self-accomplishment."

Many backpackers hike with companions or spouse. One veteran told me, "If you hike with more than two or three other people, it's not really hiking." Other serious hikers express the need to be off by themselves every so often. For what? For contemplation. To ponder life and its values free from such intrusions as people and telephones. To set one's priorities in proper perspective.

A writer-hiker friend, more articulate than most, told me he thought the hiking experience helped him to feel more comfortable with himself. "It gives you breathing space and time to consider where you've been and where you're going. And all the while you plod on ahead along the trail, your body in tune with your mind, no easy state to achieve in the bustle and hubbub of city existence."

I know of a woman who expresses the need to be surrounded at all times by other people. It's almost a compulsion with her. She makes dates, sets appointments, throws parties on an ongoing basis. I don't pretend to be a psychiatrist. But I can't help wondering about this woman. I get the feeling she's afraid of being alone, that she's fearful of self-confrontation. Why? I don't have the vaguest idea, nor is it any of my business. And I could be completely off base. But my instincts tell me the woman has deep-seated psychological problems.

I think the need for "space," the time and freedom to communicate with yourself, to get to know and like yourself better, is helpful to one's mental outlook and philosophy. The outdoors provides an ideal natural environment in which to accomplish this purpose.

Another hiker I know, a woman executive in her forties, told me, "Getting away from the concrete and glass jungle occasionally helps me keep from taking myself for granted. It's so easy to grow complacent with all the comforts and conveniences. Do you know I actually had a canopy built from my detached garage to the side door of my house twelve feet away so I wouldn't get wet when it rained. And I've got one of those electric gizmos that opens the garage door automatically so I don't have to get out of the car. My goodness! To what extent can you pamper yourself?"

This woman admitted she wouldn't think of trading the comforts of suburban life for rustic living. But its unnaturalness gets to her. She takes to the wilds periodically, she says, to reassert her identity. She hates the hardships and inconveniences of backpacking, but something drives her to keep doing it. "No," she confesses, "I couldn't begin to explain it rationally. It's like a debt that has to be paid off."

Hikers hike for a variety of reasons even in hiking families that have been doing it for years. Gene Slade is a veteran outdoorsman who has explored areas of the U.S. and northern Canada where even experienced hikers would be reluctant to venture. Asked why he subjects himself to the hardship and danger, he referred to Sir Edmund Hillary's famous reply when asked why he climbed Mount Everest: "Because the s.o.b. is there!"

Gene's wife June is far less rugged, but no less enthusiastic about hiking. She loves the sport for the feeling of exhilaration and happiness it gives you when all the factors are right, when you feel good physically, when you're in the right frame of mind. "You can't describe it with words," she says. "How can you explain the way you feel when you reach the crest of a hill and are smitten by the trees and the sky, or a lonesome pine silhouetted against the horizon? A lot," she adds, "depends on the scenery."

Son Don Slade, in his twenties, enjoys backpacking for the feeling of self-sufficiency it gives him, for the scenic beauty, and for the sense of peace he feels in the wilderness. There are people benefits too, he says. On the trail with a couple of friends, there's an intimacy you experience that would be hard to match. "Hiking," he adds, "also brings people with common interests together and gives them a chance to compare and share knowledge."

The Music Within. The 18th century mystic and philosopher Novalis, referred to nature as an Aeolian harp, a musical instrument, whose tones are the re-echo of higher strings within us.

Karl Humboldt, the philologist and statesman, wrote: "Natural objects themselves, even when they make no claim to beauty, excite the feelings, and occupy the imagination. Nature pleases, attracts, delights, merely because it is nature."

Hitting the trail may mean special things to many people, and different things to different people. But if there is one thing all hikers share in common it is the awakening of the senses in response to the glories of nature, the reverberations of the music within. It is a symphony of sounds and feelings and sights.

Walking along woodland trails, along paths bordering bodies of water flanked by flowers and trees, far out of sight and hearing of city streets, power lines, and automobile noises, your awareness of the environment is automatically heightened. Little used senses come suddenly to life. You turn alert to the transitory beauty of a strange cloud formation and devote a moment to wondering if any human eyes but yours could be seeing exactly what you are seeing from your exact vantage point. Or did God create this sight for your eyes alone?

Your nostrils quiver and perk to the scent of forest dampness with wildflower flavoring. The gurgle of a clear, clean and cool stream bubbling out from a wooded hillside delights ears too long abused by harsh city sounds. From somewhere nearby the warbled trill of a lark provides counterpoint to the melodic theme like a flute solo playing on cue. You hear small animals and birds chattering away with each other in a wondrous secret language no cryptographer could decode. Your appreciative eyes widen to the riotous reds, russets and golds as the seasons change and you suddenly realize that this tired old world is bigger and grander and more beautiful than you ever dreamed it could be. And you realize too that you're hooked.

If you're a fisherman, your taste buds are pampered as well. One outdoorsman told me a campsite alongside a trout-laden brook represents for him the world's most unique and exclusive dining place. He wouldn't trade it for the Four Seasons or Antoines. And if the fish is done properly, no gourmet meal ever prepared could surpass the flavor and taste of a freshly caught trout.

As Wild Or Tame As You Wish. Another benefit of wilderness walking is that it can be tailored to the individual desire and need. Trails are graded according to their length and difficulty. Depending on your personal preference you can choose a short two or three mile hike, or a rugged backpacking expedition that could last days. You can walk alone, with a companion or two, or with groups of forty or more along easy trails which, sadly, are all too often as littered with refuse as with people, usually left by inconsiderate Sunday picnickers. You can select hiking areas where no human ear would hear you if you fired a gun or shouted at the top of your voice.

Your mode of escape from civilization is entirely up to you. Parks and wooded areas are within easy access of most communities. The Manhattan tenement dweller can for the most part screen out the concrete jungle by visiting Central Park, a few minutes away. A quick bus trip will take the San Franciscan to glorious Golden Gate Park where he can immerse himself in another world inhabited by birds, flowers and trees. Rock Creek Park is nearby for most Washingtonians; Prospect Park is in the middle of Brooklyn. St. Louis, Detroit, Los Angeles, Boston, Atlanta and every other major U.S. city maintain attractive parks of substantial acreage where you can walk or hike to your heart's content.

What about trail hiking for exercise? It's ideal for pace walking if the "wilderness area" of your choice is a flat and smooth surfaced city park. Hiking or backpacking along other trails is difficult to assess as an exercise since so much depends on the amount of exertion and strain you put into the effort, the terrain itself, and the degree to which you make your cardiovascular system work.

Justice Douglas defines trails along ridges, through valleys, or down old country roads as "an exciting gymnasium." "Most gyms," he says, "are dingy and crowded, filled with the odor of sweat. The trail leading through woods or across meadows is filled with the fresh fragrance of the outdoors. There are no weights to lift, no bicycles to ride, no oars to pull. But the ups and downs of the average trail exercise most of the muscles and man ends his hike tired but renewed."

THE NATIONAL PARKS

America is blessed with its fair share of the world's magnificent scenery. The first National Park was created in 1872 when Congress, through the Yellowstone Act, set aside a wilderness area in Wyoming about two-thirds the size of Connecticut. A primary purpose of the Act and subsequent designations all over the country was to provide beautiful and historical areas for the pleasure and benefit of the public and, at the same time, preserve the natural environment to the maximum extent possible.

Today the United States Forest Service supervises 155 national forests encompassing 187 million acres and maintains well over 100,000 miles of trail. Over 14 million acres of this land has been designated wilderness area. That means they contain no man-made improvements other than the trails, retain their primeval appearance and character, and display a negligible amount of evidence of man's intrusion.

The National Parks were established by Congress to preserve outstanding scenic, recreational and historical areas for the enjoyment and use of the public. Featuring well paved roads, they attract millions of hikers and campers each year. Thousands of backpackers leave their cars for days on end to head for the well-marked trails—or those that aren't so well marked, depending on their personal preference. Of course, the further from the main roads and popular trails you venture, the further behind you will leave civilization and the crowds.

The National Park Service employs a force of rangers who patrol assigned areas in an effort to protect both the environment and its inhabitants, four-footed and human. Experienced guides are on hand to lead visitors through the park and give lectures on its various features and points of interest. Free public camping grounds are maintained in all National Parks except Carlsbad Caverns. Both inexpensive and moderate lodging and restaurants, as well as shops and transportation are also available. Some of the more popular National Parks are listed below:

PARK	ACRES	LOCATION	MAIN FEATURE
Bryce Canyon	36,010	Southern Utah	Colorful rock formations and pinnacles.
Carlsbad Caverns	49,447	New Mexico	Network of connected caverns with unusual rock formations.
Everglades	1,499,428	Southern Florida	Swamplands; swamp foliage and animal life.
Grand Canyon	673,575	Northern Arizona	Spectacular crater and brilliantly colored rock walls and ledges.
Great Smokey Mts.	510,393	Tennesse/ North Carolina	Virgin forest and high mountain ranges.
Mammoth	51,354	Central	Network of caves

Cave		Kentucky	and underground river. Limestone caverns.
Petrified Forest	101,927	Arizona, Painted Desert area	Petrified trees.
Sequoia	386,560	Eastern California	The tallest trees in the world.
Shenandoah	211,210	Northern Virginia	Scenic beauty of the Blue Ridge Mountains.
Wind Cave	28,059	Black Hills of South Dakota	Limestone caverns; old buffalo country.
Yellowstone	2,221,772	Wyoming/ Montana/ Idaho	Scenic beauty, wildlife, and geysers.
Yosemite	760,951	East-Central California	Yosemite Falls, Mirror Lake, scenic beauty.
Zion	143,254	Southern Utah	Zion Canyon, the "Rainbow of the Desert."

Information Is Yours for the Asking. If one of your aims is to avoid vacation crowds, you may prefer visiting the National Parks in the spring or fall of the year when they're not swarming with tourists. Planning ahead will make your trip more enjoyable and avoid dissapointments. If you intend visiting one of the National Parks, here are some helpful suggestions from William J. Whalen, Director of the National Park Service.

- Visiting hours and season openings and closings vary park-by-park. Generally, park areas are open every day of the year except Christmas or New Year's Day, but winter weather limits activities in some parks. You may write to the park for specific information about visiting hours and length of the season. Advance contact also can provide details about parking conditions and transportation services available to and within the park.

- Most parks have a visitor center. Stop there first. Free literature, and often exhibits, movies, and slide presentations are available to help you better understand the area and use it safely.
- Observe the common sense rules of safety. Natural hazards abound in outdoor areas, but visiting the National Parks can be a safe experience if you use ordinary precautions. Never approach wild animals. If you swim or climb or take hiking trips, do it with a partner and let park personnel know where you will be.
- Entrance fees usually of $2-$3 per vehicle are charged at many parks. If you plan frequent visits, the $10 Golden Eagle Passport, good for one calendar year, may save you money on entrance fees. If you have reached age 62, you are eligible for a free, lifetime Golden Age Passport which covers admission and provides a 50 percent discount on campground and other user fees. Both passports are available at park entrances.
- Very few campgrounds operated by the National Park Service can be reserved. Almost all are on a first-come, first-served basis.
- Special restrictions sometimes apply to backpackers using environmentally fragile back-country areas. Free permits to use certain trails and areas are issued by Park Rangers at the park. Applications usually are made in person, but you can write the park where you plan to hike for further information.
- Information on both National and State parks can be obtained from State Travel Directors in capital cities.
- If you want to avoid crowds, you might want to visit one of the National Park System's "lesser-used" areas. "Visit a Lesser-Used Park," (Stock No. 024-005-00589-7), a guide listing these areas, is available for $1.30 from the Superintendent of Documents, U.S. Government Printing Office, Washington, D.C. 20402.

Day-Hiking. In the National Parks, and in back-country and wilderness areas, you are free to take overnight hikes, or trips covering several days. This way you are really "roughing it," and getting away from all signs of civilization. Many backpackers would consider no other alternative.

However, depending on your desires and goals, there's a great deal to be said for day-hiking. Carrying a heavy pack on your back containing sleeping bag, tent, equipment and provisions, can seriously limit the pleasure of walking. Equipped with a simple light knapsack, you can get much better exercise, move and breath more easily, and cover a good deal more distance. In addition, assuming you use a motel or lodge in the park as your home base, after returning from a hard day of hiking, there's nothing like the luxury of a hot shower followed by a good meal eaten in comfort. You may not be practicing the art of survival planning day trips instead of camping out under the stars, but as one hiker told me, "Day-hiking is for me because it gives you the best of both worlds."

THE HIKING CLUBS

Scores of hiking clubs are located throughout the U.S. and Canada. Some of the larger clubs play an active role in protecting and preserving the environment colored by their activities and programs. To describe each one individually would require a good-sized book of itself. Clubs—the larger ones in particular—usually offer one or more of the following services and benefits:

Companionship. All hiking clubs provide an opportunity for their members to get together for meetings, lectures or organized hikes. Joining the club of your choice is a good way to meet people and find others who share common interests with you.

News. Most clubs publish newsletters or announcements outlining and describing organized hikes, providing members with information of local interest, and keeping up-to-date about happenings in the world of hiking, backpacking and outdoor life.

Trails. Many clubs participate in and help promote the

exploration, mapping and development of hiking trails.

Shelters. Some clubs build weather shelters and huts alongside trails.

Information. Centers are maintained with personnel who respond to inquiries from the public about hiking, backpacking and other outdoor activities. They also provide up-to-date information about back country and wilderness uses as well as weather conditions.

Publications. The larger clubs provide a variety of guide books, periodicals and maps at moderate cost. Some publish their own magazines. Subject coverage ranges from information about specific areas and trails to literature about skiing, winter hiking, first aid, canoeing, backpacking, natural history, survival and route finding. A few clubs stock and maintain libraries with books and journals of interest to the outdoors person.

Films. Film rental service is provided by the larger hiking clubs. Subjects include hiking, climbing, backpacking, camping, canoeing, outdoor safety and skills.

Guided hikes. Professional club personnel skilled in natural history, outdoor skills and safety, lead organized hikes during which education is combined with the sport.

Educational programs. Club-sponsored speakers are available to address private groups for a moderate fee. Lectures are conducted at many club centers. Some of the larger clubs sponsor teacher and youth leader workshops, and a variety of programs on outdoor living and life for the young.

Camps. Club-supervised camping facilities range from campgrounds where members can pitch tents in mountain, riverbank and lakeside locations to full-service camps, vacation lodges and inns where lodging and meals are provided in a rustic setting, with rates discounted for members. Many hikers use cabins and lodges as a home base from which to hit the hiking trails and other recreational facilities.

UNBIBLIOGRAPHY

This book is about all major forms of walking, and covers aspects of general interest. Since so many walkers are also hikers, a chapter on "Hitting the Trail" is clearly warranted. But it merely covers some of the highlights. A detailed writeup of the subject would take hundreds of pages and defeat the overall objective of this work. Hopefully, some of the information here will help whet your appetite and, if you are not yet an experienced hiker, encourage you to seek more information on hitting the trail.

I wouldn't recommend after reading this chapter that you take off on a backpacking trip to a back country or wilderness area. This is one sport where it will pay you to be as well informed as you can before getting started. It's an activity where some good solid knowledge could save you a whole lot of hardship, possibly even your life.

If you plan to do any serious trail hiking or backpacking, I would strongly recommend that you not only read up on the subject but study it diligently. What books do I recommend? My initial intention was to include a bibliography of books on trail walking and backpacking, but after visiting the library I decided this would be a disservice. There are simply too many good books to list. What would you like to know about hitting the trail? Whatever aspect of hiking, backpacking, camping or outdoor life in general you might be interested in, you can be sure there are dozens of books available that discuss the subject in depth.

Your best bet, I believe, would be to visit a well stocked public library with a checklist in hand. Assuming, for example, that you have backpacking in mind, such a list would most certainly include:

- What to wear
- Equipment to carry
- Food and how to prepare it
- Safety and first aid
- Personal hygiene
- How to pitch a tent
- How to pack a backpack
- How to avoid getting lost
- What to do in inclement weather
- Planning your trip

- Good manners along the trail
- Bedding down for the night
- Where to go and how to get there

My library checkout disclosed dozens of shelves loaded with hundreds of books discussing in great detail all the items listed above and a great deal more. Rather than attempting to pick two or three books from a recommended list, I think you would be better served to browze along the bookshelves, checklist in hand, examine several books briefly after scanning the table of contents, and check out five or six that are most clearly tailored to your requirements.

FACING REALITIES

Let's not kid ourselves. Backpacking and trail hiking are about as healthful, satisfying, invigorating and rewarding as almost any sport you could name. But like water skiing, sky diving, or circus acrobatics, you have to know exactly what you're doing to avoid getting hurt. One need merely refer to the nation's press for an insight into the number of hikers and backpackers who starve, poison themselves, freeze to death, or get mauled by wild animals every year because they failed to heed common sense safety tips and precautions.

The 17th century English author Francis Quarles once wrote, "Let the fear of a danger be a spur to prevent it; he that fears not, gives advantage to the danger." Excellent advice for the backpacker.

What follows are some basic pointers for the inexperienced hiker to consider *before* taking off on that trip:

* Don't try to become a Daniel Boone overnight. If you've never done rugged backpacking, plan simple hikes that are within your capability to begin with. Don't play the veteran hero until you're a veteran. Like any other sport or skill, results are usually measured in terms of experience. Backpacking is no exception. There's safety in numbers; three is good, four is better.

* Many areas require fire permits for hikers who leave

the main trails. They're given free of charge and serve to identify backpackers in the area and heighten awareness of the danger. The hazards of fire have been too widely publicized to require repetition here. Any hiker who uses fire should learn all there is to know about starting a fire properly, and dousing it thoroughly when he is done with it.

One backpacker I talked with told me the most embarrassing experience of his 28 years occurred while in a back country area of Virginia's Shenandoah National Park. One morning, an hour or so after leaving their campsite, he and his two companions were stopped on the trail by a park ranger. The ranger asked them to accompany him back to their campsite. When they arrived there they found a substantial part of the campsite area burned out.

"Fortunately and by sheer coincidence," the ranger told them, "I happened to be close enough by to see the smoke."

The backpackers sheepishly averted their eyes and replied, "We thought we put it out."

Where fire is concerned, thinking isn't enough. You've got to make sure.

* The chief anxiety that plagues the novice backpacker is the fear of getting lost. The fear is largely groundless if you learn how to use a compass and map and stick to well marked trails. It becomes a very valid worry for the inexperienced hiker who ventures into unknown areas before acquiring the knowhow to do so. Hiking along trails and through wooded areas, your perceptions are automatically sharpened. Gradually you will get into the habit of noticing such landmarks as mountain peaks, bodies of water, trail crossings, and fallen or oddly shaped trees.

Early in his backpacking days a now-experienced hiker I know recalls a time he was hopelessly lost in the back country and describes it as a terrifying experience. ("As night approaches, you start imagining all kinds of things.") Fortunately, his more experienced friends found him before darkness set in, which calls an important point to mind. First of all, as we said, don't hike alone until you're experienced enough to have mastered the basics of following trails and backtracking when you stray off course. When backpacking with a group, prearrange a signal to use—shout, whistle, bell, flashing light—as a call for help. If you are lost despite all precautions, stay put when darkness comes. Build a carefully contained fire against a big rock if possible to get maximum heat, and put on those extra clothes to stay warm.

* Hopefully, you'll enjoy ideal hiking conditions when you backpack. But be prepared for the worst. Count on bad weather when you pack. If the temperature drops, have the bedroll and clothes to adjust to it. Read up on frostbite. Learn how to avoid it and how, in emergency, to treat it.

* Under ordinary circumstances, the advice you hear about bears applies: They won't bother you if you don't bother them. But bears can be temperamental and unpredictable creatures, especially if injured or sick. To keep your distance is a good general rule; if one acts strangely or appears to be hurt, double your distance. And never pick up or play with a baby animal, no matter how cute or how much alone it may appear to be. Mama may be hovering nearby and misinterpret your intentions.

When camping, burn food scraps and unwanted leftovers. Bears and other wild animals are foragers and will be attracted by food left at campsites. Many hikers hang backpacks on high tree limbs out of reach of hungry prowlers. If a bear should materialize when food is at hand and decides to go after it, don't argue with him.

Generally speaking, wild animals are more afraid of you than you are of them. But in the back country it's not always a good idea to speak generally. Grizzlies, while relatively rare on most trails, constitute a definite peril for hikers. Considered by many hunters to be the most dangerous of all North American wild animals, they are much larger, more ferocious, and far less timid than their more common black cousins. Though many grizzlies have been destroyed in this country, some still roam the national forests and parks of the west hunting for food day and night in all kinds of weather.

Plant Engineering magazine editor and backpacking

afficionado Lea Tonkin once told me how she ran into one while she and her husband were on the trail to Hidden Lake in Montana's Glacier National Park. Having been informed by a park ranger they were in bear country, they took care to make plenty of noise as they walked through wooded areas, an old hiker's ploy to avoid surprising wild animals. They finally reached the lake, after having given wide berth to a wolverine encountered along the way, and sat down on the shoreline to enjoy the magnificent view.

What they didn't realize is that they had stumbled on a favorite habitat for bear fishing—where a stream flows into a lake. After several moments of silently appreciating the scenery, they suddenly heard a Mack truck engine starting up. Except that it wasn't a Mack truck at all; it was a gargantuan yellow-brown grizzly. Lea said, "We started talking loudly and banging our gear on the rocks, and after debating the issue, Mack turned tail and crashed back through the woods. You can be sure we didn't stop talking, singing and whistling for the rest of that trip."

She added gravely that others weren't so lucky. Shortly after, a party of hikers surprised a female grizzly and her cub on a nearby trail, and several of them were severely mauled.

* A time to be especially wary, and preferably absent, is in the fall when deer hunting season is literally in full blast in many parts of the country. This doesn't apply to the National Parks, however, where hunting is generally prohibited.

* Before planning a trip, it's a good idea to check the insect situation in the area for which you're headed. Certain times of the year and in certain locations mosquitoes, gnats, ticks, chiggers and other winged pests can constitute more than a minor problem. Even under favorable conditions it pays to carry insect repellant, and a snake-bite kit as well. You may not feel those insect bites at all when they occur, but they could have you itching and chafing for weeks.

* What about romping along the trail with your fun-loving dog? It conjures up a nice and warm picture. But, when hiking the back country or wilderness areas, you're better off

leaving Rags at home. A prime danger is the provoking of wildlife or visa versa. For this reason, dogs are prohibited in many hiking areas.

* Another contingency to provide for is that planned short hikes sometimes inadvertently turn into long ones. Thousands of trails wind through America's and Canada's park and wilderness areas, and while the Park Service, rangers and participating hiking clubs do an outstanding job, you can't always count on the trail signs' accuracy. It makes sense to prepare for an extended hike you didn't necessarily anticipate.

Lea Tonkin recalls a time in Banff provincial park in the Canadian Rockies when she and her husband decided to take a walk before breakfast. They didn't even bother to put on their hiking boots.

The turnoff for the lookout point they were headed for wasn't marked. They kept walking and walking—and walking —and hours later ended up at a place called the Ink Pots, a beautiful meadow where springs bubble cold and clear from deep in the earth. It had been uphill all the way. They had no food with them, having planned to be gone no more than two or three hours at most. "Fortunately," Lea says, "some fellow hikers we met on the way back were kind enough to share some of their food with us. But the trek down the mountain would have been far less taxing had we worn hiking boots."

She adds, "It also calls to mind the importance of remembering that at high altitudes even a short trip can be tiring, and take much longer than anticipated."

Also, the higher you climb, the cooler it gets. I can recall quite vividly a hike I once took in Colorado's Rocky Mountain National Park. The temperature was comfortably mild when we started out, and expecting to be back within four or five hours, all I had with me was a light knapsack containing lunch and a light sweater. The "walk" took longer than we expected, and after three hours of uphill climbing, light sweater and all I was shivering.

* Many of the hundreds of books in the library on

hiking, camping and backpacking, offer excellent advice on the best kind of first aid kit to purchase and the items to include. After reading all about the aspects that interest you most, go back and read this section again two or three times. The best kind of hike is the one where you never open your first aid kit. But when the need for it occurs, it's the most important item you carry.

13

SHOULD YOU RUN?

"I do not choose to run."

Calvin Coolidge

Assuming your legs and feet are in relatively good shape, you know you can walk. But after making the sensible transition from a modest and conservative to an energetic walking program, should you stop at that point? It depends on your physical condition, your doctor's advice, and your state of mind. If you decide to go on from walking to running, what do you hope to get out of it?

WHY RUN?

Most serious walkers do it to slim down and shape up. If you exercise for the health values it brings, the first question to deal with is: What's the best exercise for you? Other exercises that rate high on the list along with walking include swimming, bike riding, skating, and of course, running, if the conditions are right. Your personal preference will, or should, depend on 3 further factors:

1. Which exercise is *safest* for you?
2. Which one gives you the most enjoyment and satisfaction?
3. Which exercise is most convenient and practical?

Personally, I engage in 3 forms of exercise primarily: Walking, swimming and tennis. Although I enjoy walking immensely, I find tennis the most fun of all. But considering the unpredictable stretches, spurts and strains inherent to the game, it's not a very safe exercise for a man in his 50s who once had a back problem. Although it helps shave down the calories, playing tennis probably isn't one of my more brilliant pursuits. My more practical side encourages me to swim a couple of times a week because I feel it's quite therapeutic. But I find swimming relatively boring and not very convenient. Walking, of course, is the safest and most convenient exercise of all, and since I like to do it in the bargain, it's the best bet as far as I'm concerned.

What about running? I've tried it and it makes me uncomfortable. I feel the jolt in my heels, knees and back. Listening to my body, I hear it tell me, "Hey, cut this out!" So my philosophy is: "Who needs it? What's the point in punishing myself?"

No point at all from my way of thinking, *which needn't be your way of thinking.* But I figure, if I can achieve my health and satisfaction objectives through walking and other means, why run? From my point of view, the only advantage I can see of running over walking is that it would save me a little time. As one doctor told me, "You get about the same cardiovascular benefit out of 30 minutes of brisk walking as you get from 20 minutes of running."

Beyond Physical Health: The Psychic Kick and the Joy. Deprive someone of the psychological stimulation he relies on and you deal him a shattering blow. Even though the dedicated non-runner may respond with dubious ear to some of the poetically fervant testimonials about running, the sheer volume of huzzas earns it a measure of credence and respect. I for one am satisfied that most running afficionados are sincere in their fervor. James F. Fixx, in his well-researched "The Complete Book of Running," interviewed innumerable runners whose eyes apparently took on a beatific glow in describing the sport. One runner, for example, told Fixx that: "To run is to live. Everything else is just waiting."

Fixx also talked with several doctors, psychologists and other professionals, some of whom give running an edge over psychotherapy and drugs in working with abnormally depressed patients, and attribute to running a host of positive results from relief of tension and anxiety to conquered feelings of shyness, improved self-esteem, and a more gratifying sex life.

Fixx also discusses the views of New Jersey cardiologist Dr. George A. Sheehan, who is to running what Mozart is to music. More than an ordinary doctor, Sheehan is a philosopher who writes up a highly readable storm on running and its philosophical implications, and is as much at ease quoting Nietzsche and Jung as he is discussing the findings of Dr. Kenneth Cooper and the feelings of greats in running's hall of fame.

One of Dr. Sheehan's main themes is that you *are* when you run. Since *being* is what life's jigsaw puzzle is all about, it follows that running should merit the highest priority. In evaluating the literature on exercise—and Dr. Sheehan's treatises are a good deal more than that—one would be hard put to find anyone more dedicated to any cause than he is to running. As Fixx defines the good doctor's position, he would surely agree with the cynic who said, "Physical fitness is just a brief stage we go through on the way to learning how to run well."

What About You? We're back where we started. Should you run? If you feel as Sheehan, Cooper, Fixx & Co. do about running, quite obviously it would merit your strong consideration.

The trick, however, may lie in becoming honestly and sincerely convinced, and not merely conned. The problem is that when any idea or concept gets rolling with the avalanche-like momentum of running in America, it's bound to attract a motley crew of crackpots and con artists along with the honest believers. The more articulate of the me-too exponents usually succeed in cashing in on the fallout by angling off on new tangents and possibly even organizing subcults of their own which, if nothing else, sell a whole lot of books. The crackpots? What they're up to is anyone's guess.

Following the peak of the running craze many of these self-appointed pundits, guru-like in their pronouncements, attributed a patchwork of mystical qualities to the sanctified exercise. One strategy is to hook up with an already confusing and fairly far-out concept and tie it together with running. Holism, for example, is the theory that reality is made up of organic or unified wholes that are greater than the simple sum of their parts. Now that in itself is a mouthful to swallow. Hence "holistic running," the inevitable linkage. One author describes the ecstatic and trance-like state he goes into after a few miles of holistic running.

Another writer describes "inner running" as the ultimate natural high, an interesting concept. This author urges his readers to "do nothing but run when you run." Others assure us with missionary zeal that running leads us through all the different stages of man's evolutionary development. Genetic, transcendental, and euphoric significances are linked to the sport. Zen is introduced into the picture along with soul transformations and seekings after Buddha or God. Running, we are also told, awakes the unconscious mind, and hastens the evolutionary processes toward a higher state of being and knowing. It evokes childhood memories, reveals secret goals, "illuminates the inner framework of the soul," helps us articulate long-suppressed fantasies and dreams. Also ascribed to running are such ethereal experiences as feelings of weightlessness and spacelessness.

In "The Psychic Power of Running: How the Body Can Illuminate the Mysteries of the Mind," Valerie Andrews explains, "We must wonder if the biological need to run isn't an instinctive drive to recapitulate our primary genetic strengths before the next evolutionary leap into the future."

If you understand that, maybe you *should* be running.

Some runners run because through running, through driving their lungs and legs beyond their natural limits of endurance, they experience excruciating pain—and find, at that threshold, pleasure. Although the reasoning may be difficult for most of us to fathom, I believe a majority of these stoics are sincere in their goals.

They also have an impressive intellectual consensus to support their contentions. The philosopher Ebner-Eschenbach wrote, "Pain is the great teacher of mankind, beneath its breath souls develop." The psychologist William James told us, "Pain used in life gives us a new dimension of life." And Arthur Hallam stated more than a century ago that, "Pain is the deepest thing we have in our nature, and union through pain and suffering has always seemed more real and holy than any other."

"The severity of pain in running depends on the intensity of the mind-body struggle," James Fixx explains. Your body says stop, but your mind says keep going.

I consider myself fortunate that I don't have this problem. My body says, "Slow down; walk, don't run." And my mind says, "Right on!"

But that's me. Now what about you?

I don't mean to be irreverant. In a nation where religious freedom is one of our constitutional birthrights, you're entitled to worship at any altar you wish. So here's another factor to mull over. I sometimes get the feeling too many of us stay so preoccupied doing things that are "good for us" we wind up doing too many *right* things that bring us all kinds of benefits but too little joy.

What I am getting at is this: If you honestly and deep down believe running—or anything else—will bring you inner peace, do something uplifting and spiritual for your soul, enhance your evolutionary development (if you know what that means), or fulfill your long-suppressed fantasies and dreams, who am I or anyone else to advise you not to do it? My personal feeling, and one too often forgotten, is: If you want something badly enough, and if the gut feeling and emotion tied into the wanting are genuine, maybe you should let practicality go hang, ignore your level-headed peers who think you're a nut and, so long as you don't hurt anyone else but yourself in the process, get on with it.

The years slip away too quickly to let our dreams pass us by. If running happens to be the—sport, exercise, religion? —you feel so strongly about, perhaps you shouldn't settle for walking simply because it's the practical thing to do. Take my blessing and run.

But if you don't share this fervor, it's another matter entirely.

DECIDING FACTORS

You're a relatively normal individual, hooked on neither the pleasure of intense pain nor the transcendental aspects of otherism. Why run?

Because running, like walking, can yield impressive physical and mental health benefits. Most psychiatrists and psychologists would agree that getting away from the harrowing grind of your day-to-day duties and responsibilities from time to time and engaging in some form of physical activity can help relieve tension and anxiety, dissipate anger, and help shed feelings of gloom. As a *cure* for deep depression, few therapists would rate exercise as anything more than a useful aid. As one psychiatrist assured me, "There are few if any quick and easy remedies for the person who is seriously mentally ill."

But running, like brisk walking, offers most of the psychological benefits discussed in Chapter 9, *The Thinking Person's Exercise.* For some, depending on state of mind and outlook, it might work even better than walking to relieve tension and anxiety, and help shed anger or get rid of the blues. One walker/runner told me, "I find it much easier to blank my mind while I'm running than while I'm walking." This same person says, "When it comes to such things as decision-making and problem-solving where the idea is to ponder and not go blank, in my experience nothing beats walking."

So far as the cardiovascular benefits of running are concerned, the value of exercise that sensibly taxes your system has been discussed at length in earlier chapters. If you scored well on a stress test, get the green light from your doctor, your body gives you no adverse signals when you run, and you enjoy doing it, why not? Under ideal conditions, running ranks high on the list of beneficial exercises, according to some medical sources, number one.

In fact running has proved so beneficial for humans, they are now trying it on cows. Dr. John D. Cantwell reports that researchers at the U.S. Dairy Association have devised a jogging program for "flabby, heart disease-prone dairy cattle confined to inactive lives of eating, drinking, resting, being milked, and producing one calf a year." A mechanical exerciser with moving tailgates pushes the cows around a fenced ring. Most of the animals "respond positively" to the program. While clearly beneficial to bovine cardiovascular systems, no mention is made of the effects of the running on their anxieties, tensions and depressions.

If medical opinion is to be your key deciding factor in determining whether or not to run, the sad truth is that it all depends on which doctor you ask. Dr. Thomas Bassler, who heads the American Medical Joggers Association, contends marathon running virtually guarantees immunity from coronary disease, and attributes jogging deaths to heat stroke and other causes. Jogging is safe, he says, if performed properly under ideal conditions. "If you train under 6 miles a day or smoke," he cautions, "jogging can kill you."

Realistically, from the health risk standpoint, ideal running takes place only in a medically supervised environment where, should you collapse during the exercise as a result of heat stroke, arrhythmia triggered by anoxia, potassium shift, magnesium depletion or some other cause, medical help will be close at hand to revive you.

Cardiac joggers at Seattle's Cardio-Pulmonary Research Institute (CAPRI), for example, run with trained nurses in attendance and are monitored by portable defibrillator paddles which give electrocardiographs in a second. "Among 1,500 people since the program started in 1968," *Medical Tribune* correspondent Mark Grant was informed ten years later, "we've had 18 cardiac arrests, but all were resuscitated."

Dr. Kenneth Cooper of Dallas's Aerobics Center reports not a single death there, and no death away from it in five years. "In 2,000,000 miles," says Dr. Cooper, "we've had to resuscitate a patient once." At the Cooper clinic, close supervision takes place where potential problems exist. Certain older patients are never permitted to enter the third, unsupervised grade.

Two Sides To The Coin. Most doctors, even the running advocates among them, would think twice, then once again, before claiming that running is risk-free even under the best of conditions. Dr. Sheehan himself doesn't tell patients that running will protect them from coronary disease.

Bill Rodgers, three-time winner of the Boston Marathon is philosophic on the subject. "More people die because they don't exercise than because they do," he points out. "I like to think when I run that my heart's not going to give out on me. But who can say? Nothing's certain in this world."

One thing is certain. Innumerable runners are hurting themselves to the point where orthopedists are having a field day. In the world of running, "runner's knee" is about as common as the common cold in the outside world. On the other hand, who ever heard of "walker's knee"?

And too many runners are dying, suddenly and unexpectedly. Medical research at the University of Cape Town, South Africa, confirms six cases of myocardial infarction in marathon runners, four of them angiographically proved.

Is running a better exercise than walking? "It's a controversial question," according to Michigan cardiologist Dr. Joseph P. Bertucci. "Consult 100 cardiologists and you will get one hundred different answers."

This distinguished physician is strongly anti-running, categorizes it as a "dangerous form of activity since it destroys knee joints, ankles and feet. In my practice," he adds, "I have seen many injuries and several deaths reported as a result of strenuous jogging."

Older people, he says, are particularly vulnerable. "Take my word for it. Fast walking is more beneficial and can be performed by any age group."

That's one cardiologist's opinion based on his personal experience.

Arthur M. Sackler, M.D., international publisher of the *Medical Tribune,* echoes his caution. "Projected nationally," he writes, "the number of deaths from jogging could be considerable. Clearly, jogging has a risk/benefit ratio. Inappropriately practiced, it may fit the designation of 'imminent hazard' . . . ."

As a dramatic case in point, Dr. Sackler cites the mid-1978 death of Robert S. Summers, administrator of the Miami Heart Institute, who dropped dead while jogging in a program directed at strengthening his heart. Ironically, some years ago one of the early jogging deaths in Miami was that of a prominent physician, Dr. Edward Lauth, a proponent of the jogging program he himself helped initiate through the Heart Association.

Commenting to the *Miami Herald,* Medical Examiner Dr. Ronald K. Wright declared, "We have four or five jogging deaths a year." The victims, he added, "are usually in their 40s and they die of heart attacks."

ARE YOU TOO OLD TO RUN?

In balancing the risks against the benefits of running it's hard to know whose word to go by. The well hooked runner will run at any age in any kind of weather and sometimes in any condition. Dr. George Sheehan admitted to *Washington Post* writer Lawrence Meyer in a telephone interview that "if I had chest pains, I'd probably ignore it . . . . Running has become more important to me. It's become part of my life. I try to listen, but I can understand people not listening."

A man of 69 who has been running for years told me, "I know I should slow down to a walk. But I am seemingly unable to do so. When I slow down to brisk walking, I become frustrated. I need to feel myself running. I need to get back into the rhythm."

When I asked what made him want to slow down, he replied, "Running hurts me; it's hell on my knees."

One doctor will tell you you're too old to run if you're past 35. Another will contend that you're never too old to run.

Dr. John D. Cantwell says, "Age is no deterrent to

running." He cites a 70-year-old man who took up the sport in his early 60s and worked up to marathon distance. "His maximum oxygen uptake," notes Dr. Cantwell, "was 55 ml/kg/min., considerably higher than the reading of 42 ml/kg/min. on a halfback from Georgia Institute of Technology who was 50 years younger."

He calls to mind a 73-year-old ex-high school and college track star who had been inactive for 40 years thereafter. At age 63 he started a walking program and built up to 32 km a day. He first tried jogging at age 68 and over a 10 month period developed a tolerance where he could slowly jog to 16 km a day, a rate he has maintained ever since.

Mavis Lindgren, pictured in a Blue Cross/Blue Shield institutional ad captioned 5 MILES A DAY KEEPS THE DOCTOR AWAY, started running at age 62, with her doctor's blessing. Prior to that she had been subject to chest colds all of her life, had whooping cough at age two, tuberculosis at 13, and suffered three bouts with pneumonia.

Still off and running at 71, Mavis says, "After I started running I never had another cold. I've been sick only once in nine years. I had a real bad flu. I had it for three hours."

The ad goes on to state that Mavis Lindgren and an estimated 10 million other joggers in America feel running keeps them healthy. So maybe it *is* for you too, whatever your age.

In a U.S. Department of Health, Education, and Welfare booklet titled "The Fitness Challenge In the Later Years," and subtitled "an exercise program for older Americans," jogging is strongly recommended, but the careful and gradual approach is stressed. "The main idea is to alternate walking and jogging bouts and to gradually increase the proportion of jogging to walking. In addition, the total distance covered can be gradually increased as well as the speed with which the distance is traversed. However, the speed element is not emphasized beyond the point of getting a good workout within a reasonable time."

In this program, prepared jointly by The President's Council on Physical Fitness and Sports and the Administration on Aging, different levels of exercise achievement are specified, with close monitoring and testing every step of the way. If you proceed from one level to the next without problems, you will eventually reach the ultimate level which includes some jogging along with a host of other exercises. The program is based on the premise that one of the most reliable experts to heed is your own body. If you try to go too far too fast, somewhere along the line your body will probably protest.

The booklet goes on to say, "There are many people around the country in their 60's and 70's who are jogging 2 to 5 miles daily. But don't set your goals this high unless you have gradually raised the distances jogged without experiencing severe reactions or extreme fatigue lasting for several days. Remember to 'taper off' by walking the last interval and moving around until your breathing and pulse rate return to near normal."

FROM A WALK TO A RUN

No law says you have to stop with walking if your body doesn't object. Dr. John D. Cantwell tells about men in their 60's at Atlanta, Georgia's Preventive Cardiology Clinic who have suffered heart attacks and can still train under medical supervision to the point where they can run competitively in a six-mile foot race.

Of course there's no point in jumping into the water before you've learned how to swim. Dr. Louis C. Galli, who heads the Medical Committee for the New York Marathon, suggests getting into a walking program before starting a running program.

The President's Council on Physical Fitness and Sports reminds us that few beginners are capable of running continuously for any distance. The "walk test" will help you determine where to begin. If you can comfortably walk three miles in 45 minutes, it's all right to start running. Or, better still, alternate running and walking. If you can't pass the test, walk three miles a day until you can.

In the beginning, the Council advises, you should

alternately run and walk continuously for 20 minutes. Speed isn't important, but the amount of time is. It takes about 20 minutes for your body to begin realizing the "training effects" of sustained vigorous exercise.

If you do decide to combine walking and running, no one can tell you just how much you should walk and how much you should run. Exercise capacity varies, even in persons of the same age and build. The Council's rule-of-thumb is, after warming up, to walk briskly until you feel you are moving easily. Then run at a comfortable pace until you begin to feel winded or tired. Resume walking until you feel like running again. Repeat the cycle for 20 minutes at the outset, gradually increasing to 30 minute stints.

Doctors recommend at least 2 daily workouts five or more times a week for people who are trying to improve their fitness and maintain a desirable level.

How fast should you walk? The "talk test" will help you find the right pace. You should be able to talk while walking. If you're too breathless to do so it means you're probably overexerting yourself.

The President's Council advises you not to get discouraged when you first begin walking. Progress will seem slow at the outset, but your strength and staying power will gradually increase. After eight or 10 weeks, if you work out conscientiously, you should be able to run the full 20 minutes at a reasonable pace, although the pace will be slower for older people. After completing the "reconditioning phase," you should be able to extend your running time to 30 minutes. The amount of time you devote to the exercise is more important to your health than the distance you cover.

Running can be gruelling or relatively easy; it depends on the demands you make on yourself. I interviewed a dentist and his wife/nurse who jog every morning before the first patients arrive. One definition of jogging is combined walking and running, although some people use it as a synonym for running. The dentist is 42; his wife is three years younger. Their jaunts last 45 minutes, alternate 10 minutes of brisk walking with 10 minutes of easy running and wind up with a 5 minute walkdown. He says, "We find it invigorating and, beyond working our systems up to the desired 70 percent of capacity, find it no strain at all.''

If you have been a very sedentary person for years, are seriously overweight, or past 50, and have been bitten by the running bug, the best advice you could get would be to start from a conservative base of walking about a half mile per day. When you can walk this briskly and comfortably, raise the distance to a mile. After a week or so of this, intersperse your walking with some easy running, in doses of no more than 14 or 15 steps at the outset. Slowly increase the number of steps on a day-to-day basis, providing the extra exertion your body needs, but not so much exertion that you find yourself gasping for breath.

One of the main goals of exercise is to increase the amount of air you can draw into your lungs. Brisk walking will help you build your oxygen intake capacity. Running will do the same thing. So will combined running and walking. And pace walking will do it to perfection. They're all on the menu. It's up to you to order the dish you prefer.

WALKING TO WIN

If you are intent on running competitively, as specials on the menu you can always find side dishes of long distance running, cross country running, or one of the highly publicized marathons like those held in New York and Boston.

But if competitive sport is your thing, you don't have to run in races to become a competitor. You can also win in a walk. Forty year old Ron Laird of the New York Athletic Club and points north, south, east and west all over the globe, has 69 national championships, 81 records, and participation in four Olympics to prove it. Laird is a race walker who prefers race walking to almost anything you could mention. Exceeding even Dr. George A. Sheehan in his zeal for his sport—he has dedicated his entire life to it—he performs odd jobs between race walking stints.

Although race walking is popular in several countries abroad, it is not very big in America. Writer Barry McDermott estimates that nationally there are no more than about

300 hard core race walkers, with Laird probably having the hardest core of all.

If walking to win strikes your fancy, you will find track meets and road walks all over the country to choose from, along with annual AAU championships and Olympic tryouts.

McDermott comments that "Race walking would appear to be easier than running, but in certain ways it is much more difficult. A runner can soar, but a walker is chained by regulations that say he must be in constant contact with the ground, and that he must straighten his supporting leg during each stride, which results in that familiar Mae West movement of the hips. While moving faster than joggers, walkers, like harness horses, are always fighting the inclination to break into a run—which confounds long-distance runners. It is far easier to run an eight-minute mile than it is to walk one."

RUNNER'S IMAGE

We're a nation of bandwagon hoppers. It would be interesting to speculate on the number of people who are running these days mainly because it's the "in thing" to do.

We are also a nation of joiners. Running, like tennis and golf, has become a kind of fraternity. Runners feel a kinship with each other. Those who run feel they belong to the club. I recently saw a bumper sticker that read, HONK YOUR HORN IF YOU'RE A RUNNER.

Running also makes a statement. The person in warm-up suit or shorts jogging down the avenue tells the rest of the community, "Hey, I'm a runner! I'm fit. I'm strong. I have power."

I mentioned this to a psychiatrist. He shrugged and said, "It might be interesting in some cases to speculate on the deeper implications of this pronouncement. How much macho could be involved? Could some male runners, for example, be encouraging the rest of the community and the female half in particular, to conclude that if this guy possesses the strength and endurance running demands, he must have the capacity to perform other physical feats as well, especially those done in bed?''

The psychiatrist smiled enigmatically. I never did find out for certain if he was pulling my leg. Yet I can't help but wonder how many people may be running mainly because, consciously or subconsciously, they believe running makes them look good. If this shoe fits your foot, unless you honestly believe you can boost your self-image or self-worth through running, some further reflection may be in order. I don't think impressing others is of itself enough of a reason to run.

Well, now that we are back to this, I never did answer the question: ''Should you run?''

Frankly, only you are qualified to answer for yourself. Personally, I would in general not recommend hard running (as opposed to a less strenuous combination of walking and running) for anyone who:

- Is over 40 years old, unless the running is medically supervised;
- Is unable to pass a stress test;
- Is unable to get his doctor's okay;
- Doesn't genuinely enjoy running for the psychological lift and/or intellectual stimulation he gets out of it.

In short, you should shoot for something more than the simple exercise value you derive, for you can get the same health benefits out of pace walking without all the jolt and the strain.

14

A NATION
OF WALKERS

**"The civilized man has built
a coach, but he has lost
the use of his feet."**
Ralph Waldo Emerson

As Dr. Matthew Guidry, who is Director of Community and Special Projects for the President's Council on Physical Fitness and Sports, states the case: "Walking will become a natural beneficiary of the fitness craze. A lot of runners are hurting their knees, complicating arthritis grief, and contributing to other physical problems. As more and more people realize vigorous walking can accomplish the same purpose as running without the danger and harm, they will turn to walking for conditioning. But," he told me, "the key emphasis must be on the word 'vigorous.' "

On top of that, as automation and technology continue to provide increased leisure, and as pressure cooker living simultaneously accelerates, a growing desire and need exists among the desk-and-machine-chained populace to escape, however briefly, to the natural environment. As awareness of this need continues to build, more trails and other walking facilities will be developed in response. This includes traffic-free shopping malls, streets where autos are banned, and bike trails and walkways within the city itself.

Oh yes, it would appear that the day of the walker is clearly at hand. The evidence speaks for itself.

Item: Hiking clubs, community groups and youth organizations throughout the United States are working with the Departments of Interior, Agriculture and Commerce on the development of new trails, and the expansion and improvement of existing trails.

In the west, concerned citizens from several organizations have interested the National Park Service in the building of a National Desert Trail system slated to run from the Mexican border through the Big Basin area, cutting across a number of states and extending all the way to Canada.

Item: Duane Enger of the National Park Service informed me of several trail cushioning programs in force to deposit tread materials—sawdust, wood chips, etc.—on rocky, hard-to-walk surfaces, and to build steps at hazardous spots. The Indiana Dunes project near Gary, Indiana is an outstanding example. Members of the Young Adult Conservation Corps (YACC) and the Youth Conservation Corps (YCC) received special training and work with representatives of the Park Service and various clubs.

Item: Enger also told of trails being built on pontoons in marshy cranberry bogs to keep them from sinking or floating away. And at Gulf Island, Florida beach areas the Park Service is constructing a trail system on wooden walkways to protect the environment. This way walkers can avoid plodding through sand which makes walking difficult, and at the same time preserve the natural terrain.

Item: Since the early 1900's when railroad popularity peaked, thousands of miles of rail beds and rights of way have been abandoned by now-defunct lines. To an increasing degree citizen groups, hiking clubs and community representatives have been urging Park and Commerce Department officials to convert these strips into scenic trails and walks. Many already have been transformed. One notable example is in Western Oregon where old tracks, formerly used to transport logs, have been converted into a fine trail facility.

Item: Increasingly, local communities are getting into the act. In Manchester, New Hampshire, a walking program featuring a simulated 50 mile walk to Boston has been dubbed WALK FOR YOUR HEALTH. Sponsored by the Park and Recreation Department, it was described as a big success in the July 1978 issue of *Parks and Recreation* magazine. All age groups participated with the byproduct benefit that a heightened sense of community was achieved in addition to the health gains.

Item: A Presidential Sports Award Program initiated in 1977 recognizes successful participants with an award certificate, emblem and pin. Under "Fitness Walking," the requirement is that a minimum of 125 miles must be walked within a four-month period. Each walk must be continuous, without pauses for rest, and the pace must be at least four miles per hour. No more than two-and-one-half miles in any one day may be credited to the total.

Item: The Department of Health, Education and Welfare is said to be planning a model physical fitness program that is being touted as one expected to surpass any other yet in existence. The word is that walking will play an important role in this project.

CORPORATE INVOLVEMENT: A DEVELOPMENT OF MAJOR SIGNIFICANCE

No sector of society holds a greater stake in physical fitness than the business community. Industry spends billions each year on insurance, medical and death benefits, and more billions are lost as a result of work disruptions and delays resulting from employee illness and death. Most large corporations today sponsor health and exercise programs for their people and for executives in particular. It is industry's concern and involvement, in fact, that in large measure fueled the past decade's revolution in fitness awareness.

Each month more and more companies, as part of their marketing services operations, or in attempting to take positive action along lines of corporate social responsibility— or a combination of both—are expanding fitness programs for the use of the public as well. This is clearly an evolutionary trend.

The trend wasn't hard to foresee, notes a spokesperson for Scholl, Inc., whose recently completed walking program appears in.Appendix D. "The mounting interest in sports," she says, "has been apparent for a number of years. On top of that was the increased number of foot problem inquiries the company was receiving. Many of them were being traced back to such sports as running, jogging and tennis, engaged in by people who were ill-equipped to participate."

Another matter of concern was the volume of material appearing in the press that stressed the importance and benefits of vigorous exercise without discussing the requirements for participation. This misled many people, encouraging them to plunge into ambitious programs without proper preparation or medical approval. Scholl, primarily in the footwear and foot products business, felt a responsibility to help offset some of the damage by setting the public straight on the facts.

The renewed interest in walking was brought on by the growing realization that to survive the stresses of our society and the sedentary lifestyle that is the byproduct of many jobs, the automobile, and automation, we must get back to the basics and rely more on ourselves and less on our machines. Also growing is the realization that many of us cannot, or prefer not to, jog or run or engage in strenuous sports like tennis, paddle ball and squash on the continuing basis required for exercise to count. But practically everyone can walk—and everyone who walks can pace walk.

Scholl's spokesperson stresses what she refers to as the "mindset approach." It's a matter of getting people to think of walking as exercise, for walking that is properly paced or performed as a sport, is the best exercise known to man.

Exercise Trail Program. "People are more likely to exercise given pleasant surroundings, direction and purpose. They like to know you're supposed to start here and finish there. It gives them a positive incentive and helps get 'em out."

So believes James Schwaninger, Assistant Director of Corporate Responsibility for J.C. Penney Company, Inc. Under his leadership, his company updated a *Par Cour* program developed in Switzerland where it was sponsored and underwritten by Zurich's Vita Life Insurance Company. The

Exercise Trail consists of 20 exercise stations along a one to two mile course.

"The ideal trail," notes Schwaninger, "runs about a mile and a half and can be built for as little as $1,000 with labor contributed by a Jaycee or other community organization. In 1978 three hundred and fifty exercise trails were set up in 47 of the 50 states. Twenty-two were built in Europe, two in Asia, one in Africa. The Air Force, which likes the idea, built 24 trails overseas and 15 domestically, constructing them within easy access of dependent housing areas so they can be used by family members as well as military and civilian personnel."

In getting a program underway, the company works with the Department of the Interior, the President's Council on Physical Fitness and Sports, the Jaycees, and the local community. The only restriction is that the Exercise Trail must be built on public land for the free use of everyone in the community. Most trails are located in parks; others are on school grounds or roadsides.

Financing can be arranged with or without the cooperation of a participating J.C. Penney store. In any case the company provides a 125 page manual containing a master plan for the layout and construction of the trail including specifications for building and other materials needed. It also supplies publicity materials required to promote public use of the trail.

Where an agreement is signed with the participation of one of the company's 1,700 stores, signs for marking the trail and exercise stations are also provided and, at the discretion of the store manager, funds for construction materials or the materials themselves. In addition, a company coordinator is made available for assistance and consultation. Under non-participating agreements, the Exercise Trail may be eligible for asistance through the Federal Land and Water Conservation Fund, administered by the Department of the Interior.

Under any agreement the local parks department must provide a suitable site for the trail. It must review the construction plan and provide engineering assurance that site and soil conditions are sound. And it must furnish a representative to work with the program, provide assistance with course layout and supervision of construction activity. Typically the package of exercise signs is the most expensive item. But even under non-participating agreements where the signs are not provided free they are available for $150, well below the actual cost.

A model trail calls for walking to eight of the 20 exercise stations and jogging to the others. But as Jim Schwaninger points out, it depends on the individual's personal preference. He can walk all the way or jog all the way. Monitored use of the pilot program in Birmingham, Alabama revealed many people choose to walk the entire course. It is particularly significant that the trails are constructed with a strong family orientation. Equipment is scaled to accommodate people from 4' 3" to 6' 6" in height.

Interested in promoting an Exercise Trail in your community? Or finding out where the nearest one is available? Contact a J.C. Penney department store manager, or write: The Exercise Trail, Public Relations—42nd Floor, J.C. Penney Company, Inc., 1301 Avenue of the Americas, New York, N.Y. 10019

"Put Pep Into Your Step." Travelers Insurance Companies, headquartered in Hartford, Connecticut, has been pushing and publicizing physical fitness for a number of years. It sponsors a variety of programs for the public and its employees on the premise that "the great American pastime is inactivity." In its small way, it is joining the lengthening parade of corporations which are taking action to revise this image. Its efforts are aimed at physical fitness with a strong family orientation. Among programs sponsored is an annual amateur bicycle race.

Travelers' PEP program is one that was developed by the Maryland Commission on Physical Fitness. It features "Swedish Walking," a variety of warmup, breathing, posture and other exercises, and winds up with a 12-week walking program that ties into the Presidential Sports Award program as described in the booklet titled, "Put Pep Into Your Step." The clear emphasis is on briskly paced walking throughout.

The basic principle of Swedish Walking as the program presents it "is to walk heel-to-toe. Simply take a nice healthy stride, really stretching the leg out so that the heel touches down first, and then roll forward on your toes into your next step. It's that simple. The stretching is good for the muscles in the back of your legs, and the entire walking program stimulates your cardiovascular system. To guide your efforts remember that an average pace for one mile is 12 minutes. A "brisk" pace, again on the average, is 11 minutes."

This is vigorous walking with a capital V for vitality. The instructions also state: "Start your Swedish Walking Exercises by walking slowly. Slowly as defined by you. Then, quicken your step over the 12 weeks, again as measured by your own pace." Travelers also cautions that in any physical fitness program, it's best to consult your family physician, especially if you are over age 40 and have not recently been physically active on a regular basis. For a detailed rundown on Travelers' 12-week PEP walking program, see Appendix C.

"Walking Tours of America." For many people city walking can be as stimulating, exciting and enjoyable as trail hiking, jogging and most other exercises. A growing number of programs in the works are being geared to make city walking a new adventure combining fitness with fun.

The Kinney Shoe Corporation, for example, is working with the President's Council on Physical Fitness and Sports to encourage Americans to explore cities on foot as an alternative to jogging. With this end in mind it has developed an appetizing menu of 60 walking tours as a public service project.

The nationwide program is broken down into four regional groups: West, South/Southwest, Midwest, and East, with brochure packets that map and describe every tour. Some are thematic; others are geographic. A typical range is from two to four miles. The city tours are comprised of a mix of landmarks, mansions, museums, bridges, unusual buildings, cathedrals, cultural centers, ethnic communities and other points of interest.

An easterner myself (New Jersey), I took a bus into Fun City to case one of the New York tours dubbed "Literary Greenwich Village." A goodly gathering had amassed around Cooper Union and I asked some of the people why they had come. A few were out-of-towners, others native New Yorkers. Regardless, the consensus seemed to be: "It's a great way to stay fit and get to know the city as a byproduct benefit." One elderly woman said, "It makes a lot more sense than riding around in a stuffy old bus."

Designed to entice Americans into reviving man's oldest form of transportation, the walking program is a celebration of American terrain by Americans—and offers a new kind of guidebook to help our citizens and foreign visitors savor this land and its people, according to Richard L. Anderson, president of Kinney.

To obtain a regional packet, write Kinney Walking Tours, P.O. Box 5006, New York, N.Y. 10022, including $1.00 per packet to cover postage and handling.

WALKING EUROPEANS ARE A GIANT STEP AHEAD

We're catching up fast, but still have a way to go. As you already noted, Travelers' walking program originated in Sweden. J.C. Penney's Exercise Trails are based on a concept developed in Switzerland. Many other U.S. programs have European roots. It isn't surprising. The forces that militate against walking are less potent on the Continent than they are in America. Europeans seem to have more respect for their feet as agents of transportation and perhaps are less dominated and controlled by the automobile and its accouterments. When a European sees his walking rights threatened or abused, he's more apt to spit fire and nails in response.

In Colchester, England, for example, a "Motorists Anonymous" organization has been formed to help drivers break the car habit. They believe this will benefit both the people and environment. "In Europe," writes Clayton Jones in *The Christian Science Monitor,* "a walkers' revolt and revelry are already well under way. Since 1963 the International Federation of Pedestrians, working out of the Netherlands, has sought to bring more meaning than 'low class' to the word 'pedestrian' by influencing highway and city planners to provide pleasant pathways and safe crossings. In Britain, the 30,000-member Ramblers Association proclaims: 'The right to walk for pleasure is in jeopardy in many parts of the kingdom'.''

Orienteering. Billed as "the thinking person's sport," orienteering is the art of finding one's way through unfamiliar terrain with the help of a compass and map.

Little known in the U.S. until recently, the sport has long been popular in Europe and particularly in Sweden where it shares the limelight with soccer as the nation's leading athletic activity. Today you will find orienteerers matching their wits against Nature in at least 23 countries, including Israel, Australia and Japan.

The man most responsible for the sport's growing popularity in North America, according to Hans Bengtsson and George Atkinson, who wrote a comprehensive book on the subject ("Orienteering," published by The Stephen Greene Press, Brattleboro, Vermont), is Swede Bjorn Kjellstrom, who helped develop a simple and accurate protractor compass, a critical tool when navigating on foot. In addition to the compass, special orienteering maps depicting such focal points as houses, roads, fields and streams are available. Developed from aerial photos, with accuracy assured through field checking, ordinary maps don't suffice.

Kjellstrom introduced and helped promote the sport in the United States and Canada. In August of 1976, note the authors of the book, a 5-day meet in Quebec drew 1,500 entries. They write, "Orienteering meets test both navigating ability and stamina as the contestants are timed as they 'locate' themselves around various courses—courses usually set in a woodsy terrain. Before each meet the projected course is marked with 'controls,' or checkpoints, consisting of small red and white markers. These control points are then plotted on each contestant's map before he or she takes to the course: the object being to find and 'punch-in' at all the controls faster than the other contestants do; rather like a sports car rally on foot, or a cross-country race without a prescribed course.''

Orienteering courses, color-graded from white for beginner to blue for expert, are geared to all age groups. The best way to understand and appreciate the sport is to attend an event. This will provide an insight into the spirit and enthusiasm shared by contestants, and by noncontestants who root for their favorites. A college senior I know got his first taste of orienteering in Germany, came home all worked up and resolved to start a club of his own. He compromised by joining an already-formed group about 40 miles from his home.

Today more than 50 orienteering clubs operate in America, largely in the east and midwest. For additional information, contact the national office: United States Orienteering Federation, P.O. Box 500, Athens, Ohio 45701.

The Volksmarsch. What if you're among the millions of Americans who long to walk out-of-doors but lack the courage, stamina or inclination to backpack over rough terrain, and don't want to exert the time, effort and apprenticeship involved in groping one's way through the woods with the aid of compass and map? Take heart, there's a sport for you too.

As author Adele S. Thompson states the case: "The latest European import to reach the shores of the United States [is] the perfect answer for less-than-seasoned outdoors lovers. You don't need any expensive equipment, just a pair of comfortable shoes, your lunch, and your senses in good working order. Begun in Germany, the *Volksmarsch,* or 'People's Walk,' is a tradition throughout Europe, where today it has become a major form of recreation."

The *Volksmarscher's* equivalent of the runner's Boston marathon takes place in Nijmegan, Holland. The annual 4-day hike through the Dutch countryside originated during World War I and today attracts thousands of afficionados from all over Europe.

Volksmarsch courses are flexible, ranging from under ten miles to forty or more at the election of the organizing group and participants. Although backpacks are required for overnight jaunts, this is a test of neither stamina nor ingenuity. It's simply a whole lot of fun, and a great way to combine exercise and the enjoyment of nature with the escape from the concrete jungle and gasoline-scented streets.

Typically, the walks carry walkers through areas of scenic or historic interest. The difference between the *Volksmarsch* and the outdoor trek you can take on your own is that the event is well planned and organized; you can take advantage of the amiable companionship of other walkers; and your walk gets a start-to-finish direction and purpose which experience proves to be a prime motivating factor in getting people out into the open. In addition, there's usually someone at hand who knows a great deal about the points of interest and scenic area covered, so that *Volksmarsching* becomes an educational venture as well.

THE PEDESTRIAN REVOLT

"Walkers of the world, arise!" urges Mary E. Frey in a *Prevention* magazine article of the same title. "Do you ever feel you're being discriminated against because you don't weigh 3,000 pounds, because your top speed (in low gear, anyway) is around four mph, because you don't screech, squeal or roar in your progress down Main Street?"

Tongue in cheek? Perhaps. But not so far in as one might imagine. An increasing number of pedestrians these days are up in arms—and on their feet—protesting out-and-out discrimination against walkers. And many of them seem set on doing something about it. In short, they're tired of being treated as second-class citizens, even those who own automobiles.

One charge is that traditionally and historically, in city layout and design, urban planners slight the person afoot. There are exceptions, of course, most notably the handful of America's experimental "new cities"—where wheels and feet are alloted separate areas offering travel alternatives to the automobile. But in large cities this is rarely the case. New York is a classic example. Here, although more than two-thirds of all surface transportation takes place on foot, a disproportionate amount of travel space is provided for no-risk walking.

A growing awareness of the problem exists. Under terms of a U.S. Department of Transportation contract, for example, the city of Miami and Dade County, Florida are cooperating in a demonstration program budgeted at over a million dollars aimed at reducing pedestrian accidents. And in Phoenix, Arizona the mayor broadcast a public appeal in an effort to find ways to cut down on car use. So while the signs look encouraging, we still have a long way to go.

One thrust of crusading walkers is to convert drivers —by persuasion or mandate—from bullies behind the wheel to respecters of pedestrians. California drivers, for the most part, are advanced in this respect over drivers in most other states. There pedestrian crossings are better marked and more frequent. If a person steps off the curb intending to cross the street, an approaching vehicle is apt to grind to a screeching stop, as opposed to New York, Chicago or Boston drivers, who view such situations as a contact sport.

Consider the word 'pedestrian' itself. It has two meanings. One is "a person traveling on foot"; the other is a put-down: "Commonplace, ordinary, dull, hence prosaic." Well, there's nothing dull about walking, and a growing body of walkers is determined to prove it.

J.I. Rodale, the founder of *Prevention* magazine, notes: "Today, the word *pedestrian,* in that second sense, has outlived its value. The heart muscle thrives on movement. It loses its efficiency in lethargy. Walking, therefore, is far better than being carried in some kind of conveyance."

The Walking Association. A backpacker I spoke with was dismayed by the condition of portions of the Appalachian Trail. He told me of beer cans and garbage strewn all over the place, shelters vandalized, signs torn down or defaced.

Most of those who abuse the trails, National Park Service official Duane Enger informed me, are individuals who don't belong to the clubs. The biggest problem is beer cans and bottles, and vandals who use signs for target practice or firewood. The Park Service and other authorities do their best to monitor trails. They urge hikers to burn garbage, or crush it and take it out with them. They issue pamphlets and conduct educational programs in an effort to hammer across to trail users that the environment they are abusing is *their* environment.

But it takes more than officials and policemen to cope with the problem. The public must become involved as well, to clamp down on abusers and demand tougher penalties for those who are caught.

Within the cities themselves there's a great deal of work to be done to promote and encourage the use of the feet. And the word must be spread. People must be made to understand that walking means fun and good health, that inactivity is debilitating, and that foot travel is plain common sense. People should be proud to walk instead of being embarrassed by it. And motorists passing walkers should be envious, reminded that they should be walking too.

The energy crisis of the early seventies did not go away with the gas lines; it has been steadily worsening. Increasingly there is talk of gasoline rationing and mandatory service station closings. Needless to say, even if every American went on a walking rampage it wouldn't solve the energy problem. *But it would help.* If enough people walked their one or two-mile errands (which constitute a substantial portion of wheeled transportation), it would at least ease the energy shortage.

Within the city itself, many pedestrian crossings are unsafe and more crossings are needed. Much more could be done to protect the walker from his arch enemy, the automobile. Shopping malls, sports arenas and other public places should be designed with the walker in mind. Walking surfaces could be made more comfortable, more creature comforts (such as water, toilets, benches and shelters) provided. Although progress has been made in the past against ugly signs and other roadway blemishes, most notably when Lady Bird lived in the White House, we still have a long way to go before beautification on a nationwide scale can be achieved. Pedestrian islands are needed in shopping and traffic areas. And what's needed more than anything else are people who care. Fortunately, such a group of people exist. They call themselves The Walking Association.

Walker Power. Groups of walkers organized nation-wide into a vast pedestrian army is a concept whose time has come. The Walking Association could conceivably develop into an organization of this scope, given the fervor of its founder and the mushrooming popularity of walking for health, fun and sport. A still-small group which started in 1977 in Arlington, Virginia, what it lacks in size it makes up in enthusiasm. Its executive director is Dr. Robert B. Sleight, a psychologist and president of Century Research Corporation.

The Association offers, according to its own press release, a way to "get America back on its feet." A non-profit organization, its goal is to encourage and promote walking in the United States. "Many nations already have organizations dedicated to walking," notes Dr. Sleight. "There is even an International Federation of Pedestrians, headquartered in the Netherlands. In America organizational support was lacking until the Walking Association was formed."

The organization poses some pertinent questions:

- What has happened to walkers' rights?
- Why is walking discouraged in the U.S.?
- Why do walkways take a back seat to highways?
- Why do wheels have priority over feet?

Services offered by The Walking Association include a regularly published newsletter which presents professionally prepared walking guides; program advice and motivational pep talks; information on legislation of concern to pedestrians; information exchange among related groups; discounts on walker accessories and literature; walking challenge charts and certificates; walking news and developments in America and throughout the world.

A major thrust of the group is to help promote and participate in research into the problems which most affect walkers today. It also plans to provide advisory services for members, information on funds available for walking programs and events, and representation on government and business committees where emphasizing the need to recognize walkers' rights would apply.

The Walking Association also offers encouragement and guidance in the establishment of local chapters throughout the U.S. Dr. Sleight stresses the great need for walkers to speak up and speak out for their rights. Only through organization in force can walker power become a reality and this end achieved.

Interested in either joining The Walking Association, or forming a chapter of your own? For information contact The Walking Association, 4113 Lee Highway, Arlington, Virginia, 22207.

THE RESEARCH NEED

A variety of questions are posed in connection with walking for which no definitive answers exist.

- What's the best surface for walking?
- What are the most healthful and beneficial rates of speed for people of different ages, male and female?
- What walking programs are best suited for senior citizens, and for individuals with various illnesses?
- What are the most effective safety procedures and devices to make cities safer for pedestrians?
- What types of equipment and facilities—tracks, treadmills, inclines, moisture generators, floor coverings, etc.—might be useful to walkers who wish to exercise indoors?
- How does load carrying, such as backpacks of varying weights, affect the health values of walking?
- To what degree does air polluted by automobile fumes and stack emissions affect healthy individuals and those with heart and lung problems? Where specifically is it beneficial to walk, and where is it of marginal or no value?

This is but a small sampling of the questions that might be asked. Today the answers can only be guessed at by medical authorities, fitness experts, safety engineers and facilities planners. According to Dr. Robert B. Sleight, this should not suffice in an affluent society such as ours. "Rather large amounts of money have been spent for study of human performance while operating the automobile," he points out. "One important motivation for such study has been the many deaths involving the automobile. But few people realize that falls, most of which occur while walking, are the second accidental killer."

It is time, he believes, for man's oldest means of locomotion, walking, to be thoroughly studied. He proposes for the purpose a research laboratory devoted to developing answers to such questions as those listed above. In a comprehensive presentation for which he is currently seeking support, he estimates that a planning study for such a lab would take about four months and constitute a good working start.

Included would be: (1) Matters needing study, (2) Equipment and facilities needed, and (3) Manning requirements. Dr. Sleight spells out the details in his proposal, with each item costed. Establishment of a manned and equipped research laboratory to study human walking behavior, he calculates, would entail a first-year cost of about $214,000. "The goal," he concludes, "would be to make walking once again a viable, healthful and cost-effective human activity."

COMMUNITY INVOLVEMENT

Barbara Ward, the economist, once described a neighborhood as somewhere that "children can grow up without being run over, where friends can meet, where that deeply neglected resource, the human legs, can be recovered and used, and where the sociability and the exchanges of human existence can take place in a civilized form."

Clearly, for this goal to be reached the community— each individual community—must play a key activist role. This becomes evident from such endeavors as J.C. Penney's Exercise Trail Program. Without community backing and participation, a trail couldn't get launched. Increasing numbers of town parks and recreation department officials are coming alive to this realization, with progressive mayors providing added momentum. In the past, many towns confined their sports and fitness involvement to the sponsorship of periodic athletic events. Today officials and politicians are branching out, taking a hard look at more generalized programs being suggested by corporations, walking organizations and clubs.

Dr. Matthew Guidry emphasizes the importance of "planting the responsibility where it belongs—with the community agencies." He sees an exciting potential for all kinds of beneficial programs with walking prominently featured. Again, he says, it's a matter of "spreading the word, publishing and distributing literature. No extensive work is involved, and very little expense."

It's the kind of thing, he adds, that isn't taught in the university. It's a question of seizing the opportunities that exist. The space is available. The idea is to generate public interest and enthusiasm with imaginative promotional campaigns. Nor do communities have to go it alone. An abundance of help is available from federal agencies; various clubs; such service groups as Rotary, Kiwanis and Jaycees; and business organizations with a public relations or corporate responsibility stake in the program.

One additional piece of advice from the Director of Community and Special Projects for the President's Council on Physical Fitness and Sports: "Stay away from paid consultants; they can be too darned expensive."

A BIT OF CRYSTAL BALL GAZING

Certainly the Great Walkers' Rebellion of the 80's will leave its imprint on the American lifestyle just as the Runner's Revolt of the 70's had its own special impact. The question is what changes and innovations can we expect as a result of:

1. The increasing awareness among citizens that inactivity produces degenerative changes in the body while exercise prolongs youthfulness and strengthens the cardiovascular system;
2. The realization that while running is beneficial to

many, not everybody can run, and not everybody would feel inclined to run even if they could;

3. The assertion by a growing body of doctors running the gamut of medical disciplines and fitness experts that pace walking can produce the same health benefits as running and other strenuous sports without the health risks and problems involved.

Projecting a year or three into the future we see:

THE PREDICTION: *More and more people over 50, 60 and 70 will be engaging in programs of continuous exercise.* Journalist Michael Clark tells about an 86-year-old woman entering and completing a 26-mile marathon, a stroke victim in her 80's who progressed from walking to running and now jogs three miles a day, a 70-year-old man who bicycles 50 miles a day on weekends and looks 20 years younger. According to Clark's findings, middle-aged and older people can engage in sports most senior citizens would never have dreamed of considering a few years ago.

He quotes Dr. Willibald Nagler, physiatrist-in-chief (a physiatrist treats illnesses using nonsurgical methods) of Cornell's Medical Center, who views walking as an almost-overlooked exercise. The German-born doctor advises long walks as an exercise. "Swing your arms," he suggests. "Move out at a brisk pace. Don't hold back. When you walk at a brisk pace with swinging arms, you expend as much energy as you do during a slow jog. In Europe, experienced hikers know when they've gotten sufficient exercise by walking. They say their arms are just as tired as their legs."

THE PREDICTION: *In many homes walking will soon supersede television watching as the most popular family pastime.* The trend is already under way. J.C. Penney, Travelers and other programs stress the joys and values of physical fitness activities on a community basis combining companionship and exercise. Increasing numbers of corporate health programs are being made available to the family as well. The President's Council on Physical Fitness and Sports places a strong emphasis on total family participation encompassing all ages from six to 96.

THE PREDICTION: *Thousands of American walkers will soon be united to stand up for their rights.* Counterparts to such organizations as the International Federation of Pedestrians and England's 30,000-member Ramblers Association will spring up all over the United States. Politicians and government leaders, sensing the trend and political clout potential of organized hikers and walkers will, in deference to Walker Power, support actions and studies designed to enhance the cause of pedestrians.

THE PREDICTION: *Corporations will stress the benefits of walking to a greater extent in their employee fitness programs.* A recent Gulf Corporation message in its *Oilmanac* publication, for example, features the value of walking: "It *is* true that one must walk 35 miles to lose one pound of fat, but the 35 miles need not be walked at one time. Walking an additional mile each day for 35 days also will take off that pound." The article goes on to quote the calorie-burning value of walking as compared with other exercises; Walk 1½ miles in 30 minutes, burn 100-149 calories; 3 miles in 45 minutes, burn 200-249 calories; 5½ miles in 1 hour, 36 minutes, burn 350-399 calories; 7 miles in 2 hours, 20 minutes, burn 450-500 calories. (Quoting Dr. Kenneth H. Cooper, from his book "Aerobics for Women.")

THE PREDICTION: *Walk-a-thons will become even more popular and widely attended than marathons are today because everyone can participate.* They will be sponsored by local communities, corporations and clubs, linked to charity drives and other causes. In such events modest registration fees will be charged, with prizes going to winners, and the bulk of the receipts turned over to organizations like The American Heart Association, American Cancer Society, and American Arthritis Foundation.

THE PREDICTION: *We will soon see the return of the walking stick.* Industries engaged in the manufacture of pedometers and other walking accessories will boom.

THE PREDICTION: *Many city streets will become safer thanks to walking.* Crime tends to decrease in neighborhoods where sizable numbers of people are up and about.

THE PREDICTION: *Cities and towns will become more livable thanks to the accouterments of walking.* We will see a rash of nature paths, arcade malls, and auto-free zones mushrooming in cities large and small throughout the nation.

Dr. Matthew Guidry, of the President's Council, predicts some growing trends of his own: Long scenic hikes becoming commonplace; intercity tours that will center on shopping; a profusion of city tours geared to scenic spots and points of interest; more and more family walks, with the whole family participating; more social calls made on foot instead of on wheels, especially appealing where senior citizens play the host.

Dr. Guidry has a dream that is dear to him. "What I'd like to see," he told me, "is a Walk America Program that will include the whole family in communities all over the U.S. Medals would be awarded for the completion of prearranged goals. It could excite widespread national interest and substantially boost the level of fitness in America."

When might this dream become a reality? That's up to you. What's at stake is *your* heart, *your* body, *your* life.

So, walkers of the world—unite!

APPENDICES

What is the ideal walking program for you? Most doctors recommend 40 to 60 minutes of brisk walking per day, the kind of walking that makes your heart pump harder and expands your oxygen intake capacity.

Pace walking encourages you to set the rate of speed and energy output individually suited to your personal needs and capabilities. (See Appendix A.)This permits you to design your own individual walking program. Or you might wish to apply your personal pace to other organized programs in which you might like to participate.

For your interest and consideration, the appendices include three popular walking programs already in force. Appendix B outlines a series of three subprograms contained within a master program presented by the President's Council on Physical Fitness and Sports. This will be of interest to the beginning walker who wishes to go on from a walking program to one that combines walking and jogging, and possibly from there to a jogging program.

Appendix C is a detailed breakdown of the 12-week walking program prepared by Travelers Insurance Company. Appendix D is the Scholl, Inc., "Walking-for-Exercise" program just recently introduced to the nation. Appendices E through J present additional items of interest to walkers and hikers.

APPENDIX A

THE COMPLETE BOOK OF WALKING'S
10-STEP PACE WALKING PROGRAM

Note: If you are a beginning walker, complete all 10 steps. If you have been walking for exercise at least 30 minutes per day, skip steps 3 and 4.

Step 1: Show this program to your doctor and get his okay.

Step 2: Spend 5 minutes doing two or three of the warmup exercises in Appendix E or warmup exercises of your own choice.

Step 3: Walk at your accustomed walking pace for 20 minutes each day in one or two segments. Time yourself using the sweep second hand of your watch, or a pedometer, to determine number of steps per minute. Repeat for 4 to 6 days.

Step 4: Walk at your accustomed walking pace for 30 minutes each day in one or two segments. Repeat for 4 to 6 days.

Step 5: Lengthen your stride and quicken your step a little but not too much so that your walking pace is increased by about 5 to 7 steps per minute. Time yourself as you walk to make this determination. Walk 30 minutes per day. Repeat for one week or until you are absolutely comfortable walking this rate. Don't be afraid to swing your arms with gusto as you walk.

Step 6: Walk at this new rate, increasing the time you walk to 40 minutes per day, in one to three segments. Repeat for 4 to 6 days.

Step 7: Lengthen your stride and quicken your step to your *maximum natural walking rate.* Continue for 15 minutes, then slow down to your previous (Step 5) rate for 5 minutes. Walk your maximum rate another 15 minutes, then slow down for 5 minutes. Total walking time: 40 minutes. Repeat for one week or until you are absolutely comfortable walking this rate. For your own interest and information, time yourself as you walk to determine how many steps per minute your maximum natural rate is.

Step 8: Continue your maximum natural rate, increasing your walking time to 40 minutes per day, in one to three segments. Repeat for one week.

Step 9: Increase your maximum natural walking time to 50 or more minutes per day, in one to three segments. Continue this exercise on a daily basis for no less than 5 days per week.

Step 10: Warmdown. Repeat Step 2 above.

Congratulations! You have now accomplished your goal. All that remains from here on in is to walk your way to good health the natural pace walking way. In time, as your muscles tone up and strengthen and your oxygen intake capacity increases, you may be able to boost your maximum walking rate (steps per minute) even more. But this is of small importance at this point. What matters most is that you are taking advantage of the best possible exercise known to man.

APPENDIX B

RED, WHITE, AND BLUE EXERCISE PROGRAM
Prepared By The President's Council on Physical Fitness and Sports

RED — WALKING PROGRAM

Week	Daily Activity

1   Walk at a brisk pace for 5 minutes, or for a shorter time if you become uncomfortably tired. Walk slowly or rest for 3 minutes. Again walk briskly for 5 minutes, or until you become uncomfortably tired.

2   Same as Week 1, but increase pace as soon as you can walk 5 minutes without soreness or fatigue.

3   Walk at a brisk pace for 8 minutes, or for a shorter time if you become uncomfortably tired. Walk slowly or rest for 3 minutes. Again walk briskly for 8 minutes, or until you become uncomfortably tired.

4   Same as Week 3, but increase pace as soon as you can walk 8 minutes without soreness or fatigue.

When you have completed Week 4 of the **RED** program, begin at Week 1 of the **WHITE** program.

WHITE — WALKING-JOGGING PROGRAM

Week	Daily Activity

1   Walk at a brisk pace for 10 minutes, or for a shorter time if you become uncomfortably tired.

Walk slowly or rest for 3 minutes. Again walk briskly for 10 minutes, or until you become uncomfortably tired.

2   Walk at a brisk pace for 15 minutes, or for a shorter time if you become uncomfortably tired. Walk slowly for 3 minutes.

3   Jog 20 seconds (50 yards). Walk 1 minute (100 yards). Repeat 12 times.

4   Jog 20 seconds (50 yards). Walk 1 minute (100 yards). Repeat 12 times.

When you have completed Week 4 of the **WHITE** program, begin at Week 1 of the **BLUE** program.

BLUE — JOGGING PROGRAM

Week	Daily Activity
1	Jog 40 sec. (100 yds.)—Walk 1 min. (100 yds.) Repeat 9 times.
2	Jog 1 min. (150 yds.)—Walk 1 min. (100 yds.) Repeat 8 times.
3	Jog 2 min. (300 yds.)—Walk 1 min. (100 yds.) Repeat 6 times.
4	Jog 4 min. (600 yds.)—Walk 1 min. (100 yds.) Repeat 4 times.
5	Jog 6 min. (900 yds.)—Walk 1 min. (100 yds.) Repeat 3 times.
6	Jog 8 min. (1200 yds.)—Walk 2 min. (200 yds.) Repeat 2 times.
7	Jog 10 min. (1500 yds.)—Walk 2 min. (200 yds.) Repeat 2 times.
8	Jog 12 min. (1700 yds.)—Walk 2 min. (200 yds.) Repeat 2 times.

APPENDIX C

12-WEEK WALKING PROGRAM
Prepared By The Travelers Insurance Companies in Cooperation With The Maryland Commission on Physical Fitness

(permission for use given)

Please note: The program includes the following features:

* Swedish heel-to-toe walking as described in Chapter 14.

* The West Point Posture Exercise: Pull your abdomen in, bring your shoulders back, and your chest out. Do it so that you are comfortable, not stiff. This will improve your respiratory function.

* Deep breathing exercise: Lift your arms over your head as you take a deep breath, inhaling through your nose, and exhaling through your mouth. You should breathe like this frequently along the route.

* Simple stretching exercises as depicted below, described by the program as "the third facet of Swedish Walking."

1. Hand Squeeze: Put your hands out, palms down, and squeeze your fingers into a fist. Do this five times, then turn your hands over, palms up and repeat. Finally, just shake your hands five times to get the circulation all the way out to the fingertips.

2. Shoulder Rolls: Beginning with your arms at your side, roll your shoulders forward in full circle, slowly, five times; reverse by rolling shoulders backwards in a circle, slowly, five times. Then, shrug shoulders up and down five times.

3. Arm Rotations: Swing your right arm forward five times; reverse motion, rotating arm backward five times. Repeat with left arm. With both arms together in a windmill fashion, swing forward five times; then reverse direction, again five times.

4. Arm Thrusts: Bring arms to chest height, elbows out, make fists, then thrust arms forward, bring back; thrust sidewards, bring back, then thrust arms upward and down. Repeat three times.

5. Arm Circles: Put your arms out at your sides, and rotate your arms forward in small circles as you walk. Then reverse your arm motion making circles larger as you increase revolutions. Repeat five times.

6. Wing Stretchers: Bring your arms up to chest height, elbows up, and as you're walking, pull your elbows back as far as you can. This is particularly good for the chest and shoulder muscles as well as the upper back. Repeat five times.

7. Scissors: Start with your arms out at your side, at chest height. Bring them forward, and crisscross them in front of you in a scissors fashion. Crisscross them five times each.

Before You Take A Step: Some people will complete this program sooner than others. If you're in good physical condition, you can certainly progress as fast as you wish. Remember, you're not competing against anyone, so start walking three times a week for better health.

FIRST WEEK: Session 1 — 3/4 Mile
Learn how to walk heel to toe.
Learn how to deep breathe.
Learn correct body posture, including movement of arms.
Perform deep breathing exercises every 200 yards or so.
Walk at a relatively slow pace.

Session 2 — Same

Session 3 — Same

SECOND WEEK: Session 1 — 7/8 Mile
Gradually lengthen your stride, varying the pace from slow to medium. Continue deep breathing exercises and emphasize correct body posture.

Session 2 — Same

Session 3 — Same

THIRD WEEK: Session 1 — 1 Mile
Again lengthen your stride. Add the West Point posture exercise while walking for 25-50 yards. Then alternate the pace, at times slow, at times a little faster, and then yet a little faster. At this time emphasize heel-to-toe walking, so that you will be walking normally with a heel-to-toe stride.

Session 2 — Same

Session 3 — Same

FOURTH WEEK: Session 1 — 1 1/8 Miles
Continue everything stressed in the first three weeks, and add for the first time exercises #1-5 while walking. Gradually lengthen the stride again. At this point, you should be walking at a medium pace at all times.

Session 2 — Same

Session 3 — Same

FIFTH WEEK: Session 1 — 1 1/4 Miles
Continue as in the 4th week, adding exercises #6 & 7 to your routine while walking. Again, lengthen your stride.

Session 2 — Same

Session 3 — Same

SIXTH WEEK: Session 1 — 1 1/2 Miles
Increase your pace to a brisk walk. Alternate the pace, varying among slow, moderate, and fast speeds. Include arm and shoulder exercises #1-5.

Session 2 — 1 1/2 Miles
Alternate fast and slow walking and the various exercises #1-7.

Session 3 — Same as #2

SEVENTH WEEK: Session 1 — 1 5/8 Miles
Walk briskly for 1/2 mile, then alternate slow, medium, and brisk pace for the rest of the distance.

Session 2 — 1 5/8 Miles
Walk a little more than a half-mile at a brisk pace; then alternate slow, medium, and brisk walk the rest of the way.

Session 3 — 1 5/8 Miles
Walk 3/4 of a mile briskly, then follow same variations as in Session #2. All week long, strive to practice breathing, West Point posture, and simple stretching exercises.

EIGHTH WEEK: Session 1 — 1 3/4 Miles
Walk briskly for 7/8 of a mile, vary pace between slow and moderate for the balance of the distance. No more brisk walking during the second half of your walk.

Session 2 — 1 3/4 Miles
Walk biskly for 1 mile; then finish the distance with slow and medium-pace walking.

Session 3 — Same as #2
Concentrate on deep breathing, West Point posture, and simple stretching exercises.

NINTH WEEK: Session 1 — 1 7/8 Miles
Walk briskly for 1 1/8 miles, vary pace between slow and moderate for the balance of the distance.

Session 2 — 1 7/8 Miles
Walk briskly for 1-1/4 miles, then finish the distance with slow and medium-pace walking.

Session 3 — Same as #2
Remember to concentrate on your posture as well as performing the exercises you enjoy doing.

TENTH WEEK: Session 1 — 1 1/2 Miles
Walk briskly for 3/4 of a mile. In the past few weeks, we've steadily increased distances so that your body has had to con-

tinually acclimate itself to the extra work. Now, we're shortening the distance *and* the amount of brisk walking to give your body a chance to build up some reserve strength for the longer distances of the next two weeks. Don't forget to vary your pace from slow to medium for the remainder of the distance, and do your exercises as you walk.

Session 2 — Same

Session 3 — Same

ELEVENTH WEEK: Session 1 — 1 5/8 Miles

Walk briskly for as much of the distance as you possibly can. If you feel you must, reduce your pace to a medium walk.

Session 2 — 1 3/4 Miles

Session 3 — 2 Miles

Remember to do all the things you have learned during the previous part of the program.

ONLY 1 WEEK TO GO!

TWELFTH WEEK: Session 1 — 2 Miles

Walk briskly for as long as you can. You should be able to complete the entire 2 miles at this pace. If you can't, don't feel as if this hasn't worked for you.

Session 2 — 2 1/8 Miles

Walk briskly for 1/2 mile, then moderate pace for 1/2 mile, then brisk pace for 3/4 of a mile. Finish the distance at a moderate pace. Do your breathing and posture exercises.

Session 3 — 2 1/4 Miles

Graduation day! Walk briskly the entire distance as best you can.

APPENDIX D

SCHOLL'S "WALKING-FOR-EXERCISE" PROGRAM

Note: The program, developed by Scholl, Inc.'s fitness consultant, kinesiologist Maurita Robarge, is being conducted on the occasion of the company's 75th anniversary as part of its "Walk-for-Health" campaign. Before beginning any exercise program, Scholl advises, check with a doctor for a "clean bill of health." A body that's unused to exertion may require a special, individualized walking plan.

STEP ONE:
BEGINNING A WALKING EXERCISE PROGRAM

A—Short Daily Walks

The average person walks about ½ mile during each day's routines—or about 3½ miles each week. To increase the fitness value of this activity, concentrate on good walking style while mailing a letter or "making the rounds" at the office or at home. Make sure to spend a *minimum* of 15 minutes daily on this portion of the program.

Tips for "Fitness Walking":

* A good walking style begins with good posture. Hold your head up, pull in your stomach, straighten your back. Keep toes pointed straight ahead, with weight resting chiefly on the ball of the foot.

* Concentrate on rhythm as you walk. A good arm-swing will help improve your gait by equalizing your balance and eliminating waste-motion. Try extra arm movements—moving arms in a circle or arc—to increase the

exercise action. (You'll be surprised to discover how much more strenuous walking can be with added arm movement.)

* Walking quickly will promote cardiovascular fitness: The more exertion your system can sustain, the more capacity your body will have for prolonged physical exertion. Brisk walking will increase your heartbeat rate, pumping more blood through your system, and will increase the flow of oxygen in and out of lungs.

* A fast walk of 3⅓ mph. (equivalent to doing one mile in 18 minutes), will burn up about 300 calories per hour, while a more leisurely rate of 2½ mph. (one mile in 24 minutes) only uses about 210 calories per hour. A quick step is actually less tiring, because the continuous forward momentum of a brisk walk literally will take some of the gravity-induced weight off your feet.

B—Sustained Walks Every Other Day

Prolonged walking—*at least* 30 minutes every other day, or about five miles per week—is an important aspect of a beneficial exercise plan. Warmup exercises are the key to comfortable, safe distance-walking.

Stretching exercises help prevent muscle strain, decrease stiffness around the joints, and give the walker a wider range of motion. It's especially important to stretch lower back leg muscles: They're the main source of push-off power for feet, and are often the first muscles to "complain" of strain during a long walk.

Before any long walk, spend a few minutes warming up with these exercises:

* Stand upright in your best posture, then slowly let your upper body fall forward until your hands and arms hang to your toes. Hold for 30 seconds; slowly straighten up into a stand. Repeat 5 times.

* Do push-aways from a wall. Stand with feet 16-18 inches away from the wall. Keeping heels flat on the floor at all times, alternately straighten and bend elbows to push away and approach the wall. Repeat 10 times. (You should be able to feel pull at the back of lower-leg muscles. If you can't, stand farther away from wall.)

* With arms out at sides for balance, stand on left leg. Bend right leg at knee. Upper right leg should be parallel to floor. Point toes as forcefully as possible toward ground. Hold for 5 seconds; relax. Repeat 10 times with each leg.

Once your muscles are limbered up, head outdoors and walk—quickly, purposefully, and with good posture. If a 60-minute walk every other day is beyond your current capabilities, work up to it gradually with a week-by-week plan to increase endurance:

Begin by walking 10-15 minutes, alternating 5 minutes at a brisk pace with several minutes of more leisurely steps. Continue three times weekly until you feel comfortable with the pace and distance.

Then, "push" yourself to increase the pace over the entire walk. Eventually, as your fitness level increases, you'll be able to walk the full 15 minutes quickly and comfortably.

Gradually work to increase distance, then pace, until you can walk 30 minutes at a fast walk.

Note: Trembling muscles, labored breathing, or headaches, all indicate over-exertion. Slow down or rest, and walk a shorter distance until your body develops more stamina. If symptoms persist, consult your doctor.

STEP TWO:
AUGMENTING THE PROGRAM

As your fitness level increases through daily exertion, you may want to supplement a walking program with exercises, greater distance, or faster walking speed.

— Start by increasing the amount of time spent on "routine walking": Opt for stairways rather than escalators; park the car several blocks from your destination and walk the rest of the way; take a walk during coffee breaks, before lunch or dinner.

— Incorporate simple isometric exercises into your walk:

* Contract abdominal muscles forcefully for 10 seconds; relax; contract again.

* Strengthen lower back muscles while you walk by rotating your pelvis forward . . . or "tucking your tail under."

— Continue to increase the distance and pace of long walks, until you can walk briskly and comfortably for 30-60 minutes. To reap extra fitness rewards, enjoy these long walks daily instead of every other day, or alternate walking with jogging.

— Spend extra time on warmup exercises, and end a long walk with several minutes of warmdowns.

APPENDIX E

STRETCHING EXERCISES

To minimize the chance of injury or soreness, warm-ups and warmdowns should be taken before and after any athletic activity. The more energetic the activity, the more important stretching exercise is to avoid excess strain. In attaining the following positions suggested by The President's Council on Physical Fitness and Sports, stretch slowly and easily avoiding any jerking or bouncing.

Achilles Tendon and Calf Stretcher

Stand facing wall approximately three feet away. Lean forward and place palms of hands flat against wall. Keep back straight, heels firmly on floor, and slowly bend elbows to hands, and tuck hips toward wall. Hold position for 30 seconds.

Repeat exercise with knees slightly flexed.

Back Stretcher

Lie on back with legs straight and arms at sides with palms down. Slowly lift legs, hips, and lower part of back and attempt to touch toes to floor behind head. Keep legs straight and hold position for 30 seconds.

Straddle Stretch

Sit on floor and spread straight legs about twice shoulder width. Slowly lean forward from waist, sliding hands along floor, as far forward as you can. Hold for 30 seconds.

Return to starting position. Slowly stretch forward over right leg, sliding both hands down to right ankle. Try to keep knee straight and touch chin to right knee cap. Hold for 30 seconds.

Return to starting position. Repeat second step of exercise to left side.

Leg Stretcher

Sit in same position as in preceding exercise. Rest left hand on left thigh and grasp inside of right foot with right hand. Keep back straight and slowly straighten right leg, letting it raise to about a 45 degree angle. Hold position for 30 seconds.

Repeat exercise with other leg.

Thigh Stretcher

Stand arm's length from wall with left side toward wall. Place left hand on wall for support. Grasp right ankle with right hand and pull foot back and up until heel touches buttocks. Lean forward from waist as you lift. Hold for 30 seconds.

Repeat exercise with opposite hand and foot.

Hurdler's Stretch

Sit on floor with one leg extended straight ahead. Upper part of other leg should be at right angle to body, with heel close to buttocks. Slowly slide hands down extended leg and touch foot. Hold position for 30 seconds. Keeping legs in same position, slowly lean back and rest elbows on floor. Hold for 30 seconds.

Reverse position and repeat both stages of exercise.

APPENDIX F
A DAILY CONDITIONING EXERCISE PROGRAM
— DR. ASA'S MAGIC 12 —
12 Exercises in 12 Minutes — Every 12 Hours

As a good supplement to "pace walking" (which improves your cardio-pulmonary fitness), Dr. Maxim Asa, a noted physiologist, recommends the following scientific formula involving 12 exercises for stretching, strengthening, and general conditioning to be executed in the sequence in which they appear below.

1. *Warm up*—Jog in place 150 times.

2. *Stretching*—Position: Sit on the edge of a chair with your legs straight. Action: Bend forward and slide hands along shins.

3. *Stretching*—Position: Sit on floor with straight legs. Action: Grasp ankles and attempt to touch forehead to knees, bob down.

4. *Conditioning*—Skip rope.

5. *Abdominals*—Position: Lie on your back with legs resting on a chair, hips and knees at 90° flexicon, hands behind neck. Action: Lift head and shoulders (sit-up) attempting to touch elbows to knees.

6. *Posterior muscles*—Position: On hands and knees. Action: Bend one knee to touch forehead, then extend leg and raise head. Hold and repeat with other side.

7. *Posterior muscles and upper back*—Position: Lie on stomach, hands under forehead, elbows raised. Action: Raise chest off floor, hold and return.

8. *Anterior muscles*—"Push-ups" with straight back and legs.

9. *Trunk muscles*—Position: On your knees. Action: Sit to one side, knees together, then to the other side.

10. *Leg muscles*—Position: Stand in front of a stable chair. Action: Step up on chair without a thrust.

11. *Stretching*—Position: Straddle stance, arm to side. Action: Touch toes of opposite straight leg and return. Repeat to other side.

12. March around the room singing out loud.

APPENDIX G

HIKING CLUBS

Adirondack Mountain Club
172 Ridge Road
Glen Falls, N.Y. 12801

American Alpine Club
113 East 90th Street
New York, N.Y. 10028

Appalachian Mountain Club
5 Joy Street
Boston, Ma. 02108

Appalachian Trail Conference
P.O. Box 236
Harper's Ferry, W. Va. 25425

Chicago Mountaineering Club
Speck Memorial Library
739 Forest Avenue
Glen Ellyn, Il. 60137

Colorado Mountain Club
2530 West Alameda Avenue
Denver, Co. 80219

Finger Lakes Trail Conference
c/o Mary C. Kendall
Bald Hill Road
Springwater, N.Y. 14560

Green Mountain Club
P.O. Box 889
43 State Street
Montpelier, Vt. 05602

Hawaiian Trail & Mountain Club
P.O. Box 2238
Honolulu, Hawaii 96804

Idaho Alpine Club
P.O. Box 2885
Idaho Falls, Id. 83401

Iowa Mountaineers
P.O. Box 163
Iowa City, Iowa 52242

Keystone Trail Assn.
P.O. Box 144
Concordville, Pa. 19331

Mazamas
909 N.W. 19th Street
Portland, Ore. 97209

Mountaineering Club of Alaska
700 Fifth Avenue
Anchorage, Alaska 99501

Mountaineers, Inc.
719 Pike Street
Seattle, Wash. 98101

New York & New Jersey Trail
    Conference
P.O. Box 2250
New York, N.Y. 10001

Potomac Appalachian Trail Club
1718 N Street, N.W.
Washington, D.C. 20036

Randolph Mountain Club
R.F.D. 1
Berlin, N.H. 03570

Sierra Club
530 Bush Street
San Francisco, Ca. 94108

Smoky Mountains Hiking Club
201 South Purdue
Box 1454
Knoxville, Tn. 37901

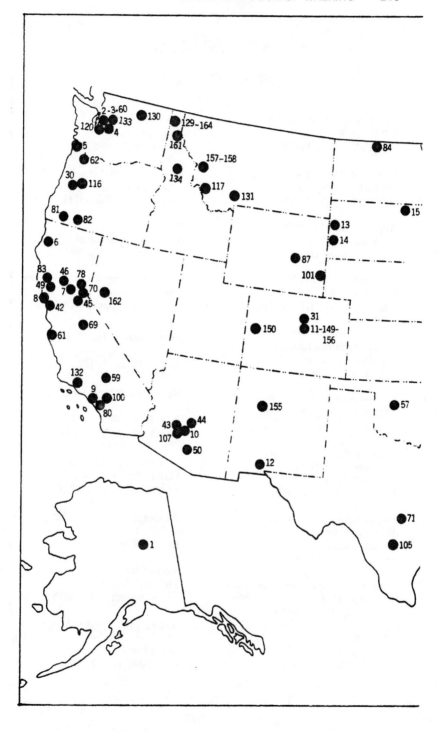

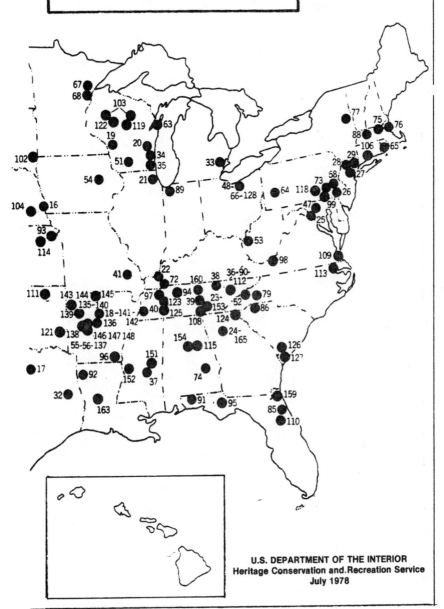

NATIONAL TRAILS SYSTEM
National Recreation Trails

U.S. DEPARTMENT OF THE INTERIOR
Heritage Conservation and Recreation Service
July 1978

APPENDIX H

TRAILS INDEX

Legend: B-bicycle; F-foot; H-horse; M-motorized, general; SM-snowmobile; WC-wheelchair; XC-cross-country ski

Index
No. State: Name of Trail: Length: Type of Trail: Administering Agency

1. Alaska: PINNELL MOUNTAIN TRAIL (24 miles) F, Bureau of Land Management, U.S. Dept. of the Interior, Washington, D.C. 20240

2. Washington: LAKE WASHINGTON BICYCLE PATH (3.2 miles) B-F, City of Seattle Dept. of Parks and Recreation, 610 Municipal Building, Seattle, Wa. 98104

3. Washington: LAKE WASHINGTON SHIP CANAL WATERSIDE TRAIL (.25 miles) F, U.S. Army Corps of Engineers, Seattle District, 1519 Alaskan Way South, Seattle, Wa. 98134

4. Washington: FRED CLEATOR INTERPRETIVE TRAIL (1.3 miles) F-WC, Washington State Parks and Recreation Commission, P.O. Box 1128, Olympia, Wa. 98504

5. Oregon: TILLAMOOK HEAD TRAIL (6 miles) F, Oregon State Highway Div., State Parks and Recreation Branch, State Highway Bldg., Salem, Or. 97310

6. California: KING RANGE TRAIL (10 miles total; 2 segments) F-H, Bureau of Land Management, U.S. Dept. of the Interior, Washington, D.C. 20240

7. California: SOUTH YUBA TRAIL (6 miles) F-H, Bureau of Land Management, U.S. Dept. of the Interior, Washington, D.C. 20240

8. California: EAST BAY SKYLINE TRAIL (14 miles) F-H, East Bay Regional Park District, 11500 Skyline Boulevard, Oakland, Ca. 94619

9. California: GABRIELINO TRAIL (28 miles) F-H, Forest Service, U.S. Dept. of Agriculture, Washington, D.C. 20250

10. Arizona: SOUTH MOUNTAIN PARK TRAIL (14 miles) B-F-H, Phoenix Parks and Recreation Dept., Phoenix, Az. 85236

11. Colorado: HIGHLINE CANAL TRAIL (18 miles) B-F-H, South Suburban Metropolitan Recreation and Park District, 1800 West Littleton Blvd, Littleton, Co. 80120

12. New Mexico: ORGAN MOUNTAIN TRAIL (8.7 miles) F-H, Bureau of Land Management, U.S. Dept. of the Interior, Washington, D.C. 20240

Legend: B-bicycle; F-foot; H-horse; M-motorized, general; SM-snowmobile; WC-wheelchair; XC-cross-country ski

Index

No.	State:	Name of Trail:	Length:	Type of Trail:	Administering Agency

13. South Dakota: BEAR BUTTE TRAIL (3.5 miles) F, South Dakota Dept. of Game, Fish and Parks, Div. of Parks and Recreation, Pierre, S.D. 57501

14. South Dakota: SUNDAY GULCH TRAIL (4 miles) F, South Dakota Dept. of Game, Fish and Parks, Div. of Parks and Recreation, Pierre, S.D. 57501

15. South Dakota: TRAIL OF SPIRITS (.5 miles) F, South Dakota Dept. of Game, Fish and Parks, Div. of Parks and Recreation, Pierre, S.D. 57501

16. Nebraska: FONTENELLE FOREST TRAIL (3.9 miles) F, Fontenelle Forest Assn., 620 Continental Bldg., Omaha, Neb. 68103

17. Texas: GREER ISLAND NATURE TRAIL (3 miles) F, City of Fort Worth Parks and Recreation Dept., 3220 Botanic Garden Dr., Fort Worth, Tx. 76107

18. Arkansas: SUGAR LOAF MOUNTAIN NATURE TRAIL (1 mile) F, U.S. Army Corps of Engineers, Greers Ferry Lake, P.O. Box 310, Heber Springs, Ark. 72543

19. Wisconsin: ELROY-SPARTA TRAIL (30 miles) B-F-SM, Wisconsin Dept. of Natural Resources, Bureau of Parks and Recreation, Box 450, Madison, Wis. 53701

20. Wisconsin: ICE AGE TRAIL (25 miles) F-SM, Wisconsin Dept. of Natural Resources, Bureau of Parks and Recreation, Box 450, Madison, Wis. 53701

21. Illinois: THE ILLINOIS PRAIRIE PATH (27.76 miles) B-F-H, The Illinois Prairie Path, Inc., P.O. Box 1086, 616 Delles Rd., Wheaton, Il. 60187

22. Kentucky: LONG CREEK TRAIL (.25 miles) F-WC, Tennessee Valley Authority, Div. of Forestry, Fisheries and Wildlife Development, Norris, Tn. 37828

23. Tennessee: LAUREL-SNOW TRAIL (8 miles) F, Bowaters Southern Paper Corp., Calhoun, Tn. 37309

24. Georgia: STONE MOUNTAIN TRAIL (6.5 miles) F, Stone Mountain Memorial Park Assn., P.O. Box 778, Stone Mountain, Ga. 30083

25. District of Columbia: FORT CIRCLE PARKS TRAIL (19.5 miles total) B-F, National Park Service, U.S. Dept. of the Interior, Washington, D.C. 20240

26. Pennsylvania: FAIRMOUNT PARK BIKE PATH (8.25 miles) B-F, City of Philadelphia, Fairmount Park Commission, Memorial Hall, West Park, Philadelphia, Pa. 19131

Legend: B-bicycle; F-foot; H-horse; M-motorized, general; SM-snowmobile; WC-wheelchair; XC-cross-country ski

Index
No.   State: Name of Trail: Length: Type of Trail: Administering Agency

27. New Jersey: PALISADES LONG PATH (11 miles) F, Palisades Interstate Park Commission, Administration Bldg., Bear Mountain, N.Y. 10911

28. New Jersey: PALISADES SHORE TRAIL (11.25 miles) F, Palisades Interstate Park Commission, Administration Bldg., Bear Mountain, N.Y. 10911

29. New York: HARRIMAN LONG PATH (16 miles) F, Palisades Interstate Park Commission, Administration Bldg., Bear Mountain, N.Y. 10911

30. Oregon: WILLAMETTE RIVER TRAIL (EUGENE SECTION) (1.84 miles) F-B-WC, Eugene Parks and Recreation Dept., 777 Pearl St., Eugene, Or. 97401

31. Colorado: HIGHLINE CANAL TRAIL (13 miles) F-B-H, Aurora Parks and Recreation Dept., 1470 Emporia St., Aurora, Co. 80010

32. Texas: CARGILL LONG PARK TRAIL (2.5 miles) F-B, Longview Parks and Recreation Dept., P.O. Box 1952, Longview, Tx. 75601

33. Michigan: BELLE ISLE BICYCLE TRAIL (.9 mile) B, Detroit Parks and Recreation Dept., 735 Randolph St., Detroit, Mi. 48226

34. Wisconsin: LAKE PARK BICYCLE TRAIL (3.1 miles) B, Milwaukee County Park Commission, 901 N. 9th St., Milwaukee, Wis. 53233

35. Wisconsin: WARNIMONT PARK BICYCLE TRAIL (1.5 miles) B, Milwaukee County Park Commission, 901 N. 9th St., Milwaukee, Wis. 53233.

36. Tennessee: NORTH RIDGE TRAIL (7.5 miles) F, City of Oak Ridge, Municipal Bldg., Oak Ridge, Tn. 37830

37. Mississippi: SHOCKALOE TRAIL (23 miles) F-H, Forest Service, U.S. Dept. of Agriculture, Washington, D.C. 20250

38. Tennessee: HONEY CREEK TRAIL (5 miles) F, Bowaters Southern Paper Corp., Calhoun, Tn. 37309

39. Tennessee: VIRGIN FALLS TRAIL (8 miles) F, Bowaters Southern Paper Corp., Calhoun, Tn. 37309

40. Tennessee: HONEYSUCKLE TRAIL (.5 mile) Braille, Tennessee State Park Dept., 2611 West End Ave., Nashville, Tn. 37203

41. Missouri: ELEPHANT ROCKS BRAILLE TRAIL (1 mile) Braille-F-WC, State Park Board, P.O. Box 176, 1204 Jefferson Bldg., Jefferson City, Mo. 65101

Legend: B-bicycle; F-foot; H-horse; M-motorized, general; SM-snowmobile; WC-wheelchair; XC-cross-country ski

Index
No.   State: Name of Trail: Length: Type of Trail: Administering Agency

42. California: PENITENCIA CREEK TRAIL (5.5 miles) F-H, San Jose Park and Recreation Dept., San Jose, Ca. 95110

43. Arizona: SQUAW PEAK TRAIL (1.2 miles) F-H, City of Phoenix Parks and Recreation Dept., Phoenix, Az. 85236

44. Arizona: NORTH MOUNTAIN TRAIL (.9 mile) F-H, City of Phoenix Parks and Recreation Dept., Phoenix, Az. 85236

45. California: JEDEDIAH SMITH TRAIL (26 miles) B-F-H, Sacramento County Parks and Recreation Dept., 1416 9th St., Sacramento, Ca. 95814

46. California: CALIFORNIA AQUEDUCT BIKEWAY (67 miles) B-F, California Dept. of Water Resources, 1416 9th St., Box 388, Sacramento, Ca. 95814

47. Maryland: TOUCH OF NATURE TRAIL (.3 mile) Braille, Maryland Park Service, Tawes State Office Bldg., Annapolis, Md. 21401

48. Ohio: HARRIET L. KEELER WOODLAND TRAIL (.5 mile) F-WC-Braille, Cleveland Metroparks, 2000 Northern Ohio Bank Bldg., Cleveland, Oh. 44113

49. California: YORK TRAIL (3.5 miles) F-H, City of Oakland, Office of Parks and Recreation, 1520 Lakeside Dr., Oakland, Ca. 94612

50. Arizona: HUNTER TRAIL (2.3 miles) F, Arizona State Parks Board, 1688 W. Adams St., Phoenix, Az. 85007

51. Wisconsin: SUGAR RIVER STATE TRAIL (23 miles) B-F-SM, Wisconsin Dept. of Natural Resources, Bureau of Parks and Recreation, Box 450, Madison, Wis. 53701

52. North Carolina: BOB'S CREEK TRAIL (8 miles) F. Bowaters Carolina Corp., P.O. Box 7, Catawba, S.C. 29704

53. West Virginia: THE GENTLE TRAIL (.4 mile) Braille-F, The Huntington Galleries, Inc., Huntington, W. Va. 25701

54. Iowa: SAC AND FOX TRAIL (5 miles) F-H-B-XC, Cedar Rapids Park Dept., 2nd Avenue Island, Cedar Rapids, Iowa 52401

55. Arkansas: CEDAR CREEK SELF-GUIDING TRAIL (1.5 miles) F, Arkansas Dept. of Parks, 149 State Capitol, Little Rock, Ark. 72201

56. Arkansas: SEVEN HOLLOWS TRAIL (3.5 miles) F, Arkansas Dept. of Parks, 149 State Capitol, Little Rock, Ark. 72201

Legend: B-bicycle; F-foot; H-horse; M-motorized, general; SM-snowmobile; WC-wheelchair; XC-cross-country ski

**Index
No.   State: Name of Trail: Length: Type of Trail: Administering Agency**

57. Oklahoma: RED STICK TRAIL (1.5 miles) F-WC, Oklahoma City Parks and Recreation Dept., 200 N. Walker Ave., Oklahoma City, Ok. 73102

58. Pennsylvania: WISSAHICKON TRAIL (5.4 miles) F-H-B, Fairmount Park Commission, Memorial Hall, West Park, Philadelphia, Pa. 19131

59. California: TWENTY MULE TEAM TRAIL (12 miles) F-H-B, California City Park and Recreation Dept., 10400 Heather Ave., California City, Ca. 93505

60. Washington: DISCOVERY PARK LOOP TRAIL (2.8 miles) F-B, Seattle Parks and Recreation Dept., 610 Municipal Bldg., Seattle, Wa. 98104

61. California: TORO RIDING AND HIKING TRAILS (6 miles) F-H, Monterey County Parks Dept., P.O. Box 367, Salinas, Ca. 93901

62. Oregon: WILDWOOD PARK TRAIL (14 miles) F-H, Portland Park Bureau, 2115 S.E. Morrison St., Portland, Or. 97214

63. Wisconsin: AHNAPEE STATE PARK TRAIL (15 miles) F-B-SM, Wisconsin Dept. of Natural Resources, Bureau of Parks and Recreation, Box 450, Madison, Wis. 53701

64. Pennsylvania: FLOUR SAK BATTLE BICENTENNIAL TRAIL (1 Mile) F-Braille, Pennsylvania Historical and Museum Commission, Box 1026, Harrisburg, Pa. 17108

65. Rhode Island: CLIFF WALK (3.5 miles) F, City of Newport, City Hall, Newport, R.I. 02840

66. Ohio: ROCKY RIVER BICYCLE TRAIL (5 miles) B, Cleveland Metroparks, 2000 Northern Ohio Bank Bldg., Cleveland, Ohio 44113

67. Minnesota: CONGDON CREEK PARK TRAIL (.75 mile) F-XC, Duluth Parks and Recreation Dept., City Hall, Duluth, Mn. 55802

68. Minnesota: LESTER PARK NATURE TRAIL (1 mile) F-XC, Duluth Parks and Recreation Dept., City Hall, Duluth, Mn. 55802

69. California: LOST LAKE NATURE TRAIL (2 miles) F, Fresno County Dept. of Parks and Recreation, 6725 W. Kearney Blvd., Fresno, Ca. 93706

70. California: WESTERN STATES PIONEER EXPRESS TRAIL (50 miles) F-H, California Dept. of Parks and Recreation, 1416 9th St., Sacramento, Ca. 95814

71. Texas: TOWN LAKE WALK AND BIKEWAY (9.75 miles) F-B, Austin Parks and Recreation Dept., P.O. Box 1088, Austin, Tx. 78767

Legend: B-bicycle; F-foot; H-horse; M-motorized, general; SM-snowmobile; WC-wheelchair; XC-cross-country ski

Index
No.   **State:**   **Name of Trail:**   **Length:**   **Type of Trail:**   **Administering Agency**

72. Kentucky: HILLMAN HERITAGE TRAIL (10 miles) F, Tennessee Valley Authority, Div. of Forestry, Fisheries and Wildlife Development, Norris, Tn. 37828

73. Pennsylvania: UNION CANAL WALKING AND BICYCLE TRAIL (2.3 miles) F-B, Berks County Parks and Recreation Dept., Box 272, R.D. 5, Sinking Spring, Pa. 19608

74. Alabama: BARTRAM TRAIL (1 mile) F, Forest Service, U.S. Dept. of Agriculture, Washington, D.C. 20250

75. Massachusetts: DR. PAUL DUDLEY WHITE BICYCLE PATHS (6.5 miles) B-F, Metropolitan District Commission, 20 Somerset St., Boston, Ma. 02165

76. Massachusetts: FREEDOM TRAIL (2.5 miles) F, Freedom Trail Commission, Public Works Dept., One Beacon St., Boston, Ma. 02108

77. New York: CRANDALL PARK INTERNATIONAL SKI TRAILS (2.2 miles) XC-F-B, Glens Falls Recreation Dept., Glens Falls, N.Y. 12801

78. California: LAKE TAHOE BICYCLE AND PEDESTRIAN WAY (5 miles) B-F, Placer Cty. Dept. of Parks, 175 Fulweiler Ave., Auburn, Ca. 95603

79. North Carolina: BILTMORE CAMPUS TRAIL (1 mile) F, Forest Service, U.S. Dept. of Agriculture, Washington, D.C. 20250

80. California: SANTA ANA RIVER TRAIL (15.7 miles) F-B-H, Orange Cty., Cty. Administration Bldg., 515 N. Sycamore St., Santa Ana, Ca. 92701

81. Oregon: BEAR CREEK BIKEWAY AND NATURE TRAIL (3.4 miles) B-F, Medford Parks and Recreation Div., Dept. of Community Development, Medford, Or. 97501

82. Oregon: LINK RIVER TRAIL (.75 mile) F, Pacific Power and Light Co., Public Service Bldg., Portland, Or. 97204

83. California: MUIR WOODS INTERPRETIVE TRAIL (.88 mile) F-WC-Braille, National Park Service, U.S. Dept. of the Interior, Washington, D.C. 20240

84. North Dakota: OLD OAK TRAIL (3 miles) F-SM-XC, North Dakota State Park Service, 900 East Blvd., Bismarck, N.D. 58501

85. Florida: RICE CREEK TRAIL (3 miles) F, Hudson Pulp & Paper Corp., P.O. Box 1040, Palatka, Fl. 32077

86. South Carolina: TABLE ROCK TRAIL (9 miles) F, South Carolina Dept. of Parks, Recreation and Tourism, 1205 Pendleton St., Columbia, S.C. 29201

Legend: B-bicycle; F-foot; H-horse; M-motorized, general; SM-snowmobile; WC-wheelchair; XC-cross-country ski

Index
No. State: Name of Trail: Length: Type of Trail: Administering Agency

87. Wyoming: LEE McCUNE BRAILLE TRAIL (.3 mile) Braille-F, Natrona Cty. Parks Board, P.O. Box 1507, Casper, Wy. 82601

88. Massachusetts: NORTHFIELD MOUNTAIN TRAIL SYSTEM (30 miles) H-F-XC, Western Massachusetts Electric Co. Contact: Northeast Utilities Service Co., P.O. Box 270, Hartford, Conn. 06101

89. Indiana: CALUMET TRAIL (9.2 miles) B-F, Indiana Dept. of Natural Resources, Div. of Outdoor Recreation, 608 State Office Bldg., Indianapolis, In. 46204

90. Tennessee: RIVER BLUFF TRAIL (3.1 miles) F, Tennessee Valley Authority, Div. of Forestry, Fisheries and Wildlife Development, Norris, Tn. 37828

91. Florida: JACKSON TRAIL (21 miles) F, Florida Dept. of Agriculture and Consumer Services, Blackwater River State Forest, Rte. 1, Box 77, Milton, Fl. 32570

92. Louisiana: RED RIVER TRAIL (5.25 miles) B-F, City of Shreveport Parks and Recreation Dept., 800 Snow St., Shreveport, La. 71130

93. Kansas: INTERNATIONAL FOREST OF FRIENDSHIP TRAIL (.56 mile) F-WC, City of Atchison, City Hall, 515 Kansas Ave., Atchison, Ks. 66002

94. Tennessee: OLD HICKORY TRAIL (1.66 miles) F, U.S. Army Corps of Engineers, Nashville District, P.O. Box 1070, Nashville, Tn. 37202

95. Florida: APALACHICOLA BLUFFS TRAIL (.8 mile) F, Florida Dept. of Natural Resources, Div. of Recreation and Parks, 202 Blount St., Tallahassee, Fl. 32304

96. Arkansas: LEVI WILCOXON DEMONSTRATION FOREST TRAIL (.75 mile) F, Georgia-Pacific Corp., Crossett Div., P.O. Box 520, Crossett, Ark. 71635

97. Tennessee: FORT HENRY HIKING TRAILS (26 miles) F, Tennessee Valley Authority, Div. of Forestry, Fisheries and Wildlife Development, Norris, Tn. 37828

98. Virginia: CASCADES TRAIL (4 miles) F, Forest Service, U.S. Dept. of Agriculture, Washington, D.C. 20250

99. Pennsylvania: KELLYS RUN—PINNACLE TRAIL SYSTEM (4.75 miles) F-H, Pennsylvania Power & Light Co., Land Management Office, Holtwood, Pa. 17532

100. California: SANTA ANA RIVER TRAIL (10 miles) F-H, Riverside Cty. Parks Dept., 4080 Lemon St., Riverside, Ca. 92509

101. Wyoming: GRASSROOTS TRAIL (.94 mile) F-B, Torrington Parks Dept., Torrington, Wy. 82240

Legend: B-bicycle; F-foot; H-horse; M-motorized, general; SM-snowmobile; WC-wheelchair; XC-cross-country ski

Index
No. State: Name of Trail: Length: Type of Trail: Administering Agency

102. South Dakota: WOODLAND TRAIL (1.33 miles) F-XC, South Dakota Dept. of Game, Fish and Parks, Div. of Parks and Recreation, Pierre, S.D. 57501

103. Wisconsin: ICE AGE TRAIL (Kettle Bowl Segment, Lumber Camp Segment, Old Railroad Segment, Parrish Hills Segment, Chippewa Moraine Segment, and Blue Hills Segment) (62.5 miles total) F-XC-SM, Ice Age Park and Trail Foundation of Wisconsin, Inc., 780 N. Water St., Milwaukee, Wis. 53202

104. Nebraska: WILDERNESS PARK HIKING TRAIL (13 miles) F-XC, Lincoln Parks and Recreation Dept., 2740 A St., Lincoln, Neb. 68502

105. Texas: SAN ANTONIO RIVER TRAIL (8 miles) F-B, San Antonio Parks and Recreation Dept., P.O. Box 9066, San Antonio, Tx. 78285

106. Connecticut: SLEEPING GIANT TRAILS (25 miles) F, Connecticut Dept. of Environmental Protection, 165 Capitol Av., Hartford, Ct. 06115

107. Arizona: SUN CIRCLE TRAIL (68 miles) F-H-B, Maricopa Cty. Parks and Recreation Dept. 4701 E. Washington St., Phoenix, Az. 85034

108. Tennessee: BLUE BEAVER TRAIL (10.5 miles) F-H (H: 1-mile segment), National Park Service, Southeast Region, 1895 Phoenix Blvd., Atlanta, Ga. 30349

109. Virginia: SEASHORE STATE PARK NATIONAL AREA TRAILS SYSTEM (23 miles) F-B, Virginia Div. of Parks, 1201 State Office Bldg., Capitol Sq., Richmond, Va. 23219

110. Florida: OCALA TRAIL (68 miles) F, Forest Service, U.S. Dept. of Agriculture, Washington, D.C 20250. (Maintenance assistance is received from the Florida Trails Assn. through a cooperative agreement.)

111. Oklahoma: PATHFINDER PARKWAY (4.7 miles) F-B, City of Bartlesville, P.O. Box 699, Bartlesville, Ok. 74003

112. Tennessee: THIRD CREEK BICYCLE TRAIL (2.3 miles) B-F, City of Knoxville Recreation Dept., City Hall Park, P.O. Box 1631, Knoxville, Tn. 37901

113. North Carolina: HISTORIC EDENTON TRAIL (1.9 miles) F, Town of Edenton, Edenton, N.C. 27932

114. Kansas: PERRY LAKE TRAIL (10 miles) F, U.S. Army Corps. of Engineers, Perry Project Office, Rte. 1, Box 62, Perry, Ks. 66073

Legend: B-bicycle; F-foot; H-horse; M-motorized, general; SM-snowmobile;
WC-wheelchair; XC-cross-country ski

Index
No.   State: Name of Trail: Length: Type of Trail: Administering Agency

115. Alabama: PINHOTI TRAILS SYSTEM (2 segments—28 miles total) F,
Forest Service, U.S. Dept. of Agriculture, Washington, D.C 20250 (26
miles on Talladega National Forest lands); and Alabama Div. of Parks,
Dept. of Conservation and Natural Resources, 64 N. Union St., Mont-
gomery, Al. 36130 (2 miles within Cheaha State Park)

116. Oregon: McKENZIE RIVER TRAIL (13 miles) F, Forest Service, U.S.
Dept. of Agriculture, Washington, D.C. 20250

117. Montana: BIG HOLE BATTLEFIELD TRAIL (.5 mile) F-H, National Park
Service, Rocky Mountain Region, P.O. Box 25287, Denver, Co. 80225

118. Pennsylvania: HARRISBURG RIVERFRONT BIKEWAY (4 miles) B-F,
Harrisburg Dept. of Parks and Recreation (with assistance from the
Harrisburg Bicycle Club), Municipal Bldg., 423 Walnut St., Harrisburg,
Pa. 17101

119. Wisconsin: ICE AGE TRAIL (Kronenwetter Segment and Leathercamp
Segment) (15 miles total) F-XC-SM, Ice Age Park and Trail Foundation
of Wisconsin, Inc., 780 N. Water St., Milwaukee, Wis. 53202

120. Washington: BAYSIDE GREENBELT TRAIL (2.5 miles) F, City of
Tacoma, Dept. of Public Works, 930 Tacoma Ave. S., Tacoma, Wa.
98402

121. Oklahoma: INDIAN NATIONS TRAIL (20 miles) F, Oklahoma Tourism
and Recreation Dept., 500 Will Rogers Bldg., Oklahoma City, Ok. 73105

122. Wisconsin: ICE AGE TRAIL (40 miles) F, Forest Service, U.S. Dept. of
Agriculture, Washington, D.C. 20250

123. Tennessee: RED LEAVES OVERNIGHT TRAIL (30 miles) F, Tennessee
Dept. of Conservation, 2611 West End Ave., Nashville, Tn. 37203

124. Georgia: BARTRAM TRAIL (2 segments—22 miles total) F, Forest Service, U.S. Dept. of Agriculture, Washington, D.C. 20250

125. Tennessee: LADY FINGER BLUFF TRAIL (2.7 miles) F, Tennessee
Valley Authority, Div. of Forestry, Fisheries and Wildlife Development,
Norris, Tn. 37828

126. South Carolina: EDISTO NATURE TRAIL (1.5 miles) F, Westvaco Corp.,
Timberlands Div., P.O. Box WV, Summerville, S.C. 29483

127. South Carolina: HUNTING ISLAND MARSH BOARDWALK TRAIL (.25
mile) F, South Carolina Dept. of Parks, Recreation and Tourism, Div. of
State Parks, Edgar A. Brown Bldg., 1205 Pendleton St., Columbia, S.C.
29201

128. Ohio: CUYAHOGA VALLEY TOWPATH (2.8 miles) F-H, Cleveland
Metroparks, 2000 Northern Ohio Bank Bldg., Cleveland, Oh. 44113

Legend: B-bicycle; F-foot; H-horse; M-motorized, general; SM-snowmobile; WC-wheelchair; XC-cross-country ski

Index
No. State: Name of Trail: Length: Type of Trail: Administering Agency

129. Idaho: HANNA FLAT TRAIL (.25 mile) F-WC-XC, Forest Service, U.S. Dept. of Agriculture, Washington, D.C. 20250

130. Washington: RAINY LAKE TRAIL (.8 mile) F, Forest Service, U.S. Dept. of Agriculture, Washington, D.C. 20250

131. Montana: PALISADE FALLS TRAIL (.33 mile) F-Braille, Forest Service, U.S. Dept. of Agriculture, Washington, D.C. 20250

132. California: PIEDRA BLANCA TRAIL (18.2 miles) F-H, Forest Service, U.S. Dept. of Agriculture, Washington, D.C. 20250

133. Washington: ICE CAVES TRAIL (.9 mile) F, Forest Service, U.S. Dept. of Agriculture, Washington, D.C. 20250

134. Idaho: MAJOR FENN NATURE TRAIL (.6 mile) F, Forest Service, U.S. Dept. of Agriculture, Washington, D.C. 20250

135. Arkansas: PRAIRIE CREEK JOGGING TRAIL (1 mile) F, Resident Engineer, Dardanelle Office, U.S. Army Corps of Engineers, P.O. Box 1087, Russellville, Ark. 72801

136. Arkansas: TOLLANTUSKY TRAIL (1.4 miles) F-WC, Park Manager, Toad Suck Ferry, U .S. Army Corps of Engineers, Rte. 5, Box 199, Conway, Ark. 72032

137. Arkansas: CEDAR FALLS TRAIL (2.2 miles) F, Superintendent, Petit Jean State Park, Rte. 3, Morrilton, Ark. 72110

138. Arkansas: FOREST HILLS TRAIL (1.5 miles) F, Resident Engineer, Nimrod Lake, Blue Mountain Resident Office, U.S. Army Corps of Engineers, Plainview, Ark. 72857

139. Arkansas: SUMMIT PARK SELF-GUIDED TRAIL (1.75 miles) F, Superintendent, Mount Nebo State Park, Rte. 2, Box 160-A, Dardanelle, Ark. 72834

140. Arkansas: BRIDGE ROCK TRAIL (1 mile) F, Resident Engineer, Dardanelle Office, U.S. Army Corps of Engineers, P.O. Box 1087, Russellville, Ark. 72801

141. Arkansas: BUCKEYE TRAIL (.1 mile) F-WC, Resident Engineer, Greers Ferry Office, U.S. Army Corps of Engineers, P.O. Box 310, Heber Springs, Ark. 72543

142. Arkansas: MOSSY BLUFF TRAIL (.7 mile) F, Resident Engineer, Greers Ferry Office, U.S. Army Corps of Engineers, P.O. Box 310, Heber Springs, Ark. 72543

143. Arkansas: YELLOW ROCK TRAIL (2 miles) F, Director, Arkansas Dept. of Parks and Tourism, 1510 Broadway, Little Rock, Ark. 72202

Legend: B-bicycle; F-foot; H-horse; M-motorized, general; SM-snowmobile; WC-wheelchair; XC-cross-country ski

Index
No.´ State: Name of Trail: Length: Type of Trail: Administering Agency

144. Arkansas: DEVIL'S DEN SELF-GUIDED TRAIL (1.5 miles) F, Director, Arkansas Dept. of Parks and Tourism, 1510 Broadway, Little Rock, Ark. 72202

145. Arkansas: ROBINSON POINT NATURE TRAIL (3 miles) F, Resident Engineer, Mountain Home Office, U.S. Army Corps of Engineers, P.O. Box 369, Mountain Home, Ark. 72653

146. Arkansas: DAM MOUNTAIN TRAIL (4.5 miles) F, Lake Catherine State Park, Rte. 1, Box 722, Hot Springs, Ark. 71901

147. Arkansas: HORESHOE MOUNTAIN TRAIL (3.5 miles) F, Lake Catherine State Park, Rte. 1, Box 722, Hot Springs, Ark. 71901

148. Arkansas: FALLS BRANCH TRAIL (2 miles) F, Lake Catherine State Park, Rte. 1, Box 722, Hot Springs, Ark. 71901

149. Colorado: HIGHLINE CANAL TRAIL (17-mile extension) F-B-H, Colorado Div. of Parks and Outdoor Recreation, 1845 Sherman, Denver, Co. 80203

150. Colorado: CRAG CREST TRAIL (11 miles) F-H, Forest Service, U.S. Dept. of Agriculture, Washington, D.C. 20250

151. Mississippi: BURNSIDE PARK NATURE TRAIL (2 miles) F, Philadelphia-Neshoba Cty. Parks and Recreation Commission, Rte. 6, Philadelphia, Ms. 39350

152. Mississippi: RIVERSIDE PARK NATURE TRAIL (2 miles) F, City of Jackson Parks and Recreation Dept., P.O. Box 17, Jackson, Ms. 39205

153. Tennessee: PINEY RIVER TRAIL (10 miles) F, Bowater Southern Paper Corp., Calhoun, Tn. 37309

154. Alabama: GEORGE WARD PARK EXERCISE TRAIL (1.5 miles) F, Birmingham Park and Recreation Board, 700 City Hall, Birmingham, Al. 35203

155. New Mexico: PASEO DEL BOSQUE BICYCLE TRAIL (5 miles) B-F-WC, Albuquerque Parks and Recreation Dept., 1801 Fourth, N.W., Albuquerque, N.M. 87107

156. Colorado: PLATTE RIVER GREENWAY TRAIL (7 miles) F-B, Div. of Parks and Outdoor Recreation, 1313 Sherman St., Denver, Co. 80203

157. Montana: BLUE MOUNTAIN EQUESTRIAN AND HIKING TRAIL (6 miles) H-F, Forest Service, U.S. Dept. of Agriculture, Washington, D.C. 20250

Legend: B-bicycle; F-foot; H-horse; M-motorized, general; SM-snowmobile; WC-wheelchair; XC-cross-country ski

**Index
No.   State: Name of Trail: Length: Type of Trail: Administering Agency**

158. Montana: BLUE MOUNTAIN NATURE TRAIL (.25 mile) F, Forest Service, U.S. Dept. of Agriculture, Washington, D.C. 20250

159. Florida: UNIVERSITY OF NORTH FLORIDA NATURE TRAILS (12 miles) F-WC (¼-mile WC), University of North Florida, P.O. Box 17074, Jacksonville, Fl. 32216

160. Tennessee: BEARWALLER GAP HIKING TRAIL (6 miles) F, U.S. Army Corps of Engineers, Nashville District, P.O. Box 1070, Nashville, Tn. 37209

161. Idaho: COEUR D'ALENE RIVER TRAIL (14 miles) F-H-M, Forest Service, U.S. Dept. of Agriculture, Washington, D.C. 20250

162. Nevada: GRIMES POINT PETROGLYPH TRAIL (.37 mile) F, Bureau of Land Management, Carson City District, 1050 E. William Street, Carson City, Nevada 89701

163. Louisiana: WILD AZALEA TRAIL (30 miles) F, Forest Service, U.S. Dept. of Agriculture, Washington, D.C. 20250

164. Idaho: LAKESHORE TRAIL (7 miles) F-WC-XC, Forest Service, U.S. Dept. of Agriculture, Washington, D.C. 20250

165. Georgia: BUSH MOUNTAIN TRAIL (.75 mile) F, Atlanta Bureau of Parks and Recreation, 260 Central Ave., S.W., Atlanta, Ga. 30303; and Outdoor Activity Center, 1442 Richland Rd., S.W., Atlanta, Ga. 30310

APPENDIX I

SOME GUIDELINES FOR BACKCOUNTRY HIKERS AND CAMPERS

(Courtesy of Appalachian Mountain Club.)

The *Appalachian Mountain Club* offers these guidelines to assist you in preserving our mountain country. Please follow these simple rules so the backcountry will remain for all to enjoy.

Campers: Bring Your Own Tent Or Shelter

Fixed shelters are often full, so each group (and individual) should carry all needed shelter, including whatever poles, stakes, ground insulation, and cord are required. Please: *We can no longer cut boughs or branches for bedding.*

Camp Off The Trail

Help preserve both the solitude and beauty of our trails by camping 200 feet from the trail edge. Leave no traces of your camp when you leave.

Limit The Size Of Your Group

Please try to limit your group to a size leaders can safely handle and backcountry sites can easily accommodate (recommended ratio, one leader to eight people).

Use A Portable Stove

There is simply not enough wood left for everyone to have a wood fire. But please use your stove with care—it can be dangerous.

Help Preserve Nature's Ground Cover

If a shelter is full, try to choose a clear, level site on which to pitch your tent. Today's heavy use means the wilderness just can't survive site-clearing and ditching around tents.

Drink From The Water Supply, But—

Please don't wash in it. Wash your dishes and yourself away from and below all sources of drinking water. Dispose of waste water away from streams and springs.

Think About Human Waste

Stay away from (and below) the water supply. Camping groups: If no toilets are nearby dig a trench 12 inches deep, covering it completely when you break camp.

Carry In—Carry Out

Please carry out leftover food. Leave the mountains cleaner than you found them—bring a refuse bag and carry out *more* than you carried in.

Use Special Care Above Timberline

Extreme weather and a short growing season make these areas especially fragile. Just footsteps can destroy the toughest natural cover, so please watch where you tread. (And, of course, please don't camp above timberline.)

FOR A BETTER (AND SAFER) TRIP

Plan Your Trip

Have the latest guidebook and maps. Check them thoroughly before you leave and know you have mastered all the options for time, alternative routes, and weather. Remember the shorter daylight hours in fall and winter.

Tell Others Where You Are Going

Always leave your trip plans with someone in the family or a close friend.

Ideal Climbing Party—Four People

Four is the smallest number of people who can make sure your hiking plans succeed. Do not hike alone!

Mountain Weather Is Unpredictable

The northeastern United States lies in two major storm paths, so check your radio or t.v. weather forecasts, and listen to regional and local radio stations on your car radio for the latest mountain weather. Bad weather in the mountains hits fast and clears slowly. Think twice if storms or fronts are predicted. In the mountains, the higher you go, the worse the weather.

Carry Extras: Clothing, Food, Knowledge

Extra clothing—windbreakers, wool jackets, hats, gloves, and other warming items—are useful in every season. High-energy food such as hard candy, Lifesavers, and chocolate bars should always be in your pack. So, too, should fruit and liquids. Insurance extras such as first aid supplies, aspirin, compass, maps, and guidebooks must always be there (as should the knowledge of how to use them). But avoid carrying too much gear—it can become a burden.

Watch Stream Crossings

Melting spring snows and sudden storms swell mountain streams and brooks quickly. Be careful in any season of valley trails that include stream crossings.

Mountain Mishaps Are Rare

But should one occur in your party, the most important thing is to remain calm. If you become lost, stay where you are and keep warm. Or, remember that in the mountains, following running water downhill will nearly always bring you to helpful signs of man.

If a member of your group becomes lost, note details of his clothing and appearances, the time and location, and report these to authorities.

In case of an accident, at least one person should remain with the injured person. Others should note carefully the location and contact the State Police, the Fish and Game Department, or the U.S. Forest Service.

These suggestions are intended only as basic hints, and are by no means to be regarded as complete, infallible guides to mountain safety.

APPENDIX J

WALKING POINTS

Good brisk walking is the best exercise there is.
—*Dr. Joseph Bertucci*

To find new things, take the path you took yesterday.
—*John Burroughs*

Today I have grown taller from walking with the trees.
—*Karle Wilson*

I have two doctors, my left leg and my right.
—*G.M. Trevelyan*

Nature gives to every time and season some beauties of its own.

—*Charles Dickens*

Physical fitness is vital for the optimal function of the brain, for retardation of the onset of serious atherosclerosis which is beginning to appear in early adult life, and for longevity, and a useful and healthy life for our older citizens.
—*Dr. Paul Dudley White*

Two or three hours walking will carry me to as strange a country as I expect ever to see.
—*Henry David Thoreau*

All walking is discovery. On foot we take the time to see things whole.

—*Hal Borland*

To travel on foot is to travel like Plato and Pythagores.

—*John Davis*

Nature is the living, visible garment of God.
—*Johann Wolfgang von Goethe*

Of all exercises walking is the best . . . . Walking the plantation of Monticello always stimulated my imagination.
—*Thomas Jefferson*

The principle of a sound mind in a sound body is still the basis of excellence in living.
—*Dr. Thomas B. Quigley*

I find that the three truly great times for thinking thoughts are when I am standing in the shower, sitting on the john, or walking. And the greatest of these, by far, is walking.
—*Colin Fletcher*
(from "The New Complete Walker")

I used, when I was younger, to take my holidays walking. I would cover 25 miles a day, and when the evening came I had no need of anything to keep me from boredom, since the delight of sitting amply sufficed.
—*Bertrand Russell*

People should have a right to walk to work, to school, to stores, under safe, pleasant, and healthy conditions.
—*Simon Brienes & William J. Dean*
(from "The Pedestrian Revolution:
Streets Without Cars")

I feel very strongly that vigorous physical exercise for at least one hour daily is essential as a preventive measure for sickness and disability in later life.
—*Dr. Hans Kraus*

Nature is man's teacher. She unfolds her treasures to his search, unseals his eye, illumes his mind, and purifies his heart.
—*Alfred Billings Street*

I travel not to go anywhere, but to go.
—*Robert Louis Stevenson*

Walking is the only way to get the "feel" of a city, to really experience all it has to offer.
— *Juliann Skurdenis & Lawrence Smircich*
    (from "More, Walk Straight Through the Square")

The swiftest traveler is he that goes afoot.
                    — *Henry David Thoreau*

If you pick 'em up, O Lord, I'll put 'em down.
                    — *Prayer of the Tired Walker*

INDEX